THE MAKING OF A
BESTSELLER

THE MAKING OF A
BESTSELLER

SUCCESS STORIES FROM AUTHORS AND THE
EDITORS, AGENTS, AND BOOKSELLERS BEHIND THEM

BRIAN HILL ▪ DEE POWER

Dearborn™
Trade Publishing
A **Kaplan Professional** Company

Vice President and Publisher: Cynthia A. Zigmund
Acquisitions Editor: Michael Cunningham
Senior Project Editor: Trey Thoelcke
Interior Design: Lucy Jenkins
Cover Design: Design Solutions
Typesetting: Elizabeth Pitts

© 2005 by Brian Hill and Dee Power

Published by Dearborn Trade Publishing
A Kaplan Professional Company

Printed in the United States of America

05 06 07 10 9 8 7 6 5 4 3 2 1

Library of Congress Cataloging-in-Publication Data

Hill, Brian E. (Brian Edward), 1955–
   The making of a bestseller : success stories from authors and the editors, agents, and booksellers behind them / Brian Hill and Dee Power.
      p. cm.
   Includes index.
   ISBN 0-7931-9308-7
   1. Best sellers—United States—History—20th century. 2. Publishers and publishing—United States—History—20th century. 3. Books and reading—United States—History—20th century. 4. Popular literature—United States—History and criticism. 5. Authorship. 6. Authors, American—20th century—Interviews. I. Power, Dee II. Title.
   Z1033.B3H55   2005
   381′.45002′09730904—dc22

                                                        2004022940

Dearborn Trade books are available at special quantity discounts to use for sales promotions, employee premiums, or educational purposes. Please call our Special Sales Department to order or for more information at 800-621-9621 ext. 4444, e-mail trade@dearborn.com, or write to Dearborn Trade Publishing, 30 South Wacker Drive, Suite 2500, Chicago, IL 60606-7481.

Contents

PART TWO
Publishing

PART THREE
The Author

The authors wish to express their appreciation to all the publishing industry professionals—authors, editors, agents, publicists, booksellers—who took the time to talk with us about their experiences. For our purposes, a *bestselling author* is defined as an author who has had one or more books reach the *New York Times* or *Publishers Weekly* bestseller lists or the *USA Today* Top 50 list. When we began writing *The Making of a Bestseller,* our major concern was whether bestselling authors, who have enormous demands on their time and receive many interview requests, would be willing to share their success stories with us. Happily, we found out that they were not only willing but eager to talk to us, giving their readers an inside look at the life and career of a bestselling author, as well as passing on their knowledge and wisdom to the next generation of authors.

We wish to begin, then, with a special salute to all the authors who are quoted in this book:

Mark Bowden	Barbara Taylor Bradford
Dan Brown	Sandra Brown
Harlen Coben	Catherine Coulter
Barbara Delinsky	Linda Fairstein
Rachel Gibson	Laurell K. Hamilton
Anna Jacobs	Sabrina Jeffries
Iris Johansen	Dr. Spencer Johnson
Stephanie Laurens	Brad Meltzer
Christopher Paolini	Carly Phillips
Susan Elizabeth Phillips	Christina Skye
Bertrice Small	Nicholas Sparks
Peter Straub	Stuart Woods

And we very much appreciate the contribution of screenwriter Kirk Ellis.

Many of these authors have sold tens of millions of books over the course of their careers. But, as we will see in the pages that follow, their incredible success is not due simply to their individual efforts. No matter how talented an author is or how unique their voice, ideas, or storytelling ability, a bestseller is always the result of the contributions and dedication of a host of people, some inside the publishing houses, some outside—and ending with the readers themselves.

We also wish to thank our attorney, Helen Wan, at Frankfurt Kurnit Klein & Selz in New York, for introducing us to several of the literary agents we interviewed.

We would be remiss if we didn't thank all the agents, editors, experts, and booksellers for their valuable contributions:

Agents:

Matt Bialer

Richard Curtis

Joel Gotler

Heidi Lange

Margret McBride

Scott Miller

Editors:

Lee Boudreaux

Paula Eykelhof

Janice Goldklang

Karen Kosztolnyik

Jennifer Enderlin

Jonathan Galassi

Daniel Halpern

Neil Nyren

Publishing industry experts:

Lyn Blake, Amazon.com

Michael Cader, *Publishers Lunch*

Rick Frishman, Planned TV Arts

Lawrence Shapiro,
   Book of the Month

Gene Taft, Publicaffairs.com

Toby Usnik, New York
   Times Company

Fauzia Burke, FSB Associates

Jim Cox, Midwest Book Review

Theresa Meyers, Blue Moon
   Communications

Meg Smith, Book Sense

Sam Tanenhaus, *New York Times
   Book Review*

Booksellers:

John Bennett, Bennett Books

Cindy Dach, Changing
   Hands Books

Mitchell Kaplan, Books & Books

Michael Powell, Powell's Books

Gayle Shanks, Changing Hands
   Books

Carol Chittenden, Eight
   Cousins Children's Bookstore

Daniel Goldin, The Harry W.
   Schwartz Bookshops

Barbara Meade, Politics and
   Prose

We must also thank the over 100 literary agents and publishing editors who took time to participate in our editors and agents survey, as well as the many, many independent booksellers who gave us their input.

Finally: A well deserved thank you to our own editor at Dearborn Trade Publishing, Michael Cunningham, and his great staff.

After conducting the more than 50 interviews that went into this book, we came away with this conclusion: all of these people truly love the publishing industry. Being involved in publishing provides much more to their lives than just a paycheck, no matter how large that paycheck may be.

It all begins with a passion for books—and a never-ending admiration for the authors who have that special gift with words.

1

THE INCOMPARABLE THRILL

A MOUNT OLYMPUS FOR AUTHORS
FIRST THE STRUGGLE, THEN THE THRILL
TREMENDOUS REWARDS BUT TREMENDOUS PRESSURE

A MOUNT OLYMPUS FOR AUTHORS

Bestselling authors are the gods and goddesses of the publishing industry. They occupy a special place, and the air is truly rare up there. They don't run into many other people where they live. The Spago restaurant on Authors' Mount Olympus always has a table waiting for them, and someone else always picks up the tab. The phrase, *It's lonely at the top,* has never been more applicable than to the world of the bestselling author.

For a lucky few authors, the rise to the bestseller list is meteoric—they might even achieve it with their very first book as did Allison Pearson, Brad Meltzer, and Jennifer Weiner. For most, though, a writing career builds slowly and painstakingly, and reaching the bestseller lists comes much later—after two, five, or even ten books.

DAN BROWN, *Author*

Dan Brown's *The Da Vinci Code* has experienced phenomenal success. It has been on the *New York Times* bestseller list for more than 86 straight weeks, primarily in the number-one position, becoming one of the most widely read books of all time. Worldwide, sales are almost 15 million copies. In every country where *The Da Vinci Code* has so far been translated and published, it has either debuted at or climbed to number one. In early 2004, after the publication of *The Da Vinci Code,* Dan's previous books—*Digital Fortress, Deception Point,* and *Angels and Demons*—all held spots on the *New York Times* bestseller list during the same week.

How did you feel when you found out for the first time that
The Da Vinci Code has made the bestseller list?

Stunned. I was all alone in a coffee shop in Seattle (my first stop on my book tour) when my editor called with the news that *The Da Vinci Code* would debut at number one. After falling off my chair and spilling my coffee, I remember wandering the streets of Seattle in a daze for a couple of hours. At some point I remember realizing that no matter what happened in the following weeks, I would forever have a number-one bestseller to my name. Of course, never in my wildest dreams did I imagine that *The Da Vinci Code* would still be number one more than a year later.

Other than the money, how has having a book on the bestseller
list changed your life?

A lot more pressure. A lot less privacy.

Whatever the timeline—blazingly fast or agonizingly slow—the first thing you realize when you talk to a number of bestselling authors is the passion, the zeal for writing, they share. The bestselling author-to-be is not the professor you overhear at the coffee house saying, "Ahh, if only I didn't have all these time-draining teaching responsibilities, I could sit down and become the next (Faulkner, Hemingway, fill in your favorite)." The bestselling author of five years from now is getting up at 4:00 AM and writing for three hours before she has to go to work. If we could somehow interview this undiscovered talent, she would say, "I don't want to be the next (whoever). I want to be the first and only *me*. My voice is unique, and it needs to be heard."

JONATHAN GALASSI, *President and Publisher*
Farrar, Straus, & Giroux, LLC

What makes a great literary voice?

A great literary voice is always something new—a voice that is *sui generis* expertly makes use of language to put across a particular way of seeing. Often, you can tell this right away, in the first sentences or paragraphs. It has nothing to do with what the book is ostensibly "about." What it's really "about" is the mind of the writer. Needless to say, other factors enter in later—accessibility, coherence, consistency, subject matter, etc. But the impact of a real voice is immediate and often overwhelming. It doesn't happen terribly often, needless to say.

FIRST THE STRUGGLE, THEN THE THRILL

Bestselling authors are not necessarily immediately recognized as having work with great commercial potential. They generally go through the same difficult process as nearly all authors do to get their first work into print. After the momentary ecstasy of seeing their first book in the stores, an apprentice period lasting a number of years, and a number of books, can follow before the author reaches even the lowest rung on the bestseller list.

CATHERINE COULTER, *Author*

Catherine Coulter is an incredibly prolific and versatile novelist, at home in the suspense/thriller genre as well as historical romance and contemporary romance. In 1988, she first appeared on the *New York Times* bestseller list with *Moonspun Magic,* the third novel of the *Magic* trilogy. She has continued to hit the *New York Times* bestseller list more than 59 times in a row, as well as the *USA Today* and *Publishers Weekly* lists. More than 40 million copies of her books are in print. Among her most popular books are her FBI series thrillers featuring married FBI agents Dillon Savich and Lacey Sherlock. Some of Catherine's popular titles include *Blowout, Blindside, The Cove, Hemlock Bay,* and *Riptide.*

How did you feel when you first made the bestseller list?

Hitting the bestseller list means hitting the *New York Times* bestseller list for the first time, not the *USA Today* list or the *Publishers Weekly* list or any of the other big newspaper lists. It's a very mysterious thing to me why the publishing industry set up the *New York Times* as the torch bearer for bestsellerdom, but at some point in the past they did, and now we all have to live with it. How did I feel? It's a moment you'll remember until you croak. Everyone remembers exactly what they were doing, what they were feeling. It is a very, very big thing psychologically. For me, it was in August 1987 at 7:30 in the morning when my editor called me. "You made the *New York Times*." It was a total surprise, although it shouldn't have been because my numbers had grown so that reaching critical mass was just a matter of time. You could have drowned in the champagne that day.

Stephen King's *Carrie* was the fifth novel he'd written. James Patterson's first mystery was turned down by 31 publishers (but later won an Edgar Award). Mary Higgins Clark's first story took 6 years and 41 rejection slips before it was finally published. Her first novel was, as she puts it, "a commercial disaster." Her second, *Where Are the Children?*, was a bestseller. Janet Evanovich's first three attempts were, in her own words, "sucky unsellable manuscripts." Time and time again, bestselling authors have learned the same lesson: with great diligence and unwavering devotion to the craft of writing, "sucky" can eventually turn into sublime.

Peyton Place, by Grace Metalious, which became the number-three bestseller for all of 1956 and raised the bar for spicier romantic fiction, was rejected by more than a dozen publishers before it found a home. Ayn Rand's *The Fountainhead*, still popular and topical 60 years after publication, initially faced rejection. So did the Harper Lee classic, *To Kill a Mockingbird*, which was later made into a movie for which Gregory Peck won an Academy Award and is still on every child's school reading list. The legendary *Joy of Cooking* was initially self-published and didn't cause editors to boil over with enthusiasm. Even Dr. Seuss's first book faced rejection. Horton may have heard a Who, but unfortunately he didn't hear from a publisher for a long time.

The difference is that after the first big success, the doors to the publishing houses are forever open to the authors who make the bestseller list. Instead of pursuing editors at the major houses, the authors become the ones being pursued. Looking back, they don't recall their early career as characterized by rejection; it seems more like "success delayed."

The defining difference between the would-be author and the bestselling author-to-be occurs at that critical moment when it is easiest to say, "To hell with it. I don't need all this pain. I'll go do something else." That is the moment the bestselling author-to-be simply shrugs and returns to the word processor, relatively unscathed by whatever negative comments the gatekeeper (agent, editor) or even the marketplace might have said.

No one can take away the joy of putting the beautiful words on the page. That joy is the sustaining element. Years later, the same negative comments that lacerated the authors who gave up become humorous cocktail party stories for the author celebrating a 17th straight appearance on the *New York Times* bestseller list.

You also notice that these perennially bestselling authors have more words inside of them, bursting to get out, than the average author. Their output is amazing. Recall the episode of the TV series *Frasier* where the Crane brothers had the opportunity to meet one of their beloved authors from their college years, T. H. Houghton (Robert Prosky), who had written exactly one book, was hailed for his literary genius, and then spent the next 20 years wondering if he had anything more to say. Finally, he came out with his next manuscript, which he didn't like and threw out the window of Frasier's condo. While this fictional writer of fiction was ruminating for 20 years, probably in the same coffee house as the professor we met earlier, real-life mystery author Patricia Cornwell has had 17 books published. Danielle Steel has produced 60 novels, 10 children's books, and 2 nonfiction books. Jude Deveraux has written over 40 books.

Surprisingly, becoming a bestselling author was not necessarily the goal of the writers who have gotten there, and it certainly wasn't their primary motivation for pursuing a writing career. J.K. Rowling has sold several *hundred million* copies of her Harry Potter books. She has said repeatedly in interviews that she greatly appreciates all the fame, fortune, and movie deals that have resulted from the books. But she maintains that the greatest thrill was simply finding out the first book, *Harry Potter and the Sorcerer's Stone*, was going to be published. To be able to say she was a published author was her dream from childhood, a dream she didn't let go of, even though she wasn't actually published until she was past 30.

Even if you don't quite believe the romantic, if rather Dickensian, story of the struggling but plucky single mum in Edinburgh, Scotland, who had to type extra copies of her manuscript to send out to prospective agents because she didn't have enough money to go to the local Kinko's—you still have to admire the fact J.K. Rowling persevered over a period of five long years to complete her first book and find her delightful literary voice.

STUART WOODS, Author

Stuart Woods is one of America's most successful mystery writers. He has created enduringly popular series characters, including jet-setting lawyer Stone Barrington and tenacious small-town chief of police Holly Barker. His bestselling recent titles include *Reckless Abandon, Capital Crimes, Dirty Work,* and *Blood Orchid.* Stuart flies his own airplane to book signings and spends time aboard a vintage motor yacht.

Is there a certain amount of luck involved in reaching the top of the fiction writing profession?

You've got to write good books that appeal to people. It's certainly possible to get a lucky break. A good review at the right time helps. I'm not conscious of having especially good or bad luck along the way. My sales have grown steadily over a period of many years. I haven't had the explosive growth some authors get with one or two novels.

Then there's the story of Alice Sebold, whose first novel, *The Lovely Bones,* became the literary phenomenon of 2002 and much of 2003. All she managed to do was sell nearly three million copies of this first novel. It reached number one on Amazon.com six weeks before it was published, spurred by a recommendation by author Anna Quindlen on NBC's *The Today Show.* Publishing industry insiders had difficulty finding a comparable book that has rocketed to the top of the bestseller lists so quickly.

MARK BOWDEN, Author

Mark is perhaps best known for his bestselling book *Black Hawk Down,* an intense, harrowing account of the 1993 U.S. Army Rangers' mission in Mogadishu, Somalia, that resulted in a drawn out firefight.

The book was made into a very popular motion picture directed by Ridley Scott. He is also the award-winning author of *Bringing the Heat* (named one of best sports books of 1994, by the *New York Times*), *Doctor Dealer,* and *Killing Paulo,* and he has been a reporter at the *Philadelphia Inquirer* for 19 years. He also writes for many national magazines and is a national correspondent for *The Atlantic Monthly.*

How did you feel when you first saw *Black Hawk Down* in the bookstore with the banner, "*New York Times* bestseller," next to it? You'd written other books prior to that . . .

Which were purchased by members of my immediate family.

Black Hawk Down's success was a huge thrill. I can remember getting the news when it made the *New York Times* bestseller list. It's the kind of thing that attaches to your name—bestselling author.

At first, to tell you the truth, you feel a little fraudulent. You haven't done anything different than you did before, with your previous books. Suddenly, you are just given this information, from the publisher, that this book you've written has become bestselling. It's enormously satisfying. The full implications of it aren't immediately understood.

You don't feel like you're suddenly a better writer, better at what you do. It's almost as though you're walking down the street, and somebody comes up to you and tells you you're descended from royalty. You aren't a different person, but suddenly everyone's calling you "Prince."

TREMENDOUS REWARDS BUT TREMENDOUS PRESSURE

Bestselling authors sleep well at night, not just because of their large bank accounts and investment portfolios, and because they have the luxury of getting up in the morning and doing what they have always dreamed of doing—writing. They also sleep well because they have another asset, one that does not necessarily depreciate over time and one that the IRS has not yet found a way to tax: a loyal readership. They know that the public will likely gobble up whatever they write next.

Authors newly arrived on the bestseller list quickly learn of an additional great reward: the publisher wants to keep you there and is willing to invest significant financial and creative resources to do so.

For these fortunate authors, their latest title's marketing program is planned out months before the book is completed, and the publisher backs it with significant amounts of money when it's released. This is important, because bookstores want to know what kind of marketing campaign is behind the book to decide how many copies to order. Tyndale, the publisher of Tim LaHaye and Jerry B. Jenkins' *The Remnant,* shipped an amazing 2.4 million copies of the book to bookstores prior to the publication date and was said to have committed $3 million to the book's marketing campaign. Not surprisingly, the book made its debut on the *Publishers Weekly* bestseller list in the number-one position.

Perpetually bestselling authors are expected to produce at least one title per year, and the publishing house's marketing and promotion machine goes into motion on their behalf. Certain authors' books are even released each year on pretty much the same date because of that date's perceived attractiveness to the author's loyal audience. The goal for these upper-echelon books is sales of a million or more copies; thus, the stakes for the authors and their publishing houses continue to get higher. Twenty years ago, selling 250,000 to 500,000 hardcover books was considered terrific.

MATT BIALER, *Literary Agent*
Sanford J. Greenburger & Associates

When you have a client who becomes a breakout author, how does it make you feel personally?

It's a great feeling. You know your instincts were correct. It makes you optimistic about the industry. At our agency, we had *The Da Vinci Code,* an example of a book where everything fell in place: the right author with the right book who found the right agent who found the right editor and the right publisher.

Reviews, feature stories about the author, advertising campaigns, and author appearances on TV are all planned to reach a crescendo when the book is shipped to stores. The publisher must ship enough copies so that every chain bookstore can have stacks available when the customers begin pouring in to ask for them. In our instant gratification society, bookstores that do not have enough copies in stock can lose sales; the customer may not come back again. The bookstore can return books that don't sell to the publisher but still faces the risk of using valuable retail space for a book that turns out to be a dud.

When a first printing of a book is huge, the risk is that much greater for the publishing house, because so much capital goes into the printing costs and then to the marketing campaign (and the author has already received a huge advance).

Nonfiction is, to some extent, also celebrity-author driven with big names from politics, sports, entertainment, and self-help gurus. But the nonfiction list is more likely to include "new" authors who do not yet have a big following. A riveting topic, event, or unusual approach to the self-help genre can allow a relatively unknown author to crack the nonfiction list. At any given time, the mix of authors on the nonfiction list can seem strange, to say the least. Take 1996, for instance: Dilbert, Dennis Rodman, Walter Cronkite, and the Duchess of York all appeared on the *Publishers Weekly* annual bestseller list—in that order.

LEE BOUDREAUX, *Senior Editor*
Random House

What personal satisfaction does an editor get from seeing one of their authors make it to the bestseller list?

Well, it's hugely satisfying! I was thrilled when *Black House* was number one on the *New York Times* list. Last summer, Adriana Trigiani's *Lucia, Lucia* hit the list. Random House published her first novel in 2000, and this was the culmination of a lot of hard work by a lot of people. It's great to know that a book like that is going to reach the wide audience it deserves.

Given the long odds, how does a new author crack the bestseller fiction list? It is something of a mystery, even to veteran editors at the largest publishing houses and, as a result, difficult to repeat with the next "new" author with great talent who comes along. Editors have no idea why an unknown writer sometimes immediately strikes a chord with book buyers. It was certainly not because the author benefited from the kind of massive marketing campaign that the "sure thing" bestselling authors receive.

The challenge faced by the first-time bestselling author is to turn a successful first bestseller into an enduringly successful career. With one success, an author is left to ponder whether it was just a fluke. Perhaps the subject matter just happened to be particularly compelling or topical. Or the work was just something the marketplace was looking for at that one moment in time, and the publisher did a terrific job at marketing. With the second success comes more confidence.

JOHN BENNETT, Owner
Bennett Books, Wyckoff, NJ

How often do you see a surprise bestseller?

Every season. I did not anticipate the success of *The Da Vinci Code* or *South Beach Diet*. The bestseller lists are not exclusively dominated by the familiar names—first-time authors or authors that never had a big success before can make it, too. Dan Brown published several books that never approached the popularity of *The Da Vinci Code*. You try to figure out what will be the next big seller, and it is difficult. It might be easy to predict that the next *Harry Potter* book will be a success. It's not as easy to have predicted Dan Brown's emergence.

The top of the bestseller list, the Author's Mount Olympus, is not a peaceful, sun-splashed park where you can snooze in a hammock all afternoon. It is a precarious place to which all those people you left behind on the way up are still climbing—they've read your most recent bestseller and think they can write something better. Publishers expect the sales of a new book by a bestselling author to exceed sales of all that author's previous books. The pressure builds.

SANDRA BROWN, Author

Sandra is a suspense novelist who began her career in 1981. Among her more than 50 *New York Times* bestsellers are *White Hot, Hello Darkness, The Crush, Envy,* and *The Switch*. This Texas native has 70 million copies of her books in print worldwide and is translated into 30 languages. In an earlier career, Sandra worked as a feature reporter for the nationally syndicated TV program *PM Magazine*.

Every one of your books since *Mirror Image* has made the list—do you feel pressure to continue making the list?

Oh absolutely, the competition is more intense. There are so many brand-name authors who have a loyal readership. When their books come out, their fans are eager to buy them. I know when scheduling a book to come out, I'm constantly looking to see, "Well, who is coming out that same week, what's the competition going to be?"

There's an implied competitiveness with myself as well. If I made number two on the list last year, then I'd like to make number one this year. If I was on the list for six weeks last year, I'd like to be on the list for eight weeks this year. You're always looking to ratchet it up if you can.

It's not only book sales. I also feel even more pressure to provide new and interesting stories to my readers. It would be a severe downfall for any author to start concentrating on strictly the market, on sales, on making the bestseller list. You expend a lot of energy and time that could otherwise go into your creative process.

I feel more pressure to tell a good story to my reader. There are some things I can't do anything about. I can't do anything about John Grisham, Tom Clancy, and Stephen King all coming out the same week I'm coming out. What I can do something about is write the best story I know how to write. That's what I really try and focus on.

NEIL NYREN, *Senior Vice President, Publisher, and Editor-in-Chief*
G. P. Putnam & Sons

So how does a book get to be a bestseller?

The main thing to remember is there is no one way to a bestseller. There are an infinite number of ways to get there—not to mention an infinite number of ways to fail. Sometimes a concentrated burst of publicity will do it, sometimes word of mouth, sometimes it's a slow build, sometimes great reviews. There are times when everything happens just the way you expect it to and other times when a book comes out of nowhere.

And we *love* that. It gives us all hope: that good books can become bestsellers purely because they're just good books.

Why are some books gobbled up by insatiable readers while others meet an ugly fate in the remainder bin? What makes a bestseller happen? Is the author subject to the whims of a capricious marketplace, or are there solid reasons for a book's success that can be replicated? Do bestselling authors approach the craft of writing and the marketing of their books differently than those who are perpetually on the outside looking in? Let's find out. We'll probably encounter a number of surprises along the way.

"Success comes to a writer, as a rule, so gradually that it is always something of a shock to him to look back and realize the heights to which he has climbed."

P. G. WODEHOUSE, *Louder and Funnier*

2

MAKING THE LIST
How They Work

AGAINST THE ODDS
A BRIEF HISTORY OF HOW THE BESTSELLER LIST BEGAN
HOW THE LISTS WORK

Bestsellers bring prestige, power, and—let's not forget—profits to their publishing houses. A house with a history of bestsellers has demonstrated that they are tuned in to what readers want to buy and have marketing savvy, industry connections, and a shrewd business sense. Authors know that these publishers have the financial capability to pay large advances, print runs in the hundreds of thousands, and the clout to get their titles in the chain stores.

HEIDE LANGE, *Literary Agent*
Sanford J. Greenburger Associates, Inc.

Are some publishers better at generating bestsellers?

I think what levels the playing field in this area—whether it's a big house whose imprints regularly appear on the lists or a small house that only occasionally appears—is when all members of a publisher's team work together to the best of their ability. It's not enough to have a fabulous book that is only prized by the acquiring editor. That editor, together with the active support of the agent, has to convince the rest of the house to play their roles as creatively and aggressively as possible.

When one or two departments drop the ball, especially if one of these is the publicity department, this could seriously affect the performance of a book. However, when everyone is committed to it and conveys that to important people outside the house—the "big mouths" in the industry, including other successful authors, key people in the bookselling community, and the media—then a strong book has the best chance of rising to the top. Of course, an experienced publishing house will better know how to read the early signs and be prepared to take all the appropriate steps in order to further build momentum. This may take the form of store placement, expanding an author's tour, and taking out ads—in other words, proceeding aggressively. The agent should be ensuring that all of this occurs.

AGAINST THE ODDS

The statistics regarding success in the publishing industry are daunting, and it's best that most aspiring writers pay them no mind. Otherwise, a lot of what we now hail as great literature would never have been attempted. Bowkers estimates that 175,000 new titles are now published annually. It is believed that less than 1 in 100 books that are submitted for publication actually end up in print; some experts place it at 1 in a 1,000 books.

It has been estimated that only 10 percent of books published ever end up selling enough copies to earn back the advance paid to the author. In other words, the author will never have the happy experience of finding a royalty check from a publisher in their mailbox. How many become bestsellers? Fewer than .3 percent. *Writers Digest* has said that 24 million people in the United States describe themselves as creative writers. Less than 5 percent of these writers have ever been published.

A notion is promulgated in a lot of those "How to Become a Fabulously Successful Author" books that, with enough grit, perseverance, and, of course, using the marketing techniques outlined in the book, anyone can become a bestselling author. Well, especially in fiction, the statistics reveal you can't. Most of the seats at that table already have reservation cards.

Let's look at the *Publishers Weekly* fiction bestseller list for a ten-week period. With 15 slots on the list, over ten weeks there are 150 positions available. Seemingly.

The truth is, over that time only 40 different books appeared on the list. Just 10 books occupied 48 percent of the available positions (72). Eighteen books took up nearly 70 percent of the positions.

The banner headline we have all seen in the bookstore, "21 Weeks on the Bestseller List!!!," translates into the list being dominated primarily by the same few most popular authors. To the author trying to get on the list, the other writer's 21-week streak of success just means 21 fewer spaces available for their own, perhaps equally wonderful book.

Another way of looking at these results is that, if 40 books made the list over a 10-week period, an average of 4 new books per week appeared on the list, or 208 for the entire year (in fiction). Truly, not many authors ever get to enjoy "the thrill" described in Chapter 1.

Considering the numbers of novels published each year—upwards of 17,000—a new author really only has a tiny chance to secure a spot, even position 15, on the list. But it does happen: eight first novels made the bestseller list in 2003, and eleven made it in 2002.

New per-title sales records were set in 2003: Dan Brown's *The Da Vinci Code* sold an unprecedented 5.7 million copies, and Rick Warren's *The Purpose-Driven Life* sold 11.3 million copies. According to *Publishers Weekly,* 30 hardcover fiction titles sold more than 400,000 copies in 2003. An additional 98 sold more than 100,000 copies. Twenty-four nonfiction hardcover titles sold more than 400,000 copies in 2003, and 100 additional titles sold at least 100,000 copies.

A big success in hardcover fiction now means one million copies, rather incredible when you consider many authors are ecstatic when their book's sales top 20,000. It really is a quantum leap from *author* to *bestseller.*

Here's a strange question: does being on the bestseller list cause a book's sales from then on to increase? Alan Sorensen, a Stanford business professor, examined hardcover fiction sales for 2001 and 2002 and came up with some interesting conclusions in his study, "Bestseller Lists and Product Variety: The Case of Book Sales." He found that appearing on the *New York Times* bestseller list did indeed thereafter increase a book's first-year sales, but previously bestselling authors got the least boost from appearing on the list, while "new" or unknown authors got as much as a 57 percent jump in sales. For new authors, the list helps to advertise them to the book-buying public, Sorensen concluded. With favorite authors, such as Nora Roberts, her fans do not need to look at the bestseller list to make a decision about buying her new book.

A BRIEF HISTORY OF HOW
THE BESTSELLER LIST BEGAN

The bestseller list originated in 1895 in a publication called *The Bookman*. This list contained fiction titles only. *Publishers Weekly* began a nonfiction list in 1912, then added its own fiction list a year later, and *The New York Times Book Review* list, often referred to simply as the *New York Times* bestseller list, began to appear on a weekly basis in 1942.

How to Live on 24 Hours a Day, by Arnold Bennett, sounds like a great new time-management book for the ultraharried person of the 21st century. It was also useful in 1912, when it was published. Reviewing the lists from past decades, going back to the turn of the 20th century, you make a startling discovery—not much has really changed in terms of the types of books that make it to the top: adventure, romance, history, politics, culture, celebrities, and self-improvement.

Even the public's appetite for books by show business stars is nothing new. Appearing sixth on the nonfiction list for the year 1917 was *Laugh and Live*, by early film star Douglas Fairbanks.

Studying the historical bestseller lists, you also see that authors from the past, to whom many of the literature classes we took in high school and college were dedicated, did not necessarily appear on any lists, at least while they were alive and could still spend the royalties. Those after-death royalties seem somehow unsatisfying.

The five corporations that currently dominate the bestseller lists are Random House, Inc., Penguin USA, Simon & Schuster, Time Warner, and HarperCollins in that order. It is estimated that these five companies accounted for 75 percent of the hardcover bestselling titles for 2003 and about 72 percent of the hardcover bestsellers in 2002. Paperback bestsellers emerged from these same five houses in roughly the same proportions.

NEIL NYREN, *Senior Vice President, Publisher, and Editor-in-Chief*
G. P. Putnam & Sons

How important are bestsellers to the overall profitability of a publishing house?

It depends upon what that publishing house does. There are lots and lots of publishers who have never published a bestseller in their life, because that's not what they're trying to do. They're trying to produce a steady income. They're working on backlist books which will sell year after year after year.

That's a wiser procedure for a lot of publishers to do, because a bestseller tends to be a very front list-oriented thing. You go out, you have a big burst of sales, and then the book falls off the list, until it comes out in paperback. That's the end of it. In order to be successful you have to keep feeding the front list, and so you're always looking for new books. It's tough.

There are publishers who make an extremely good living out of producing books that will sell each and every year.

Putnam is known for its bestseller success. We tend to publish about 85 to 90 books a year, and in 2003, we placed 31 titles on the *New York Times* bestseller list, which is great. That's over a third—but that also means close to *two*-thirds of the titles we published were not *New York Times* bestsellers. There were a few of them in there that we would have liked to have been, but didn't make it, but most of them were books we knew going in were not going to be bestsellers. They were authors we were trying to build, or books with a certain market, or books that had a different sales pattern, or books that we hoped would turn out to be good backlist sellers.

A bestseller is an important part of what we do as a house and a lot of what the big houses do, but it's only a piece of what the business is about.

In nonfiction, the bestseller list is a strange neighborhood. You never know who's going to move in. Fiction writers seem to endure, appearing on the list repeatedly, even for decades, but nonfiction authors move in and out, as making those lists relies more on having a "hot topic" rather than the brand name or popularity of the author.

Gloom-and-doom books about how to cope with the end of the world appear right on cue whenever the economy worsens, but self-improvement books sit side by side with them on the bestseller list. It as though readers are thinking, "While we're waiting for the end of the world, we can at least get in better shape." Publishers tend to be behind the curve about what's happening with the economy or world affairs. By the time they get around to releasing the gloom-and-doom books, the economy has already turned, and people have gone back to being optimistic.

Consider some of the titles of bestsellers from the late '70s and early '80s.

- *Crisis Investing: Opportunities and Profits in the Coming Great Depression*
- *The Coming Currency Collapse and What to Do about It*
- *How to Prosper during the Coming Bad Years*

The authors of these books certainly prospered despite the fatal flaws in their prognostications. The 1980s are now fondly remembered as a decade of tremendous economic growth and prosperity.

Another durable trend on the bestseller list is that down the decades, though good times and bad, Americans have always sought help for their golf game.

HOW THE LISTS WORK

The recognized national bestseller lists include *The New York Times, Publishers Weekly, USA Today,* and *Book Sense.* Additionally, there are regional bestseller lists such as the *San Francisco Chronicle* and *LA Times,* chain store lists such as Barnes and Noble, and bestseller lists by genre. Then, of course, there is the bestseller list at Amazon.com.

TOBY USNIK, *Director of Public Relations*
The New York Times Company

How is the *New York Times* bestseller list compiled?

The New York Times compiles its rankings by polling many hundreds of independent booksellers nationwide (representative of about 2,000 general interest bookselling locations around the country), selected because they are willing and able to report actual unit sales on hundreds of titles week-in and week-out on a confidential basis. In addition, our panel includes about 40 wholesalers who supply books to nonbookstores (airports, hotel and hospital gift shops, grocery stores, consumer co-ops, Target, Wal-Mart, and the like). And then, of course, we poll the regional and national chains.

We also interview scores of significant online e-tailers. We are interested only in general interest outlets, where customers have equal opportunities to select from a broad range of titles, and, stated in another way, we do not poll specialty shops, as this would bias our results.

Thus, thousands of actual selling locations are interviewed by phone each week by our staff.

After the locations report their sales, what happens to the data?

All the unit sales are keypunched and run against a statistical model that tells us the weekly sales, ranks the titles for nine lists (six adult lists and three children's lists), and produces in-depth analysis (i.e., separate lists for the chains and independents, as well as regional rankings and other customized analyses). A master file carries a background description of each store, so that if any sales look peculiar, the system flags them for another interview to find out if there was any mistake or some special circumstance that we need to tell readers about. (Many business or religious books, for example, benefit from huge bulk sales, so we tell readers that with a dagger symbol after the description of the book in the published listings.) A typical large store could easily spend about seven to eight hours a week preparing our reports on a voluntary, unpaid basis, as we ask for sales on hundreds of titles in many categories in order to rank with breadth and depth. A few years ago, we began ranking as deep as 35 positions for our Web site, where we publish the expanded bestseller lists. So that is a lot of numbers each store produces for this weekly miracle.

Can you translate the rankings on the bestseller list into sales for each title?

The number of sales for any title is confidential. You can imagine why: Were we to reveal the sales magnitudes, there would be no end to the number of manipulations the lists would be subjected to by overzealous publishers, agents, and the authors themselves, scrambling to buy up their own books in order to attain a false ranking. So the only way we can really maintain the integrity of the lists is to never reveal the sales thresholds needed to step on.

So the sales necessary to qualify for a position on the list can vary?

Indeed, there really is no magic number for number 1 or number 15, for example. It is all relative to the sales that week for all other titles, in comparison to one another. Naturally, there are tremendous seasonal variations. For example, it takes a lot more sales to break onto the hardcover lists during the fall than it does during the summer. The fall is when people are buying gift hardcovers. It is harder to make the paperback lists in the summer, when people are buying vacation titles. And it is easier to get a low ranking on the hardcover fiction list, for example, if everyone is buying the number-one selling Stephen King or Danielle Steel: there are so many fewer sales down below that top spot. Without compromising any internal information, I can tell you that a wildly popular book, like the *Harry Potters,* for example, or a new John Grisham, could easily account for a quarter of a million sales in its first week in the stores.

The only way you can find out the sales rank of a specific title would be to contact the publisher. They may or may not choose to tell you— and, in fact, they may not know, as shipments may be the best number they have on hand, and this does not account for returns down the road. It may be helpful, for example, to contact Barnes and Noble headquarters or Borders, for example, and ask them for their own figures for their chains alone. That would give you a slice of information you seek. But they, too, are reluctant to share information publicly, for competitive reasons.

Publishers Weekly (http://www.publishersweekly.com) is devoted to trends and news in the publishing industry and book reviews. Each issue has several bestseller lists: fiction and nonfiction hardcover bestseller lists, trade paperback, and mass paperback bestseller lists. They also track the children's bestsellers and, on occasion, categories such as cookbooks, religion, or audio books. *PW* surveys selected bookstores, both chain stores and independents, as well as other retail sites, then uses a formula to weigh the responses and determine the bestsellers.

MITCHELL KAPLAN, *Owner*
Books and Books, Inc., Coral Gables, Florida

Are some publishers better at turning out bestsellers than others?

Some houses focus primarily on that, like Dutton and Putnam. There are some houses that are great at creating bestsellers where there were none, like Knopf has a terrific eye for spinning a book into a bestseller.

Nielsen BookScan, while not a bestseller list, does track book sales. Information is captured at the point of sale, the cash register, from about 4,500 retailers—that's about 60 percent to 75 percent of the relevant retail outlets in the industry. Wal-Mart and several supermarket chains do not report. The data can be ranked by quite a few categories and is used by publishers and distributors. Currently, the data is not available to the public but by subscription only.

MICHAEL CADER, *Publisher,*
PublishersMarketPlace.com and Cader Books

How would you say the bestseller list (whether NY *Times, PW,* or USA *Today*) has changed?

There are two kinds of bestsellers lists. The fake ones—pretty much all the lists produced by newspapers and magazines, which are not representative of the business as a whole and/or involve as much art as science—and the closest thing we have to a real one, the BookScan list (never seen by the public), which tracks actual sales. Even that only captures some sales at this point.

Overall, most lists are moving towards more of a real point-of-sale basis except, ironically, for the most followed list of all, the *New York Times* list. More and more, that list has been engineered to have less to do with the books that are actually selling the most, and its statistical accuracy has fallen in comparison to many other major lists.

Book Sense is an association of independent bookstores, those not affiliated with the major chains. They now compile their own bestseller list based on sales data from participating stores. A book receives the same point value from each store regardless of how many copies sold per store. They also publish a "recommended" list, the reviews coming from the booksellers themselves. This list includes many titles that are not bestsellers but are, in the booksellers' opinions, titles that deserve recognition. Their monthly recommendations can be seen at http://www.booksense.com.

MEG SMITH, Associate Director
Book Sense Marketing

How does the Book Sense bestseller list work?

The Book Sense bestseller lists are compiled from sales data reported by independent bookstores participating in the Book Sense national marketing campaign. An average of 475 stores nationwide report weekly, via either Nielsen BookScan or one of two American Booksellers Association developed methods. The sales data is weighted so that all stores, regardless of size, specialty, or number of units sold, equally influence the ranking of the books. The number-one selling book in every store receives the same point value, regardless of the actual number of units sold, and these point values are then combined to determine the final ranking. The same is true for the number-two selling book, and so forth.

Information is compiled on a weekly basis. Stores submit their data by 3:00 AM Eastern time each Tuesday morning. We then generate seven national bestseller lists: hardcover fiction, hardcover nonfiction, trade paperback fiction, trade paperback nonfiction, mass market, children's fiction, and children's illustrated. These lists are distributed to stores, publishers, and media outlets via e-mail by noon on Tuesday, and then officially published on our trade Web site, BookWeb.org.

How does your list differ from the *New York Times* list and the *Publishers Weekly* bestseller lists?

The Book Sense lists are immediate, accurate, and a pure reflection of the independent sector.

Book Sense lists are the "freshest" lists of the three. They are based on sales data from the week ended just two days prior to their creation.

Both *PW* and *NYT* publish their lists one or two weeks after the sales period the list represents.

The Book Sense lists are based solely on units sold in the independent stores. We do not include double sales of the same book; i.e., once at the wholesaler and once at the bookstore. They are a reliable indicator of real sales in independent stores.

The Book Sense lists naturally reflect the tastes and buying habits of the customer of the independent bookstore as well as the passion of the independent bookseller. The bestseller list is influenced by another Book Sense list, the Book Sense Picks (formerly the Book Sense 76), a monthly compendium of titles recommended and enthusiastically hand sold by the booksellers. Book Sense Picks can become a sort of grass roots marketing buzz for a title. Many Picks debut on the Book Sense bestseller list and migrate to other lists weeks later. Dan Brown's *The Da Vinci Code* (Doubleday) and Alice Sebold's *The Lovely Bones* (Little Brown) are two recent examples. Other Picks may appear primarily, but consistently, on the Book Sense bestseller list. *Book Lust,* by Nancy Pearl (Sasquatch), is one example of that phenomenon.

Incidentally, Book Sense also prepares lists for the various regional independent bookseller associations based on sales data reported by their members. We also prepare specialty lists (e.g., business, cooking, sports) and provide customized lists for several print outlets.

How can a publisher influence the Book Sense list?

Publishers influence any list only through their marketing and sales efforts.

Publishers speak to booksellers all the time about their books, through galleys, (prepublication review copies), our monthly White Box mailings [new titles sent to the stores by the publishers], personal and phone rep conversations, the convention, and forums, etc. Some publishers will focus certain of their titles for marketing efforts aimed at the bookseller nominating a book for the Book Sense Picks list. Booksellers take to certain titles because of what their sales reps tell them, or whether they like the subject matter or think their customers will, or because other booksellers are jazzed about it. If the booksellers are interested, they will communicate their passion and recommendations to their customers, and bestsellers may result.

RICHARD CURTIS, *Literary Agent*
The Curtis Agency

To what extent can a publishing house cause a bestseller to happen?

Amusingly, the only time publishers make silk purses out of sows' ears is when they're not trying and a sleeper book surprises everyone. Otherwise, a book has to have a lot of bestselling qualities in order to qualify for bestseller candidacy, such as a great author track record, heavy expenditure on advertising and marketing, a lot of media attention, timeliness, a high concept, and a handsome package. Notice I haven't said the book has to be well written. And that's the pity of the bestseller list.

3

WHAT CAUSES A BOOK
TO BECOME SUCCESSFUL?

THE MOST IMPORTANT FACTORS
PREVIOUS SUCCESS IS THE KEY INDICATOR OF FUTURE SUCCESS
LISTENING TO THE MARKETPLACE

THE MOST IMPORTANT FACTORS

As part of the research for this book, the authors surveyed over 100 editors and agents in mid-2004. Participants in our "Editors and Agents Survey" included editors at major publishing houses, university presses, and small presses, as well as agents from both small and large literary agencies. The survey was conducted by e-mail and fax. Among the questions was: "What are the most important factors in a book's success? Please select the five factors (and only five) that you think are most important and rank them from one (most important) to five (least important)."

PREVIOUS SUCCESS IS THE KEY
INDICATOR OF FUTURE SUCCESS

Looking at the average scores in Figure 3.1, "Factors in a Book's Success," agents and editors are in agreement that the fan base, whether the author's previous book was a bestseller, and the quality of writing are the keys to success. Agents attribute more of the success to the book getting good word-of-mouth promotion than editors do. Editors think

FIGURE 3.1 *Factors in a Book's Success*

	Editors		Agents
Average Score	**Factor**	**Average Score**	**Factor**
2.3	Timeliness of topic	2.2	Previous book a bestseller
2.4	Quality of writing	2.6	Word of mouth
2.7	Previous book a bestseller	2.8	Reader or fan base
2.8	Reader or fan base	2.9	Quality of writing
3.0	Author's promotional efforts	3.1	Timeliness of topic
3.0	Word of mouth	3.2	Advertising program
3.4	Reviews	3.3	Publicity
3.5	Publicity	3.3	Size of advance
4.1	Advertising program	3.3	Author's promotional efforts
4.3	Size of advance	3.8	Reviews

the timeliness of the topic is more important than agents do, although a significant number of agents (11 percent) also gave that a number-one ranking.

Agents and editors both discounted the importance of reviews to sparking sales of a book, agents ranking it last in importance and editors fourth from the last. This contradicts the advice given to "new" authors that getting their books reviewed is critical. These results could also indicate that as an author becomes more successful, has built a fan base, and has had previous bestsellers, reviews decline in importance.

The lowest score given by either group was by the editors for "size of the advance paid." Those outside the publishing industry often believe that, the higher the advance paid, the more promotional resources the publishing house will put behind the book (to make certain they recoup the advance).

For writers yet to produce a bestseller or establish a significant fan base, comfort can be taken in that both agents and editors rank quality of writing in the top four factors. Great writing wins out. Discomfort can be felt, however, in realizing that no hard and fast criteria exist about what constitutes "great writing." It comes down to subjective judgments made by individuals. We might think of the road to bestsellerdom as this immensely long conveyor belt, with hundreds of thousands of manuscripts being fed on the belt at one end and great financial success coming out the other end. Along the winding course, many pairs of hands make decisions about whether to take a manuscript off and toss it in a dark corner along with all the other failed books.

HEIDE LANGE, *Literary Agent*
Sanford J. Greenburger Associates, Inc.

Do you know when first reading a manuscript that it has bestseller potential?

It's when your own pulse quickens that you know—and hope—that a book will work. It's when you're so excited that you can't stop talking about it, to everyone, first to yourself, then of course to the author, your agency colleagues, and from there on out to editors, foreign scouts, and film scouts. This is what we're looking for. Whether we're agents or readers, we're always looking to be seduced by the next great book, whether it comes from a current client or a new writer.

LISTENING TO THE MARKETPLACE

The pairs of hands that really matter are those browsing the shelves of the bookstores, pulling out new titles and reading the back covers or even sampling the first few paragraphs to get a feel for the author's style. Think of how many books the average shopper looks at before making a selection. Then think about the vast choice from which they can select. Each time someone decides to buy your book, they are conferring an honor on you.

Publishing industry executives have the daunting task of determining what the consumer in Biloxi, Des Moines, or San Jose really wants to read.

JENNIFER ENDERLIN, *Publisher*
St. Martin's Press

How does an editor get a feel for what will work in the marketplace and what will not?

I see an editor's job as being a universal reader. What I try to do is envision myself in the place of the consumer. I ask myself, "Would I plunk down my money for this book?" You don't buy a book because you say, well, I don't like this book, but I think it will sell. As an editor, you buy it because you personally connect with the book; you can envision yourself going into a store and spending your hard-earned money on it.

What makes certain authors and certain books resonate with readers?

It all begins with a strong voice. Voice is the one thing that can't be taught. It's the author's own fingerprint, their unique storytelling style. Writers with a strong voice are the ones that emerge from the pack. Then you must have memorable characters. When people recommend their books to their friends, they talk about the characters first and foremost. They don't realize they are responding to the voice, too.

NEIL NYREN, *Senior Vice President, Publisher, and Editor-in-Chief*
G. P. Putnam & Sons

How does an editor get a feel for what books will work in the marketplace and what won't?

It's experience. If you've been in this field for a while, you know what people are reading, or you think you know what people are reading. I cast myself as a typical reader, and I buy to my own tastes, so if something works for me, I think it will work for other readers.

I try to read as much as possible. I don't read everything on the bestseller list, but I try and keep pace with what's working out there and what isn't.

What qualities do you look for in a book that you think is going to do very well?

If it's fiction, you look for a vision that's fresh; the book should be compelling and fully realized. You want it to give you something new, or something old but incredibly well done.

Nonfiction has to be based on an idea that is solid and new. The execution has to be well done. The combination of those things with the credentials of the author—then you begin to have something.

Have you ever gotten a manuscript from an unknown author that you were sure was going to be very successful?

Absolutely. There is no such thing as an absolute sure thing anymore in this business. But there have certainly been lots of times when you see something and say, "Now this, this is commercial, this ought to work." Obviously, Doubleday thought that when they signed up John Grisham.

We're all very happy when our big authors continue to do well, and we work hard to find ways to make them do even better, but most of us got into the publishing business originally for the thrill of discovery. You never know when the next submission that crosses your desk is going to be something special. And it happens. Many years ago, when I read the first *Prey* manuscript by John Sandford, I knew instantly that this guy had *it*. The book was thoroughly commercial but also extremely well written, with a great central character. There was absolutely no reason why this writer couldn't become a bestseller. The first book made the list in paperback; a couple books later, he started hitting the hardcover list as well, and now he's a number-one bestseller.

There are some writers who just have it. Many, many years ago, in a galaxy far, far away, when I was a younger editor for a different publisher, I read a manuscript called *Storm Island*. It was a World War II thriller, and it, too, just had a sure command to it. There was something about it. We wanted a more distinctive title and changed it to *Eye of the Needle* (Ken Follett), and there you are. That's what you're always looking for, what you're always hoping for.

Every editor in my position has had those experiences. And also those experiences when we were sure of it—and—it didn't work.

All literary success starts the same way, with one individual in a position of power in the publishing industry—agent, editor—reacting in an unusually positive way to a manuscript. Success may seem too much a matter of sheer luck, dependent on an author's work finding its way to just the right person who makes the very subjective judgment that it is marketable, but that's the way the industry works. Of course, when starting out, the new author has no idea who this special person might be that can turn their manuscript into a marketplace success. Somehow, the writers who achieve bestseller status manage to find them.

An unpleasant corollary to consider is the number of wonderful manuscripts that are gathering dust on closet shelves and in garages because their authors never found that impassioned advocate in the marketplace.

MARGRET MCBRIDE, *Literary Agent*
McBride Literary Agency

When you get a potential new client and you see the book proposal or the manuscript, how can you tell whether it has bestseller potential or not?

Sometimes I get chills down my spine and my stomach does these flip-flop things, or it makes me get up and walk around. It gets me excited. Sometimes I feel like singing, crying, and laughing all at the same time. It's a very visceral reaction. Thank goodness for the people who work at the agency with me, because I do most of my reading at home. And when I hear my colleagues yelp or laugh out loud—and everyone else leaps up—that says, "I think we have a winner!" It's very exiting finding a fabulous book.

MATT BIALER, *Literary Agent*
Sanford J. Greenburger & Associates

When you start reading a manuscript, can you tell it may have bestseller qualities?

I don't know if I sit there and say, "This is a bestseller." I may think to myself that this book has enormous potential. I've never gotten a book sent to me, particularly over the transom, and thought it was ready to go right there. Fiction usually needs some kind of work. Commercial fiction especially does, because there are a lot of different kinds of people writing commercial fiction, and they don't usually come out of writing schools or university programs. They are writing in a bit of a vacuum. Which is great, I like that, because they are coming to their writing career with a set of life experiences most of us haven't seen before. That vacuum they have been working in can be a very positive thing. It often means, though, there is raw talent and the book needs shaping.

I am thinking, then, this author has the potential to be a bestseller, not necessarily that book.

KAREN KOSZTOLNYIK, *Senior Editor*
Warner Books

When you get that wonderful manuscript from a new author that really excites you, what about the work stands out?

It really comes down to the voice. If an author has a really strong voice, even if they are telling a story that has been told a million times before, it can draw me in to that story. The voice is so fresh, new, original, I feel like I'm reading the story for the first time, even if it's a classic story line.

It can also come down to a high concept. The *hook*. When you are pitching to the editorial committee and sales force, you want to have your book stand out. If I can pitch the story in one or two sentences and capture their imagination immediately, that's high concept. They have so many books coming at them all the time.

A book can grab you from the first page. Karen Rose's amazing opening for her first book, *Don't Tell,* got me immediately. A woman is in a hospital bed, injured, and hears her husband talking to a nurse. He tells the nurse he has to speak to his wife. When he gets to her bedside he says how sorry he is, that he can't believe this happened to her. Then he leans in closer and says, "Next time I'll finish the job."

Karen Rose captured your interest right away. You get the hook immediately. *Bridges of Madison County* and *The Notebook* were two of our biggest bestsellers. It came down to concept and voice working together. Even with these strong elements, you can't be sure that something is an "absolutely guaranteed bestseller." You just have to trust your gut that this is something that is going to work in the marketplace.

DR. SPENCER JOHNSON, Author

Dr. Johnson is the author or coauthor of many *New York Times* best-sellers, including three number-one titles: *Who Moved My Cheese?: An A-Mazing Way to Deal with Change in Your Work and Life; The One-Minute Manager,* the world's most popular management method, coauthored with Kenneth Blanchard; and, most recently, *The Present: The Gift That Makes You Happier and More Successful, Today!* Dr. Johnson's books are available in more than 40 languages. *Who Moved My Cheese* was a true word-of-mouth sensation; its simple story of how to deal with change resonated with millions of people dealing with the stresses and uncertainty of corporate downsizing. It remained a *New York Times* bestseller for over two years—and Dr. Johnson has remained a bestselling author for over two decades.

Why do certain books succeed in the marketplace while others don't?

I believe there are three reasons a book succeeds: the book, the book, and the book. It's not because of a marketing program, which typically lasts at most 90 days, or reviews, or agents, or all the other things young writers think is important.

I remember being at Doubleday and being told a forthcoming book would be a number-one bestseller. When I asked how they knew in advance what would happen, they said because almost everybody in the publishing house who read the manuscript loved it so much that they asked for additional manuscript copies to give to their friends to read because they didn't want to wait until it was published. That's when you know a book is going to be big.

If you write a great book, one that readers think is so good they can't wait to share it with their friends, it will eventually lead to commercial success. It may not be considered a literary giant, but if it touches people so much that they either buy copies for their friends or pick up the phone and tell their friends about it, the book will succeed. That book is going to make the bestseller list more often than a book that publishers think is great, and they spend $250,000 on advertising and printing huge number of copies, but it doesn't ever catch on.

HARLAN COBEN, *Author*

Mystery/thriller writer Harlan Coben is an international bestselling author who has won the Mystery Writers of America's Edgar Award, the Private Eye Writers of America's Shamus Award, and the Anthony award—he's the first author to win all three. His first novels were about the exploits of sports agent Myron Bolitar. His latest novels are "suburban thrillers" about everyday people in extraordinary circumstances. His recent novels include *Just One Look, No Second Chance, Tell No One,* and *Gone for Good.* Harlan has a large international audience for his books. *Just One Look* reached both the *New York Times* and *Sunday London Times* bestseller lists. Readers applaud the fast-paced suspense, great storytelling, and wonderful sense of humor in his writing.

What factors caused your first big success?

If anyone knew this answer to this question, they'd be a billionaire ten times over. I'm sure you will hear about big promotional pushes or whatever, but the simple fact is, I've never seen a book truly break out without word of mouth. What causes word of mouth? Well, I'm going to go out on a limb and say it's the book itself—enjoying it so much that you tell your friends.

How do popular authors contribute to the success of their books, apart from writing the best book they can?

I'm not sure they can. There, I said it. I did the whole dog 'n' pony stuff early in my career, went to conferences, met booksellers, handed out bookmarks. Guess what? So does every other author I know. I'm not sure it works. In the United Kingdom and France, I didn't do any of that—never went to a conference, met a bookseller, etc.—and my books sell (relatively speaking) even better over there. So what does that mean? I don't know.

The only way I've truly seen a new author start to make some serious headway is by the buzz that usually comes with word of mouth.

LAURELL K. HAMILTON, *Author*

Laurell writes fantasy/horror/romance. Her first book, *Guilty Pleasures,* hit the bestseller lists in 1994. She has written nine additional Anita Blake books and, in October 2000, began the *New York Times* bestselling Meredith Gentry series for Ballantine Books. Her fascination with things that go bump in the night was fostered by her grandmother's storytelling.

What have been the most important factors in your books' success?

If I could truly answer that question, I'd make millions of dollars advising the publishing industry.

I did everything wrong. If I had set out to write a *New York Times* bestseller, I certainly never would have had mixed genres. When I first started to try and sell *Guilty Pleasures* 11 years ago, it was turned down by everyone. Mystery houses turned it down because it was science fiction. The science fiction houses thought it was horror, the horror publishers turned it down because it wasn't scary enough, because the vampires were out of the closet. The very things that made the series successful later on were the things that made it almost never sell. I was told that mixing genres was the death knell. It was a vampire novel, when vampire novels had peaked. If I had tried to write a *New York Times* bestseller, *Guilty Pleasures* wouldn't have been it.

I believe that you can't sit down and say, "I'm going to write a *New York Times* bestseller." If you have that in mind while you write, the book will read like plastic. You have to write what you want to read; you have to write what moves you. Everyone has their own special vision and voice, and once you find it, then that's what you write. I'm lucky in that what I want to write, a lot of people out there want to read as well.

I studied mystery series. It's much more difficult to find a fantasy series that has gone on much past ten books. It's easier to find a mystery series. What I found was that somewhere between book five and eight, the author usually gets tired, and it begins to show. They got bored, especially if it was a straight mystery series. I thought about what would make me bored, so I gave myself all my favorite toys. I gave myself monsters, guns, a main female character that was as tough as the men or tougher. I gave myself all the things that would keep my interest, and it worked because I'm still having a wonderful time.

I couldn't have foreseen that the *Anita* series or the *Merry* series would be as popular as they are.

4

REVIEWS

The Good, the Bad, the Ugly

THE IMPACT OF REVIEWS

HOW BOOKS ARE CHOSEN TO BE REVIEWED

NOW EVERYONE'S A CRITIC

A LAST LOOK FROM INDUSTRY PROFESSIONALS

THE IMPACT OF REVIEWS

Book reviews have an impact on book sales, if for no other reason than a review increases a title's visibility. Reviews don't cost the publisher anything except the copy of the book or galley and postage to send it to the reviewer.

Reviews in industry-related publications such as *Publishers Weekly*, *Kirkus Reviews*, and *BookList* are directed toward booksellers and librarians.

Publishers Weekly, established in 1873, is published every week both in hard copy format and online and is available by subscription. Seventy-five hundred books, audio books, and e-books are reviewed annually. Reviews appear a month or so prior to publication dates. The publication is considered the leader for the publishing industry.

Kirkus Reviews began publication in 1933 and is published every two weeks. *Kirkus* receives nearly 200 titles to review each day and selects fewer than 10 percent, or about 5,000 per year, to review. The reviews are published two to three months before the title's publication date and are available in hard copy and online by paid subscription. *Kirkus Reviews* is used by booksellers, librarians, publishers, and agents.

Booklist magazine is published by the American Library Association and includes reviews to help librarians select newly released titles for their collections. *Booklist* reviews nearly 7,000 titles per year from the 60,000 they receive. The reviews appear prior to publication.

Even though these reviews are for the book trade, they do influence the consumer-oriented publications as well. If the book is important enough to be reviewed in, say, *Kirkus Reviews,* the book editor at a major metro newspaper may feel it's important enough for the newspaper.

Authors sometimes make the mistake of saying, "My book is getting great reviews! Now I can relax. I'm going to sell tons of copies!" Not so fast, there. *Where* you get the review can be as important as the number of reviews you get. The publishing industry has certain opinion-leading publications to which nearly everyone in the industry pays close attention.

DANIEL HALPERN, *Editor-in-Chief*
HarperCollins

How important are reviews?

They can be very important—a great daily *New York Times* and a great *Sunday Times* book review can make a great difference. Big reviews like these tend to echo through the country. Obviously, a bad *Sunday Times* book review is our second favorite.

One of my happiest publishing experiences and great successes from beginning to end was doing the new *Don Quixote,* which I predict will come close to selling six figures in hard cover. The first review was in the *New York Times* by Carlos Fuentes, and it was one of the most intelligent essays that newspaper has run in the last five years; it addressed issues of translation and the importance of *Don Quixote.* The review was beautifully written and by a very important writer. That set the book up and made for many other long, serious reviews. *The New Yorker* did an amazing review, too—pages long. Those two reviews really helped sell that book. The *L.A. Times* also did a good review, and *Publishers Weekly* gave it a starred review. When it all comes together like that, reviews make a very big difference.

For an average book, how many galleys are usually sent out?

It varies a lot, from 100 to 500, unless you're doing something huge. Galleys are sent out by publicity, marketing, and editorial. We send copies for blurbs. For Nell Freudenberger, I sent galleys to reviewers whom I knew and let them know that this book was really important to me, to please take it seriously. And I called a lot of independent booksellers whom I know and asked them to think about hand selling this book.

JONATHAN GALASSI, *President and Publisher*
Farrar, Straus, & Giroux, LLC

Has the importance of reviews lessened in recent years?

Reviews are extremely important to the success of the kinds of books we publish here at FSG. Unfortunately, it's true that reviews are being squeezed out of many print media as they get "dumbed down," so publishers are having to turn to other ways—including the Internet—of trying to reach the readers who want and need their books. The Internet is very effective in reaching dedicated readers; i.e., people who know what they're looking for. It's more difficult to connect with people who don't really know what they want but are surfing or browsing.

GENE TAFT, *Vice President and Director of Publicity*
PublicAffairs

The true impact of reviews on book sales seems difficult to measure.

Authors sometimes think a review comes out and everyone runs to the store to buy their book. Suppose you hear the author being interviewed while you're driving to work in the morning and you say to yourself, "I gotta get that book." Then you get to work and there are all these crises that happen, and by the end of the day you have completely forgotten about the interview. Authors tend to be fascinated by TV, but if you think about it, TV is the least permanent of the media. On radio, you tend to be interviewed longer than on TV. Print media, magazines, may sit around for a week or so in someone's office or home, and they come back to the magazine over and over. With TV interviews, the viewer sneezes and may miss the title of the book.

But reviews in certain key publications, such as the *New York Times Book Review,* are important. *The New York Times* is still regarded as the review of record. I could mail out 500 review copies of a new book to reviewers around the country. But it's not until the *Times* reviews the book that the reviews start appearing elsewhere. This is not coincidence. Book review editors from other newspapers have significantly fewer column inches devoted to reviews than the *New York Times* does. So these other reviewers are waiting for someone to tell them, "This is an important book." Other reviewers seem to say, "If the *Times* reviews it, I should too."

A successful campaign is all about creating multiple impressions. One interview or one review doesn't do it to launch a book. Each one is a piece of the puzzle—magazines, National Public Radio, TV, newspapers. Only the most serious readers, and there aren't that many of them, would react to just one review and say, "I have to get that book." It's not until the consumer has heard about the book or the author four to five times that they remember it.

The New York Times is probably the most influential consumer-oriented book review publication, but there are several others: *The New Yorker, The New York Review of Books, New York Observer, New York Magazine* (do you see a geographic trend here?). *USA Today* provides book reviews as does the *Wall Street Journal, Los Angeles Times, Boston Globe, Philadelphia Inquirer, San Francisco Chronicle,* and the *Washington Post* to name a few. There are also a myriad of online sites such as Salon.com, Book reporter.com, CNN.com, and Myshelf.com. Magazines such as *Harpers, People, Time Magazine,* and *Business Week* regularly publish book reviews. Also, genre-oriented publications provide reviews such as *Locus* magazine for science fiction, *Romantic Times* for romance, and *Ellery Queen Mystery Magazine* for mysteries.

HOW BOOKS ARE CHOSEN TO BE REVIEWED

With literally hundreds of possibilities for a book to be reviewed, why do so few books end up with those 250 to 500 words of praise? About half the books being circulated don't qualify for a review; they are self-published or from a print-on-demand (POD) publisher, and many reviewers won't consider them. Why waste a review on a book that won't get national distribution or be in bookstores?

Unfortunately, many publications have significantly decreased the amount of space allocated to book reviews, cutting into the number of books reviewed. Sam Tanenhaus, editor of the *New York Times Book Review,* hopes to buck that trend by expanding the book review section at the *Times* to include more books and "a fuller picture of the literary scene."

SAM TANENHAUS, *Editor*
New York Times Book Review

What sets the *New York Times Book Review* apart from other major review publications?

We are the only one, that I'm aware of, that actually has a full-time staff that reads galleys as they are submitted. We examine the books; we look at them before we assign them for review. That's a huge distinction. We are not simply a conveyer belt. We are forming some impression of the books as they come in. Initially, to decide which we ought to review and then, just as crucially, who we think will review a particular book effectively. That doesn't mean the reviewer will like the book, or dislike it. But if it's a nonfiction book, the reviewer will meet the arguments presented honestly and candidly. If it's fiction, they'll begin with at least some sympathy with what the author is trying to do. That doesn't mean the reviewer will agree or approve or be moved by the results, but at least they won't go in with some kind of prejudice. It's also an exercise in fallibility. We're often mistaken in our judgments and sometimes don't agree with our own reviewers, but they can say what they think. Our job is to be sure the reviewers are being as true to the book as we can make them.

Five hundred books come in a week. Some books are automatically not going to be reviewed because they are not meant for a general audience, but often they're sent in anyway. Nothing is really excluded; some books just have a better chance than others. We don't usually do highly technical books; we tend not to review how-to or advice books. We have to make a judgment as journalists about which books are newsworthy. That's where we begin. Publishers sometimes forget that, first and foremost, we are journalists; we are reporting on books, not in the sense that we are announcing the arrival of them but that we are trying to alert our readers to what we think are the books they ought to know about.

There has been some discussion that the *New York Times Book Review* doesn't review certain genres. Is that true?

No, it's not. We are trying to expand our coverage of commercial fiction for one, because there is a very large audience for it, and it's a mistake to bypass a whole large segment of the literary world on the assumption that books written simply to entertain don't offer some news that our readers should know about. We pay close attention to mysteries, and we're going to expand our coverage of thrillers as well.

What advice would you give a small press that would help them get their books reviewed by the *New York Times Book Review*?

Publish the best material you can.

Here's something that surprises people every time. The assumption is that, if a book comes in from Knopf; Random House; or Farrar, Straus, & Giroux, it gets preference over other books. Many people think that. Yet, when we are having our discussions about the books to review, I will often ask who the publisher is, and almost every single time, we have to look at the spine of the book to see who it is.

We're not paying any attention to that. Remember, we see the books as galleys, and all the galleys look alike. That's also why I tell publishers not to worry about original paperback books; as a galley they look like any other book. We're not seeing blurbs or fancy jackets or cover artwork; we're just working from the text in the galley.

Now it's often the case, I suppose, that writers are published by smaller presses because larger presses have passed on the work they've done. Naturally, most authors prefer going to a bigger press, because they will pay more and publicize the book better.

But we are keenly aware that the big publishers often overlook worthy smaller books, so we keep our eye out for them. There is nothing more stimulating or exciting for us than to discover a new talent.

JIM COX, *Editor*
Midwest Book Review (MBR)

How is a book selected to be reviewed by *MBR*? How many books are submitted for review?

An average of 1,500 titles are submitted to the *Midwest Book Review* each month. That's an average of 50 books a day, Monday through Saturday.

A book will be screened by myself as the editor-in-chief. Those that pass the screening will then enter a 14-week to 16-week "window of opportunity" in which to achieve a review assignment. Only if the book is ultimately successful in securing a review assignment will the publisher receive a tear sheet and a publisher notification letter.

NOW EVERYONE'S A CRITIC

The Internet has caused an explosion in the number of book reviews being done by critics and readers alike. Amazon.com is the main catalyst for this explosion, encouraging readers to post reviews. One issue is the reliability of these reviews. Just read the letters to the editor section of a major metro newspaper and reflect on how many of the published letters are just rants by highly negative people. To some extent, the same holds true for Internet book and movie reviews. Having the ability to read doesn't necessarily qualify an individual to be a book critic.

LYN BLAKE, *Vice President of the vendor group*
Amazon.com

Amazon has their own in-house reviewers, and then reviews are posted by customers who have bought the book.

There are some review services we take advantage of, and occasionally we will have our own staff provide editorials. What we have found is that the best editorial content to sell books is customer reviews. Consumers trust what other consumers have to say about products.

On the opposite end of the spectrum is the *New York Times Book Review,* where book reviewers are carefully selected based on specific criteria.

SAM TANENHAUS, Editor
New York Times Book Review

How do you find the writers who do your reviews?

We have eight or nine editors who assign reviews and edit them, including myself, and we're always looking for new voices. We do it by reading other publications, by looking at the Web, following the books that come out. If we find writers whose work interests us, we'll often approach them. Not all good writers make good reviewers or even want to review. Reviewing is a strange and in some ways inexplicable gift, which some writers just seem to possess naturally and others can acquire, while others just aren't comfortable reviewing. You have to express judgments, and you have to be straightforward in your critical responses to works, and that's not something a lot of people want to do. We're looking for young writers who enjoy the act of criticism, which is not necessarily an aggressive or hostile act but an analytical one. We place a lot of store by analysis and lucid prose, and those aren't easy to find.

Many authors don't put a lot of credence in reviews, whether from a national publication, industry publication, or those posted on Amazon.com. They do pay close attention to what their fan base thinks, though.

DR. SPENCER JOHNSON, Author

What has been the impact of reviews?

Almost zero. At least half of the time, the most sophisticated reviewers don't like my books. They think they're too simple. They don't realize that "simple" is the most elegant thing there is. It's ironic that these reviewers think they're so sophisticated, but they don't understand the difference between simple and simplistic. Simplistic is naïve and not enough. Simple is enough and nothing more. As Thoreau said, "Simplify. Simplify. Simplify." Until you get down to the most powerful truths.

In an increasingly complex world, people are looking for simple answers that work, truths they can understand and use that same day at work and in their personal life. People have so many demands on their time, they don't have as much time to read as they might like.

The book reviews on Amazon.com are interesting as well. Amazon.com goes out of its way to find a negative comment about a book, because they think controversy sells books. I don't concur with that, by the way. The reader review quotes on Amazon.com are supposed to be sequenced, beginning with the most recent. But even if they have to go back a week or a month to find a negative comment, they will do so, and they'll put the negative one as the beginning quote in the reader reviews.

STUART WOODS, Author

Are the critics harder on an author as they become more successful?

There's not really much good writing done in book reviews. Other than the larger newspapers like the *New York Times*. In the hinterlands, most book reviews are a recitation of the plot with a sentence at the end that says they liked it or hated it. I might get 25 to 30 reviews on a book. One or two would be bad, the rest would range from good to raves.

STEPHANIE LAURENS, Author

Stephanie was born in Sri Lanka, has traveled extensively, had a career as a research scientist, and now lives in Australia. She is the author of eight British-style Regencies, published by Harlequin Mills & Boon, originally in the United Kingdom and subsequently in Germany, France, North America, Italy, Australia, Japan, and Russia. Stephanie has also written 14 Regency-era historical romances. Recent titles include *A Lady of His Own, The Ideal Bride,* and *A Gentleman's Honor.*

Do reviews matter much to you or to your fan base?

I don't read reviews, only those good ones friends send me and then only to extract useful quotes for my Web site. Word of mouth is important, but that's not formed by reviewers but by readers talking directly to one another. Simply the fact that you are reviewed and thus your name and title are stated can be useful, but the substance of reviews is, in reality, at bottom line, irrelevant in all segments of the entertainment industry. The audience doesn't allow any reviewer to dictate to them what they ought to like in their entertainment—the audience decides for themselves. With genre fiction, the vast (as in greater than 99 percent) majority of the audience has no idea reviews of these books even exist, wouldn't read them if they did, and even those who do, don't allow the reviewer to tell them what to read. So in genre fiction, reviews of a work are useful in the sense that they call attention to the fact the book is out there to be read, are nice and can be mutually useful if they are good, but beyond that, they don't matter. Just as with author promotion, in genre fiction, no review can affect enough readers to make a difference.

A LAST LOOK FROM INDUSTRY PROFESSIONALS

And now for the exciting conclusion. The bottom line impact of reviews on book sales is . . . ?

MICHAEL CADER, *Publisher*
PublishersMarketPlace.com and Cader Books

Do readers really care about reviews of a bestselling author's new book? Or are reviews more important for the second-tier authors trying to get more media exposure?

As with most things in publishing, no one really knows. Probably, as with other elements of popular culture (movies, music), critical opinion has little impact for the biggest projects—but popular opinion and word of mouth has a bigger impact. There's substantial anecdotal information that says reviews do little for "second-tier authors" either—in part because reviewers and review editors tend to cover a limited subset of authors that conform to their idea of what's important and/or literary (and/or published by Knopf and Farrar Straus) that consistently has little to do with the breadth of the publishing industry at large and the tastes and interests of the public.

There's no question that ink of all kind and any kind helps. But it's rare to see a book "made" because of reviews.

SAM TANENHAUS, *Editor*
New York Times Book Review

What is the effect of an unfavorable review?

The effect of an unfavorable review is a very interesting one; it's not nearly as damaging as a bland or neutral review. Readers are more sophisticated than we assume, particularly in a polarized moment such as we now inhabit. First of all, readers won't be as closely attuned to the criticism as the author and publisher, who will notice every tinge of displeasure with the book. The reader doesn't pick that up. What the reader notices is that the book is being written about. Readers tend to react to strongly critical reviews as simply strong opinions about a book, which don't necessarily carry any particular weight and may actually be more effective in interesting a reader in a book than a blandly approving review. Maybe that's because we see so much contentiousness in other media, particularly television, that we assume that if someone doesn't like something, it's as much that person's problem as the thing they don't like. It almost becomes a medium for debate, especially with nonfiction reviews.

In a way, it's a very sophisticated response, because readers are taking a broader barometer of the cultural moment and seeing that a particular book is getting a lot of attention, and that's what authors want their books to do.

"O ye critics, will nothing melt ye?"

SIR WALTER SCOTT, from *Sir Walter Scott's Journal* (1825-1832)

Take heart, contemporary authors. It seems that even *Ivanhoe* had to joust with the critics.

c h a p t e r

5

CHANGES IN READERS' TASTES

VIEWS FROM THE AUTHORS

THE CHALLENGES FOR EDITORS

THE GREAT (AND ACRIMONIOUS) DEBATE

COMMERCIAL VERSUS LITERARY

Michael Korda, longtime editor-in-chief of Simon & Schuster, discusses in his book *Making the List* how the bestseller list for each decade reflects the trends, hopes, and fears of the general American population of the day. And today's bestseller lists certainly mirror the concerns of today.

Readers' tastes change as the world around them changes. Both authors and publishers must keep abreast of these trends. Authors who have sustained popularity for 10 or 20 years, or more, do so because they consistently satisfy a mass audience. Less successful authors may turn out great work, but for whatever reason, it doesn't click with a mass audience. How closely do authors watch publishing industry trends, and do they adapt their writing to current trends or changes in reader tastes?

"An author ought to write for the youth of his own generation, the critics of the next, and the schoolmasters of ever afterwards."

F. SCOTT FITZGERALD, quoted in the *Guardian*

VIEWS FROM THE AUTHORS

PETER STRAUB, *Author*

One of the masters of the "dark fantastic" or horror novel, Peter Straub's stories are frightening, full of eerie atmosphere, gripping suspense, and an ever-building sense of dread. He has won millions of fans and critical acclaim, both for his novels *Ghost Story; Shadowland; Floating Dragon; Lost Boy, Lost Girl;* and *In the Night Room,* and also for his bestselling collaborations with the legendary Stephen King (*Black House, Talisman*). He also pens brilliantly chilling short stories.

How do changes in fiction readers' tastes affect how an author approaches writing?

In one specific way, I don't think readers are now quite as willing to stick with very long novels. I loved writing very long novels that had 900-page typescripts. That is asking too much of the readers now. My most recent novel was 300 pages long. I want to stick with that length, so I don't drive people away.

Ninety thousand words versus 200,000?

That's about right. You can write a short novel quicker than a long one. These days, no publisher would be very happy with a writer they saw as commercial taking five years between books, because they want to build on the previous book's success. They don't want readers to forget about an author. They want to encourage a certain kind of loyalty.

SUSAN ELIZABETH PHILLIPS, *Author*

This celebrated romance author is the only five-time winner of the Romance Writers of America Favorite Book of the Year Award, and she was inducted into the Romance Writers Hall of Fame in 2001—pioneered and, some say, perfected the "romantic comedy" school of fiction. Her stories sparkle with colorful characters and witty, snappy dialogue. Her recent book, *Ain't She Sweet?*, spent five weeks on the *New York Times* bestseller list, three of them in the top ten. Other recent titles of Susan's include *Breathing Room, Just Imagine,* and *This Heart of Mine.* Despite her lofty status in the romance genre, she remains a down-to-earth person with a self-deprecating sense of humor.

Have readers' tastes in the romance genre changed in the years you have been an author? How does an author adapt to these changes?

Absolutely. In the late '70s and early '80s, I loved those brutal heroes, the nastier the better. I was a good girl, and they played into my fantasies of being bad, I'm sure. Now, when I look back on those books, I can only scratch my head and wonder what in the heck I was thinking.

I don't think about adapting to changes in the marketplace. I adapt to changes in myself. I've used older characters as secondary heroes and heroines for quite a while, and I'm sure I'll do even more of that as the years pass.

BARBARA DELINSKY, *Author*

Barbara Delinsky has more than 50 titles to her credit from a writing career that began in 1981. She now has more than 30 million books in print. Prior to becoming a writer, Delinsky worked as a sociology researcher in children's services and was a newspaper photographer and reporter. She spent the early years of her life writing romance novels. By adding complexity to her stories and growing as an author, she transitioned to being a bestselling author of mainstream hardcover fiction, combining romance and suspense. Her recent bestsellers include *Flirting with Pete, An Accidental Woman,* and *The Woman Next Door.*

What changes have you seen in fiction readers' tastes over the last 20 years?

The more things change, the more they stay the same. My readers still want good writing. They want a fast-paced plot. They want sympathetic characters and a satisfying story. What's different in the last few years in commercial fiction is a taste for the unusual premise. Take the point of view of the dead girl in *The Lovely Bones, Bridget Jones's Diary,* or *The Nanny Diaries,* or the book about a dog being the sole witness to a murder. Readers flock to these novelties, but not as a steady diet. Inevitably, they return to the tried and true. At least my readers do. They like relationship books and books that are well written and well edited.

STEPHANIE LAURENS, *Author*

You have been writing since 1992. What has changed in the publishing world over the last 12 or so years?

This is the subject of a dissertation, not a simple question. Genre fiction publishing is a hugely dynamic industry—it morphs as fast as any segment of the entertainment industry. About the only constants are the storylines, and that everything else is subject to change.

What has changed in Regency-historical romances over that time period?

As noted above, genre storylines have stayed fundamentally the same, but they've stayed fundamentally the same for millennia. Literally. The audience, however, changes all the time, which means you need to change your delivery to suit—things like distance, use of point of view, pacing, character detail, structure of narrative, etc—all the technical aspects of delivery, of telling the story. Genre fiction always needs to be accessible and entertaining to the audience of now.

THE CHALLENGES FOR EDITORS

Editors at publishing houses would seem to have a particularly difficult challenge when it comes to staying current with trends in readers' tastes. Authors mainly have to be concerned with what their own readership base wants to read, with a goal also of increasing that base; editors have to look at an incredibly diverse—even somewhat polarized—population of readers and try to anticipate what books and authors will best meet their needs to be informed or entertained.

The challenge is made somewhat easier in that editors usually specialize in certain genres, or in fiction versus nonfiction. Nonetheless, they have a dual role of doing the best possible job on their own authors' books and in keeping tuned into the publishing marketplace as a whole to identify hot trends. We wanted to find out how editors do their market research. To what voices in the marketplace do they listen when deciding what books to buy?

In a publishing industry environment of cost cutting and pressure to increase profits, the price of making a mistake is high.

DANIEL HALPERN, *Editor-in-Chief*
Harper Collins

How can you tell what will sell in the marketplace and what won't?

People in publishing imagine they know what's going to sell, and sometimes they can tell. A book, for example, that we saw but did not buy is Tim Russert's *Big Russ and Me,* a pretty safe bet, which is going to sell in good numbers, given that everyone loves Tim Russert, Republicans and Democrats, and he's a very likeable, down-to-earth guy. And he's talking about his father—that's an easy one! There are other books you think are going to do well but don't do well. The truth is, unless it's very obvious, you don't know what's going to sell and what's not going to sell. Some people have a good nose for the book that is going to sell, can "sense" it has commercial possibilities. Others have a sense of "literary merit," which may or may not sell but has value beyond track. You can have a wonderful novel that sells 7,500 copies and another very good novel that sells 75,000 copies. What is it that makes a Cormac McCarthy take off, after his previous books sold poorly? Was it marketing? Was it the right book at the right time? Was it local—the West versus the South, that territory he mined so well in the early books? There are so many elements, and a huge part of it is luck.

JENNIFER ENDERLIN, *Publisher*
St. Martins Press

How do you keep up with readers' changing tastes?

I don't think readers' tastes change all that much over the years. I think they are always looking for a strong, unique voice; characters you can identify with; intriguing conflict; and interesting stories. Those have been readers' tastes for 200 years.

Have there been any significant changes in the popularity of the major fiction genres in the last, say, ten years?

Within genres, there are subgenres that come and go, but I think that is more the result of publishers trying unsuccessfully to manipulate the market rather than a true reflection of readers' tastes.

For example, in romance, five years ago people said you couldn't sell paranormal romance, then someone writes a very good paranormal romance and it sells, and suddenly publishers are saying, "Oh! Let's buy more paranormal romance." Then that subgenre is considered a hot subject area.

But that's not really how I buy. I buy based on my intuition and whether I like the actual writing; it doesn't matter to me whether it fills a slot that's in vogue or not.

KAREN KOSZTOLNYIK, *Senior Editor*
Warner Books

How do you keep up with readers' changing tastes?

Editors read a lot. We read not only the manuscripts that come in, submitted to us by agents, but also the competition's books. I look at what the current bestsellers are, because that gives me an idea of what's working and what's not. I pay attention to what's selling, trying to see if there are certain trends that are happening.

It is also really important for editors to listen to their sales force, because they are the ones out there, talking to buyers, hearing feedback all the time about what is working in their accounts and what is not. I try to ask them questions about what they see working out there. Sometimes they will mention certain authors who are working particularly well. Even when I'm having lunch with agents, I try to get a sense of what is working for them.

How quickly do sales trends change?

It can sometimes be a quick trend that is over within a year. Timing can be everything. You might have a book about Desert Storm, for example *Jarhead*, which was published right before the current war with Iraq started, and that book wound up becoming a bestseller.

Trends can be shaped by what is going on in the world. Currently, there is quite a bit of women's fiction about grieving: a husband who dies, a child who died. This could be a result of the events of 9/11. We as a country are still grappling with those issues, and we see that reflected in the works of fiction that are currently being published.

"Chick lit" seems to have found its audience. There are obviously large numbers of 20-something and 30-something young women who couldn't find books that really appealed to them since they were young girls reading Judy Blume novels. Now they find these chick lit books that speak to them, remind them of themselves, and they are voraciously reading them. This is a trend that has become a genre that is going to stick around.

What about male readers in fiction. What are their preferences now?

Women make up a higher percentage of fiction readers. Men tend to read a lot of nonfiction about current events. Not to say these books don't appeal to women. Thrillers are popular with men but also with women.

How a book is packaged affects how it can be received by the reading audience. We have an author named Karen Rose, an up-and-coming star for Warner, who writes romantic suspense in mass market paperback (*Don't Tell, Have You Seen Her?*) We package her books so they look like straight suspense, not like a romance at all. We have been hearing from bookstores that men are buying her books as quickly as women are. Part of the reason is that the packaging was designed to appeal to both men and women.

So it doesn't have that pink cover . . .

Exactly. It looks like a thriller, but it has romance in it, too.

The conclusion: it is almost impossible to predict whether a book will be a big success in the marketplace—whether it will be a perfect match to the current needs, wishes, and tastes of readers. However, everyone in a decision-making capacity in the publishing industry is expected to make this judgment.

THE GREAT (AND ACRIMONIOUS) DEBATE

Publishing houses traditionally had two goals: contributing to the culture through bringing new ideas, voices, issues, and entertainment to the marketplace—and making money. These goals were not always compatible. Some books made money, quite a few lost money, and the average ended up being the publisher's profit. Critics of today's publishing world say that within publishing houses, the marketing departments and the dreaded "bean counters" with their spreadsheets have too much power, at the expense of editors, in deciding what books should be published. The new prevailing philosophy is that *every* book should make a profit. Critics also assert that controversial voices are being stifled, because their views don't comport with those of American middle-class consumers who buy the lion's share of books.

The counterargument is that consumers now have more power, in that they "vote" for which kinds of books are being published with the dollars they spend. This is as it should be, some believe. People on this side of the debate say, "Why can't readers have what they want rather than what someone believes they *should* be reading?"

GENE TAFT, *Vice President and Director of Publicity*
PublicAffairs

How has the publishing industry changed during this consolidation phase?

The industry used to be run by bookish people who liked to read. But there are not enough book people who are good business people. Now, with the large conglomerates having taken over so many houses, a different kind of executive is involved in the industry. These are people who know how to operate a business but don't know what a good book is. One group is the MBA crowd, and the other is the English degree felt-elbow-pads group. And you hear the MBA crowd saying, "The publishing house made an 8 percent return last year. The rest of the company made a 20 percent return. You need to raise your return to that level." And the publishing people are pleading, "Wait, 8 percent was a fantastic year. The year before we did 6."

Some people in the publishing world don't believe that bestselling necessarily means best-telling. At the far end of this argument are people who say that, by increasingly catering to a "mass audience," the publishing industry is abdicating its responsibility to support voices and ideas the mass audience doesn't necessarily want to hear. At the far, far end of the debate are people who say that bestselling books are inevitably poorly written, because the mass audience has no taste.

COMMERCIAL VERSUS LITERARY

The debate is sometimes waged by dividing all fiction works into two types: *literary* and *commercial.* Like all debates that rage in our country today, this one can get a little petty, a little mean-spirited, at times.

For instance, one should be very cautious about drawing the inference that a "commercial" book is somehow less challenging to write than a "literary" one. However, the subtext of this debate sometimes seems to suggest precisely that.

Here's a celebrated author from the past who had a rather low opinion of commercial fiction (and its readers).

"The secret of popular writing is never to put more on a given page than the common reader can lap off it with no strain WHATSOEVER on his habitually slack attention."

EZRA POUND, ABC of Reading

How can you tell a "commercial" reader versus a "literary" one? Maybe one way is simply to ask the question, "What do you think of the NBA this year?"

Commercial reader's answer: "Great! I was getting so tired of the Lakers in the finals every season."

Literary reader's answer: "Great! I can't wait for the National Book Awards!"

JONATHAN GALASSI, *President and Publisher*
Farrar, Straus, & Giroux, LLC

We seem to have this divide between what is considered literary work and what is considered commercial. Is it possible to reach both audiences?

The truth is that many different kinds of books can sell extremely well. My mantra here at FSG is that literary books *are* commercial. There are hundreds of thousands of readers in this country who want and need them.

Here are a few recent examples: *The Corrections,* by Jonathan Franzen, has sold over a million copies in this country alone, *Middlesex,* by Jeffrey Eugenides, is over three quarters of a million so far, and Michael Cunningham's *The Hours* is over 1.25 million. (These are combined hardcover and paperback figures.)

Another recent example, unfortunately not published by us, is Azar Nafisi's wonderful book, *Reading Lolita in Tehran,* which has been a number-one paperback bestseller for weeks and weeks. So I would put it to you that the divide you mention is not about whether the books are commercial but about something else. Perhaps it's about whether the books in question are pure entertainment or whether they demand (and deliver) something more.

How has the decline in the number of independent stores affected the publishing industry?

The independents were very, very significant for us in helping to launch new writers. Passionate, informed booksellers who know their customers intimately are the best possible witnesses to the special qualities of something new and unexpected—which is at the heart of publishing, I think, for a house like FSG.

The chains are much less successful at this kind of interaction with customers, though they try with programs like Discover, etc. So there has certainly been an appreciable loss in this kind of influence, and hence, it's harder to make surprise bestsellers coming up from more or less nowhere. Part of the response to this is the recent trend to try to front-end the careers of "literary" writers, publishing them with a big push as if they were out-and-out commercial. This is perilous, because it's much harder to connect with literary readers using these techniques, in my view—if it doesn't work, the writer ends up in a damaged position for the future. And writers, if they are real writers, tend to write better books as they go along. They build careers—something the chancy, instant-success system does not favor.

All the midcareer writers who are the glory of our current fiction stable were developed this way—often starting modestly and building, in many cases, to very serious success. I still believe it's the right way to do it, but it's harder all the time. It takes a very sure and serious author—and an experienced agent who is secure enough to take the long view—to understand this: that a literary career is a lifelong collaboration among author, agent, and publisher. It's something achieved by working closely together—not at cross-purposes, which seems to be more the standard model these days.

With literary fiction, how important is word-of-mouth promotion?

As I've indicated above, it's extremely important. Word of mouth is the only thing in the end that will truly make a book sell. If your friends are talking about it, you're going to be interested. If not, maybe not. All books that are what we call *runaways* are so because of word of mouth. I'd say the book clubs, which are one of the marvelous spontaneous phenomena of our current culture, are a kind of institutionalized form of word of mouth.

Your authors have won countless awards. How important are awards to boosting sales of an author's work?

It varies. The major awards can be highly influential if the writer is surfing at the right point of the wave; i.e., if they have already had significant exposure, but there's still a way to go to reach word-of-mouth status. I've seen this with wonderful writers like Alice McDermott and Michael Cunningham, for instance. But if a general opinion of an author has already jelled, the impact is much less immediate. Over time, however, I believe that the imprimatur that a Pulitzer, National Book Award, or Nobel Prize grants to an author will help significantly to continue to sell their work.

PETER STRAUB, *Author*

There's always been this gulf between the writers who are deemed commercial by the critics and those who are deemed literary. You've managed to achieve recognition for both a wonderfully

**literate writing style and imaginative storytelling. What is your
view of that whole debate?**

I think that debate makes me want to lie down and put a cold cloth
on my head. At this point, people ought to know enough to take every
work of fiction on its own merits. Not prejudge it. I am different from
most of the people in my field. I started as a serious student of fiction.
My first favorites were Dickens, Fitzgerald, Kerouac—all writers who had
no connection to the genre at all. When I began writing books of that
sort, I did so with the values and strengths I had learned in what is
termed "mainstream" fiction. That made my goals and, therefore, my
books subtly different from books written by people like Stephen King
or Anne Rice.

Sometimes that's what people have noticed about my work. The
only person who ever really understood this difference fully, and very
quickly, was the author Neil Gaiman (*American Gods*), who said to me,
"You don't come from the same place as the rest of us."

LAWRENCE SHAPIRO, *Vice President and Editorial Director*
The Book of the Month Club, the History Book Club, and American Compass

---

**Why don't more books that achieve literary acclaim also achieve
bestseller status?**

The primary incentive for most people buying a book is to seek entertainment. It's not that they're resistant to literary quality, but that's
not the first thing they're looking for. In some cases, readers just want
escape entertainment, and they don't want to be challenged. By definition, literary fiction is challenging. It can also be delightful and stimulating and entertaining, and that kind of literary fiction can go head to
head in sales with any other book.

"Only a person with a Bestseller mind can write
Bestsellers; and only someone with a mind like Shelley's
can write Prometheus Unbound.*"*

ALDOUS HUXLEY in *Essays New and Old*

Important awards for literary excellence are given annually by the national book foundation and the national book critics circle. No genre author—romance, mystery—or "commercial" author ever seems to win a Best award from these prestigious organizations. Stephen King did receive the National Book Foundation 2003 Lifetime Achievement Award, and in his acceptance speech, he urged the highbrow audience at least to read some of his fellow commercial authors' books. This was viewed by some in attendance as King being "aggressive." Literary critic Harold Bloom wrote in the *Los Angeles Times* that King's award was "another low in the shocking process of dumbing down our cultural life."

BARBARA DELINSKY, *Author*

There are writers deemed commercially successful, and then there are writers who are considered literary. What is your view?

I'm from Boston. Boston prides itself on being literary, so I'm basically unrecognized here. I write commercial fiction, which isn't a bad thing at all, if you define *literary* as hard to read, slow moving, and often too dense for understanding.

There is an intellectual snobbery among some critics. A book will be billed as literary, and critics will jump on the bandwagon. But it's often a case of the emperor's new clothes; the book may be perfectly unreadable, yet critics will find something brilliant to say, lest they be thought to be unbrilliant themselves.

John Grisham actually said something quite appropriate. He said, "I've sold too many books to ever be taken seriously by critics. What I think about is making the best book I've ever written. That's my goal every time." I totally agree with this. I've been writing full time for 24 years. I'm prolific, because I don't sit looking out the window waiting for inspiration to strike. I work hard at this job. I force myself to produce, with or without inspiration. That troubles critics. It's not the image of a literary writer.

My book group often discusses what's literary and what's not, and we can't reach a consensus. There seems to be something contradictory about being commercial—i.e., selling well—and being literary. We tried the idea that literary work stands the test of time. But my books will. They capture the essence of what was happening to women in the '90s or what families were like in the early 2000s.

BERTRICE SMALL, *Author*

Bertrice Small has had one of the most enduring careers in romance writing with 32 books, including *New York Times* and *USA Today* bestsellers. She's an original "Avon Lady" and has won many awards, including most recently the *Romantic Times* Lifetime Achievement Award.

There seems to be this gulf between writers who are considered commercial and those considered literary. What is your view on this debate?

Yes, there is a gulf. Literary authors are wonderful writers, but they don't sell well, and let's face it, publishing is a business, and the purpose of business is to make a profit. And often literary books are intimidating to the average reader, which is really too bad. Publishers publish, in my humble opinion, literary books for status purposes. And thank heaven they do! As for authors of commercial fiction like myself, our books are entertaining and provide escape from the everyday world. And there are some very fine writers among our genre. Just because it's commercial fiction doesn't mean it's badly written. But that's a point that's difficult to get over.

Romance is used to sell a lot of products. Why not novels? It's always surprised me that women's fiction, written by women for women, should be so scorned by the feminist movement. But don't get me started on that subject.

Many of the authors who sold well in the distant past are now virtually forgotten, while others who were ignored in their own day are now revered. Those on the "literary" side of this debate often cite this as an example of why aiming for a mass audience is not the way to achieve immortality in publishing. Having something important to say about the age in which you lived, even if people at that time don't want to hear it—even go out of their way to ignore it, is a much better benchmark than popularity. But they take the argument too far when they suggest that something is wrong about being popular, wrong with selling millions of copies of your books. You hear that books should be "challenging, troubling, take us out of our comfort zone." What about reading being enjoyable?

SABRINA JEFFRIES, *Author*

Sabrina Jeffries moved to Thailand at the age of seven, when her parents became missionaries. She now lives in North Carolina with her husband and son. While she holds a Ph.D. in English, she gravitated to writing romances and has written over 20, including the *USA Today* best-seller, *Married to the Viscount.* Other titles include *In the Prince's Bed* and *Dance of Seduction,* and she has a new series, *The Royal Brotherhood,* to debut shortly.

What do you think of the gulf between writers who are commercial and those who are deemed literary?

Having spent many years studying "great" literature, I have strong feelings on this subject. Most people forget that some of our greatest writers wrote popular fiction. Shakespeare wrote for the masses, altering his plays to appeal to the groundlings. Dickens's novels were serialized in popular periodicals. I truly believe that, in centuries to come, our classic literature will consist of our popular fiction writers (Stephen King, for example), not our supposedly literary writers.

Why do I believe that? Because literary writers have forgotten that literature used to be about telling an entertaining story. They dismiss Aristotle's writings about plot, because it's too "contrived." Happy endings, too, are "contrived." They point out that real life isn't "contrived."

But literary fiction is no more like "real life" than commercial fiction. Whenever you craft a piece of fiction, you make artistic choices to enhance your viewpoint. You leave out the mundane (unless your point is to show how mundane life is, in which case you're choosing to include the mundane), you work over the prose, and you make the dialogue more scintillating and the observations more profound than they ever could be in real life. So I find it hypocritical of writers of literary fiction to claim that their work is superior because it's more "realistic" than commercial fiction. It's still fiction. And by definition, fiction is an artificial depiction of life.

Another phrase you might add to the above list: . . . *and generally not sell many copies.* In February 2004, veteran editor Robert Weil wrote in the *Washington Post,* "While scribblers like Dan Brown or James Patterson can, with one novel, rack up sales in the millions, it is not uncommon for noted literary novelists to sell between 3,000 and 6,000 copies of their latest work. Selling 10,000 copies in this climate would be a resplendent success."

JIM COX, *Editor*
Midwest Book Review

Why don't more books that achieve literary acclaim also achieve bestseller status?

"Literary acclaim" is the function of an educated/cultural elite. "Bestseller status" is the function of the unwashed masses who are simply looking for something to pass the time with—or solve a specific problem from plumbing to personal improvement."

It doesn't happen often, but it is also possible to cross back and forth over the great chasm—preferably under a cloak of anonymity. *Michael Crow* is the pseudonym of an award-winning "literary novelist." In 2002, he published a novel in the thriller genre, *Red Rain,* and followed it up in 2003 with *The Bite.* In a *Publishers Weekly* interview, he said, "I had written five literary novels—*the kind that are taken seriously by critics*—and it occurred to me it would fun to unleash my evil twin and write something radically different." So what happened? His thrillers met with a very positive response—in praise *and* sales—from the genre readers whom some of his literary friends look down on. In the interview, he clearly was having a great deal of fun writing these thrillers.

What if this author were at a posh dinner party at one of his "literary" friend's houses, and to his amazement, he noticed a copy of *The Bite* sitting on the bookshelf? Would he own up to having written it, or would he raise a critical eyebrow and remark, "I say, old sport, gone in for a bit of slumming, have we?"

MICHAEL CADER, *Publisher*
PublishersMarketPlace.com and Cader Books

What is your view of the controversy about literary fiction versus commercial fiction?

It's not an issue I engage in. Reading is a good thing. It's fine to read different kinds of books, and I'm not all that convinced that much of the prodigious fiction output being published these days will have tremendous lasting impact, be it "literary" or "commercial."

"I've put in so many enigmas and puzzles that it will keep the professors busy for centuries arguing over what I meant, and that's the only way of insuring one's immortality."

JAMES JOYCE

6

EDITORS AND PUBLISHERS

THE PATH TO PUBLICATION

AUTHORS AND EDITORS WORKING TOGETHER

WHY EDITORS DECLINE NONFICTION

SAYING NO TO FICTION

THE PATH TO PUBLICATION

The first step on the path to publication begins with the query letter. Nearly all the major publishing houses will not accept unsolicited submissions. So for a new author, acquiring a literary agent is mandatory. The agent sends a brief query letter and a proposal, if the book is nonfiction, or the manuscript and a synopsis, if the book is fiction, to those editors that the agent feels would be a good match.

The editor reviews the submissions and selects those book projects they feel most excited about, that fit the house's list at the time, and will sell well. At the publishing house's editorial meeting, the editors present their selections. Questions and answers follow to determine if the book has a market, if it's well written, what the competition is, and what the potential "hook" for publicity might be. Finally, a decision is made about which books will receive an offer.

The agent and editor begin negotiations for the advance, royalties, and other issues of the contract. The advance is based on how many copies of the title the publisher believes will sell. Advances for fiction can range from a few thousand dollars to seven figures for bestselling authors. The advance is paid to the literary agent, who then deducts their commission and sends a check for the remainder to the author.

Royalties are based on a percentage of either the retail price of the book or the net price the publisher receives. The author does not receive any further payment from the publisher until the advance is earned out—in other words, until the royalties earned from the book exceed the advance previously paid. However, if the book doesn't earn out the advance, the author doesn't have to repay the advance or any portion of it. Royalties, like the advance, are paid to the literary agent, who subtracts the commission and pays the author.

For aspiring writers, the title *editor* often carries with it a fearful image: the person who decides whether your book will be published at all, whether your work will flourish on the bookstore shelf or gather dust on your closet shelf. The editors, then, as a group, are the people who have the power to decide what we—as a nation—will read and, just as importantly, what we will not read. The editors must say no many more times than they say yes.

The editor is the champion of a book within a publishing house, making sure it gets a fair hearing before the editorial committee and the needed attention and resources from the marketing department.

The editor may also have a long-range advisory role for an author. A top-selling author is an extremely valuable asset to a publishing house. The editor plays a role in helping the author achieve as much success as possible—which, of course, means as much success for the house as well.

LEE BOUDREAUX, *Senior Editor*
Random House

Could you please explain the function of an editor in a major publishing house?

The editor's job in-house is enormously important, because you start building excitement for a book with your colleagues. Passion for a book is like an electrical impulse traveling down a wire, and that electrical impulse has to be strong enough affect a lot of people, from the writer to the agent to the editor. Then from the editor to the publicist who needs to get the book reviewed, the art director who is responsible for coming up with the right cover, the sales reps who sell the book to the store buyers. Then from the store's main buyer to the individual booksellers and, eventually, to the customer.

The editor has to be passionate about the book, but they also have to help articulate what's special about the book and who the intended reader is. A great deal of planning goes into every book you eventually see on the bookstore shelf.

And, of course, on the macro level, the editor's job is to get in good submissions, then convince the publisher to take a chance on them. After that, the editor edits the book, oversees the whole production process, writes the catalog and flap copy to position the book, and has a hand in the publicity and marketing strategies. Again, all of this starts when a great manuscript lands on your desk, but the process can last for years, especially when you have a long, multibook relationship with an author, which is what you're always hoping for.

How much time do you have to get the message across?

In an editorial meeting, you might talk about something for ten minutes but continue to discuss it with your colleagues for another hour afterwards. At other times, you have to streamline your pitch into a few minutes. By the time our sales rep is meeting with the bookstore buyer, a first novel might get 30 seconds. The editor is trying to help get that message into its most persuasive and most concise form. You want to separate your novel from every other novel out there, and you're competing with a lot of other books for everyone's time: the customer's, the reviewer's, and so forth.

AUTHORS AND EDITORS WORKING TOGETHER

The reader of a book doesn't notice the influence of the editor on the manuscript, save for the acknowledgement page where the author often says, "I wish to thank my awesome editor," "To my incredibly gifted and caring editor," or similar words of high praise. That's probably just fine with both editor and author. But what exactly does an editor do? Do they really plunge into a manuscript and say, "Bestselling Author, I don't like that plot twist. Please change it." Perhaps they comment, "I'm not sure that fact on page 16 is correct." Can they really tell a renowned bestselling author what to do? To what extent are the author and editor a creative team? It turns out the editor's job has many more facets than might be imagined.

BARBARA DELINSKY, *Author*

How do you work with your editors?

I'm an independent writer, so I've never relied on an editor for story ideas or plot twists. Basically, I come up with a story idea and then submit a proposal. The proposal consists of an outline, character sketches, a synopsis, perhaps the first chapter or two, even some sound bites to help with publicity. My editors say yea or nay to the proposal, but that's the extent of their early involvement.

Why? The truth is, I know my audience better than my editors do, so I'm in a better position to decide what to write. I also know my backlist better than any one editor could, which means that I know what I've already done and what I haven't. Finally, I'm the only one who knows what the creative writer-in-me needs to do next!

Once the proposal is approved, I start writing. I don't share the details of the story with my editors during the writing, because, taken out of context, those details rarely sound good. I would rather have my editors wait and read the whole book when it's done. At that point, if something doesn't work for them, they tell me and I try to accommodate.

We normally think of the editing function as one of cleaning up grammatical mistakes or perhaps making a few concise recommendations about word choice. How much involvement do they have in making a book better? You wonder if, when presented with an editor's suggested changes, an author has to restrain herself from screaming, "I've sold 20 million books in my career, and you dare to tell me how to write?"

STEPHANIE LAURENS, *Author*

How do you work with your editors? Is there lots of give and take?

Each author is different, but in my case, I tell my editor what I'm going to write (a proposal), which is her opportunity to mention if there's anything in the proposal she has any concern with—she might mention some aspect that needs to be handled carefully, but then she just leaves me to deal with it. I write, edit, and polish the manuscript. Then I submit it, and usually it goes through with no editorial comments or changes. However, if there was anything wrong or anything that could clearly be done better in the manuscript, I would expect my editor to draw it to my attention—I would then correct it. So no, there's not usually much give and take, but there's the opportunity for any necessary give and take. Usually the manuscript I submit is the final manuscript, but if they make any suggestions, I would certainly consider them but not necessarily incorporate them. Under the current standard U.S. fiction publishing contracts, there is no such thing as a publisher making changes to my work without my express consent—the author is the final arbitrator as to words within the work.

Industry critics have said that one of the problems with the publishing industry is that books are not as meticulously edited as they were in the past. The number of editorial staff is limited due to cost pressures and the need to keep churning out new titles to fit the publishing calendar. At least for the top-echelon authors, the editor gives the book lots of hands-on involvement from the moment the idea is born. (Or should we say hatched? Maybe we'll ask Michael, our editor.)

JENNIFER ENDERLIN, *Publisher*
St. Martin's Press

How much collaboration goes on between a bestselling author and an editor at the idea stage of a book?

I have an enormous amount of input. Usually the author and I have brainstormed the concept before it gets to the formal, written-down idea stage. One of the most satisfying parts of my job is the stage when I sit down with the author and we start brainstorming ideas for a new book. It doesn't mean we work the plot out then and there, but I give them jumping-off points to go and explore, and they give me feedback on my ideas. With almost all my authors, I have some kind of meeting before they decide their next book. I say to them, "Why don't you think about this kernel of an idea?" Or, "Did you ever think about this kind of conflict?" Then they take that and run with it. So I am pretty instrumental in that part of the process.

How much is committed to paper?

It is usually a conversation. Sometimes I'll say to an author, "Don't start your next book before we've had our conversation!"

Do they typically give you an outline?

It's a personal choice of the author's. Some authors like to work that way. Some authors feel like it hems them in too much, and they want the book to be more organic. So I'd say it's about half-and-half.

Let's talk about an author whose books center around a series character. How do you get them to take that character in new directions, so they aren't just doing the same book over and over?

You have to have different challenges arise for the character. You have to see the character as a living, breathing person, who meets new conflicts and challenges every day. If you keep that fresh, a familiar character is something readers really like, but the situations surrounding them must be new and varied.

Suppose an author comes up with an idea that is too much of a stretch, and you have to tell them that their readers may not go for it.

I find that if an idea is a stretch for an author, if the idea makes them a little nervous, it is usually what they *should* be writing. If the book makes you nervous, you should write it.

SANDRA BROWN, *Author*

How do you work with your editors at Simon & Schuster?

I usually come up with an idea. I will talk to Chuck (Adams) and Michael (Korda) about it and say, "This is the creative impulse I'm feeling. This is what keeps coming around in my head. I'm not sure where it's going."

For instance, *Hello Darkness* started with a character. I saw somebody who embraces darkness, who confines themselves to darkness, wears dark sunglasses all the time, works alone, lives alone, has sought anonymity and privacy to an extreme level.

So Chuck and Michael said, "Well, is it a man or a woman?" I said, "I don't know yet. This is just what I've got so far. This is just the impulse."

I thought, "What job could this person do?" So we talked through that. I finally decided a DJ at a remote radio station, and they liked that. The DJ's only relationship is with the callers, the listening audience.

It worked better for the character to be a female than a male. Both Chuck and Michael liked that very much and said go with it. So I plotted the rest of the book and put it into a synopsis and sent it to them. They came back to me with suggestions. Then I wrote the manuscript. If along the way something doesn't work, for instance, in *Hello Darkness,* the villain that I had in the synopsis did not want to be the villain. That character did not want to be the villain, but there was another character that was just jumping up and down wanting to be the villain. So I called Chuck and Michael and said "You know the person that I thought was going to be the villain just isn't. But this other person . . . ."

They said, "It's your book. If you feel that strongly about it and the character feels that strongly, then go with it." So it's very flexible; it's give and take. Sometimes we disagree.

I trust Michael and Chuck implicitly. I trust their instincts. Michael is the overall conceptual guy, and Chuck is very much hands-on. He can edit in my voice. If he changes a word, it's not a word that one of his other authors would use; it's a word that Sandra Brown would use. He's an excellent line editor for that reason.

Michael is wonderful, because he sees the big picture. He sees the whole concept of the book. If you ever start straying from that overall thematic dynamic that you had going, he'll tell you it doesn't quite fit.

This morning I was writing the preview of *White Hot* to put on my Web site, and it reminded me of a meeting I had about a year ago with Michael and Chuck in New York. We were drinking hot chocolate, and they asked me for my thoughts on the next book. I said, "Swampy." They looked at each other and said, "Swampy?" I said, "Yes. I want it hot. I want it steamy. I want it sweltering. Seedy. Decadent." And they got the picture. That was my first creative impulse for *White Hot,* that I wanted something swampy.

BERTRICE SMALL, *Author*

Is your editor important?

I love a good editor! They really make you work, but then they also make you better.

NEIL NYREN, *Senior Vice President, Publisher, and Editor-in-Chief*
G. P. Putnam & Sons

What role does an editor play?

An editor does an enormous number of tasks aside from the actual editing function.

Sometimes, the best thing an editor can do is stay out of the author's way. Just let them do what he's doing and not impose too much. At other times it's appropriate to do a little steering, if you think the author is going off the rails or trying something that is probably not going to be good for their audience. You try and guide them along.

Besides trying to get the best book possible, every editor has to be a minipublisher. It's not enough to find a book and edit the heck out of it; you have to be aware of every aspect of that book's publication. You need to know what every department in the house needs to make that book a success. And that's true whether you're trying to make the book a bestseller or just a good seller. It's true up and down the line.

An editor is really the liaison between all the departments in the house, whether it's publicity or subrights or production. You've always got to be thinking, "What does the publicity department need to do with this book? Is there a particular hook they should know about? Is there something that can get the author on television or in a newspaper? Does the author have contacts to draw on to get quotes, to write an article, set up an autographing party? Does the author have a track record? Has the author been published in a magazine—does she or he have a friendly magazine editor with whom I could discuss subrights? Is there any particular look for the book jacket that might help? The editor has to think about all of this and a lot more, in conjunction with the separate departments thinking about their specialties. The editor is the one central clearinghouse. It's very important for an editor to realize that just producing a good book is only part of the job.

DANIEL HALPERN, *Editor-in-Chief*
HarperCollins

Could you give us some insight into how the editor contributes to a book's success?

Every book is different, and your job as an editor is to help the author find the book they wanted to write and then make it happen, make the book work on its own terms. That's what any editor is always doing, trying to figure out the intent of the author and what the book needs to fulfill its mandate.

Are some authors more amenable to suggestions?

Yes. [Laughter]

What do you mean when you say "putting the right package together"?

Jackets and the covers make a very big difference in terms in the way the book is initially ordered into the stores, especially with the chains. I think people do buy based on the cover. To a large extent, I think buyers are drawn to certain covers, covers they just want to pick up. And we all know, once you get a book into their hands, the chances of selling that book go up astronomically. If you walk into a bookstore, it's interesting to see which books get picked up.

MATT BIALER, *Literary Agent*
Sanford J. Greenburger & Associates

Suppose an author delivers the manuscript and the editor suggests significant changes to the plot. Does the agent then smooth over possible disputes?

As an agent, I'm always juggling. At the end of the day, I work for my client. So I will do what they want me to do. It doesn't mean I will always agree with it. And it doesn't mean that I won't have a greater problem with it later on, if I feel like the client and I are not on the same page. You can have disagreements here and there. At the end of the day, if you're not seeing things the same way with your client and vice versa, they're not with the right agent, and you're not with the right client.

I just try to be as honest as I can. I assume we all want the same thing, the success of this book and this author. There are situations where I've seen an editor take a certain point of view that I don't agree with. I may have to step in and explain why I don't agree. But this is the last thing I want to do. I think the editor/author relationship is important. The agent should play second fiddle there, once that relationship exists. On the other hand, sometimes the editor will make a recommendation, and I agree with it, so then I have to come to the author and say I can see their point of view. "It's your book, but they're right." An agent has to be honest. You can't simply agree with the client at all times. They wouldn't want me to.

KAREN KOSZTOLNYIK, *Senior Editor*
Warner Books

Many people think of an editor as someone who changes words in the manuscript.

We don't only perform that function. Part of an editor's job is nurturing an author, helping the author develop that unique voice they have. We're not here to change the words. We have copyeditors whose job is to be adept at the technical aspects of preparing a manuscript for publication. If I see phrases in the manuscript that just don't work, I'll take my hand to it. But, as editors, we're here more to help authors, to protect and hone their voice. For instance, if the copyeditor changes something that the author says is hurting the voice, that is something I always listen to.

Is the editor involved in the strategic planning for an author's career?

An editor should be viewed as an advocate for her authors. Suppose I have a manuscript that comes in that I am incredibly passionate about. The process all starts in the editorial meeting where the editor pitches the book to the publisher. The first step is that you convince a publisher that the book is worthy of investing in. When you get the deal wrapped up and the contract is signed, your work doesn't stop there. You start working with the author, not only with the materials the author has delivered, but you also need to act as an advocate by talking that author up any chance you get.

At that point, the editor is working as a team player with other departments within the house. The art department has to come up with an incredibly strong cover for the book. The copywriting department writes tremendous copy for the back cover. You work with other departments to make certain you create a cohesive, complete package to present to customers. We also go through a series of meetings where we are pitching our authors' books to the sales force; it is our chance to show the sales force how excited we are about that author's work and to get them excited about the author. You want to give the sales force all the selling points of the book—whether it is the author's background, the hook of the story, if there is a platform we can use to help in promoting the author.

So there are a number of things an editor does beyond working with the written material itself. The main thing is being an advocate for your author.

WHY EDITORS DECLINE NONFICTION

The decision to decline a new author's manuscript is not made lightly. Any editor is afraid of turning away the next *The Da Vinci Code*. The decisions are not easy either: they have the luxury of choosing the very best books from among the very best writers—and a lot of talent is out there in America. As part of our "Survey of Editors and Agents," editors were asked: "What is the most common reason you decline a nonfiction book proposal?" The most frequently cited reasons are:

- The author's platform (media visibility and built-in marketing base) is too small.
- The book doesn't meet the needs of the publisher at that time.
- The market for the book is not large enough.
- The quality of the concept or the writing is poor.

Some of the more interesting, representative editor responses follow.

The author's platform is too small.

- "A tie: The author's platform is not established enough, and the material is not different enough from what else is out there already."
- "Subject matter is too 'small,' or the author doesn't have a platform. That is, we don't think we can sell enough copies, and the author doesn't write a newspaper column or have a radio show, etc."
- "Imitative or derivative of others; author has no national visibility or media presence—platform."

The book doesn't meet the needs of the publisher at that time.

- "The agent or the author doesn't understand what our editorial needs are. Every house has its own unique editorial perspective, and every editor has her or his own specialties."
- "We already have a similar title in our list, or the title is not appropriate for our list."
- "It's not remotely suited to what we actually publish."
- "The writer did not research our company well enough to know which subjects we do and don't publish. For example, I might get proposals on traffic safety, Wicca, and politics all in one day."
- "Author has not researched the kind of book that we publish, so the proposal is for a book that we would not really consider."

The market for the book is not large enough.

- "Usually, either there's not enough market for it, or the material itself isn't strong enough."
- "The most common reason for declining a nonfiction book proposal is, quite simply, that there is no market for the book sizable enough to make its publication profitable and, therefore, warranted."
- "The most common reason is that the book's subject matter and focus is simply something we do not feel that we can put out in the marketplace and make a profit. Many of these proposals are well written and well researched; we just don't feel that they're economically viable projects."

The quality of the concept or the writing is poor.

- "No book there; badly written; sloppily presented."

- "Not interesting to me, and author hasn't really looked into the subject far enough to convince you there's a book there that they can write."
- "Subject matter has been covered in so many other books, and there's not a new idea/fresh take in the proposal."
- "Usually not enough new and different material to differentiate it from its competition."

SAYING NO TO FICTION

Our survey also asked editors: "What is the most common reason you decline a fiction manuscript?" The answers fall into several categories, but overwhelmingly, poor writing was the most often mentioned response.

The quality of the writing is poor.
- "Most of the novels I see have plot lines that are too derivative of other novels, or the writing just isn't very good. Novelists should be seeking fresh, different, and provocative story ideas."
- "Writing quality, mostly. If there is nothing to save from it, it gets declined."
- "The writing is far below the quality of other projects on the market."

The story is not engaging, interesting, or compelling.
- "Didn't love it enough. There are plenty of submissions that are solid but not special. This has everything to do with that magical/enthralling/compelling quality we always look for as we read fiction submissions."
- "The most common reason for declining a fiction manuscript is, quite simply, because the story isn't compelling. In my experience, most fiction manuscripts submitted to and subsequently rejected by publishers are deficient of some of the most essential elements that go into solid storytelling. Often, their characters lack the necessary amount of characteristics, and the interaction of said characters lacks the necessary amount of interesting action."
- "Lackluster writing; a plot that is a) unexciting or b) hard to pitch, or c) seems to have a limited audience."

And the award for the most elegant, literary answer . . .

- "Further to this analogy of incestuous word play, just as a play-wright has the right to be playful (i.e., imaginative) when writing a play, so too does a novelist have just as much right—and some might even say duty—to employ novelty (i.e., originality by virtue of being refreshingly new) in the fabrication of a modern novel. Perhaps the most notable missing element common to all rejected works of fiction is sufficient description (of anything—characters, setting, action, you name it). A writer by definition must write, and if a writer is just another name for a scribe, then so too must a scribe describe. Thus, it is so that among many a redlined manuscript, one will find in the margins this very editorial command: 'Describe!'"

One editor coined a publishing proverb.

- "There are ever more agents but the same number of good writers."

7

LITERARY AGENTS

THE ROLE OF A LITERARY AGENT
ARE AGENTS SUPERSALESPERSONS, GATEKEEPERS, OR TALENT SCOUTS?
EDITORS' PERSPECTIVES ON THE AGENT'S PITCH
INCREDIBLE COMPETITION IN THE HUNT FOR AN AGENT

THE ROLE OF A LITERARY AGENT

Most successful authors are represented by literary agents in their negotiations with publishers. It is possible, however, to retain an entertainment/literary law firm for representation. Because an agent is paid a commission based on the advances and royalties an author receives, the plum clients for an agent are the bestselling authors. Besides the financial rewards, having one or more of them as clients lends prestige to the agent's firm and helps attract the best new talent in the literary world to sign with that firm.

DAN BROWN, *Author*

Finding an agent is one of the greatest challenges a writer faces. How did you find your agent at Sanford J. Greenburger Associates?

Heide Lange and I met through a series of synchronicities so bizarre that nobody would believe the story if I told it. I've decided it must have been divine intervention. After all, Lange is an anagram of angel—which is exactly what she has been for my career.

Why does a bestselling author still need an agent?

I need an agent now more than ever. In addition to all of the services generally associated with the best agents (contract negotiations, pursuit of subsidiary rights, passionate involvement in the publishing process), Heide now must provide additional services without which I could not continue to write. Bestsellers generate a tidal wave of media requests, publicity opportunities, and endorsement inquiries, which, while wonderful and welcome, can be all-consuming and very distracting. Nowadays, Heide directs substantial energies towards insulating me from distraction, liaising with the media, and making sure I have the privacy and quiet I need to write my next book.

Some of the glory that shines from the bestselling author's achievements is reflected onto the agent as well. To be known as the agent who just got a megastar author a fabulous new three-book deal or the agent who sold the film rights to a novel to Steven Spielberg, let's say, gives the agent individual star status.

HEIDE LANGE, *Literary Agent*
Sanford J. Greenburger Associates, Inc.

Why does a bestselling author require an agent?

For the same reasons a writer needs a good agent in the first place: to negotiate contracts that reflect the value of the author's work, to skillfully pursue subsidiary rights here and abroad, to look out for the author's best interests in every situation, and to remain actively, passionately involved in all phases of the publishing process. I make sure that everything that occurred to make the book a bestseller continues to occur.

What role does an agent play during negotiations to improve the chances of a client's book becoming a bestseller?

An agent's negotiating role has already begun when the manuscript or proposal is submitted. Based on your experience, this is when you set up and position an important book. The agent's presentation of the work alerts editors to an important offering. That positioning naturally continues into the actual negotiations, as you work out an advance that reflects a book's commercial potential and includes bestseller and performance bonuses. What is also important at this point is to solicit the publisher's promotion and marketing plans, to determine that they are prepared to position it as highly as you feel it should be. Of course, even when all this is in place, there is still a long way to go between a publisher's acquisition of a book and its ultimate successful publication, which is why an agent has to remain fully involved in all aspects of the process.

How do you go about convincing a publishing house that a new author might have bestseller potential?

As an agent, you have spent many years building a relationship with editors and publishers, which of course comes into play when you signal an important submission. Your experience and credibility are important currency. You want everyone to succeed, to have a winner. No one wants to extract a huge sum from a publishing house and then watch the book fail. You want to be sure to provide all dimensions of what is being offered: what makes the book outstanding, along with the unique qualifications of the author and ways in which the writers themselves can enhance and support the book.

Of course, once an author has published one or more books, they may have acquired, through no fault of their own, a less than stellar track record. This can pose a substantial challenge, for the author and agent as well as the publishing house. Too often, a low sales history—there for everyone to see—can thwart an author's future success. In the case of Dan Brown, as everyone now knows, we had to convince his publishers to look beyond the sales of his three previous books, to believe in his talent and bestseller potential as much as we did. Fortunately for all, they did, and the rest is bestseller history. However, this experience is not unique, and it should encourage others—authors, agents, publishers, booksellers—to have the courage to look beyond poor sales that are, after all, created by many factors having nothing to do with an author's talent.

What changes for the agent when an author reaches bestseller status?

I do the same but in greater volume. I watch the bestseller lists more carefully. It's a lot of fun—for everyone. And, of course, I try to repeat the success, for the bestselling author as well as for bestselling authors-in-the-making!

RACHEL GIBSON, *Author*

With the publication of *USA Today* bestselling author Rachel Gibson's first book, readers discovered one of contemporary romance's freshest voices. Three of her novels—*Simply Irresistible, Truly Madly Yours,* and *True Confessions*—were named among the Top Ten Favorite Books of The Year by Romance Writers of America.

Why does a bestselling author still need a literary agent?

Agents negotiate contracts. They look at each word in each contract clause and consider whether the wording is in the best interest of their client, the writer. And a good agency has a legal department, as well as foreign rights and film rights departments. Having a literary agent when you are a bestseller is, in my opinion, even more important than when you sell your first book.

Authors have, to some extent at least, a love-hate relationship with agents. Authors tend to be impatient with the slow pace of shopping a manuscript; the agent in turn is frustrated with the slow pace of response from publishers.

Agents also vary widely in their approach to the business of representing authors and manuscripts. Authors' and agents' personalities must click for the relationship to be successful and enduring. Agents' working styles can vary from gracious to bumptious, as the following unpleasant (but, fortunately, mercifully brief) discourse we had with an agent illustrates.

A Mini-Interview with a Very Nasty Agent

What is the most common reason you decline to represent an author?

They can't write. You are asking the wrong questions, so it is hard to see how your book is going to be new, different, or helpful.

Is there anything you'd like to tell us about the current state of the publishing industry?

I wish I knew what your purpose was in writing this book, because I don't see how these questions are going to get you anywhere.

Do you think the industry will be more favorable for new writers in the next 12 months or less favorable?

To my clients, much more favorable.

Just after talking with us, this agent was rushed to a New York area hospital for an emergency personality transplant. It was touch and go for a while, but we are pleased to see that the surgery appears to be a success. She was even overheard giving a nurse a compliment and was able to fly home on her broom within a week.

And now, let's get back to the gracious agents. There is much more to the agent's role than handling the negotiation phase with publishers. They are part of the creative team that carries the book forward through publication and works to make the book a success in the marketplace.

We asked literary agent Matt Bialer of Sanford J. Greenburger & Associates to give us a perspective on how an agent acts as a strategic advisor and helps the author develop his or her career.

MATT BIALER, *Literary Agent*
Sanford J. Greenburger & Associates

We've seen that it takes a team effort to cause a bestseller to happen. What does the agent contribute to that effort apart from the contract negotiations?

A good agent contributes in many ways. Often, before the editor is in the picture, it is the agent and the author working together. They have to have good rapport; there must be a lot of trust between the two. The client has to have confidence that the agent speaks with authority. Agents aren't always right, but we are always getting a sense of what the marketplace is like. We have to help our clients produce something that is true to them and their talents—but also is commercial. I spend a lot of my time trying to do that. I listen to what my clients want to do and get an assessment of their abilities, their goals. I then help them.

What other strategic advice do you give authors about their careers?

Sometimes a writer has a lot of talent but not the right attitude. There's more to building a successful career than just writing a good book. It's how fast you do your second book. How fast you do rewrites. Do you have the personality to be a successful author? There is a charm that authors need to have today that they didn't need in the past.

I think authors really need to keep track of the business. If they were in any other business, they would read the trade magazines. They should subscribe to *Publisher's Lunch* and read *Publisher's Weekly*. You see what's selling and, just as importantly, what's not selling.

In the past, certain authors were published at a certain level, say paperback originals, for years. And then, after ten books, their sales grew and they went into hardcover. It took a long time to happen. That method of reaching bestsellerdom can still occur with romance writers and women's fiction; those are huge paperback original markets. However, with thriller writers, that isn't how it happens anymore. Paperback originals are not that important to many publishers. It isn't their farm system anymore for developing talent. They need instant successes. It's a time and resource thing. Publishers don't have the patience they once did to slowly build an author's career.

Again, that's where the agent makes a difference. We're taking a new talent that we might have gotten started in paperback originals, and we have to get them to a higher level sooner. Otherwise, they don't stand as much of a chance. You have to hit the ground running.

ARE AGENTS SUPERSALESPERSONS, GATEKEEPERS, OR TALENT SCOUTS?

The agent we see in movies or on TV is usually portrayed as a silver-tongued, extremely persuasive individual, sometimes even a bit unscrupulous. These fictional agents seem always to get the deal done—on their terms. They almost mesmerize the person on the other side of the negotiating table into agreeing. We're about to see that agents do indeed have to be skilled at persuasion, but the way they get deals done for their clients is a lot more subtle than just effervescent sales hype.

Agents play an important gatekeeping role for publishers. If agents didn't exist, editors couldn't walk around their offices, because they would be up to their ears in (mostly bad) manuscripts. The agent's role was an early form of what we now call corporate outsourcing. They perform a function that the publishing houses would need thousands of employees with pay and benefits to perform. In this case, the agent doesn't even charge the publishing house. The agent's compensation comes out of the author's share of the transaction.

How much hard selling really goes on between agents and editors?

SCOTT MILLER, *Literary Agent*
Trident Media Group

How do you go about convincing a publishing house that a new author might have bestseller potential?

This is a tough question, as publishers don't like to be told anything. I think that, when you're trying to convince a publisher something like this, you have to rely on aspects other than the quality of the writing. Let's face it: the market is so tough right now that everything that is being published is pretty well written. However, an agent can use other factors to show a publisher that the book could be a bestseller.

These factors usually would be either media driven or blurb driven. By *media driven,* I mean showing the publisher that this author has a platform in the media that will help the publisher market the book. For example, I had a really media-connected first-time author. I had him draw up a sample media list, which we sent along with the manuscript. This list was designed to show the publisher just how many potential media opportunities the author could receive. The media list didn't sell the book, but it convinced the publisher to do as much as it could to exploit the media opportunities.

I also convince publishers that a new author could have bestseller potential by hyping up any blurbs by already established authors. For example, I represent a writer who is a student of a major bestselling author. When I went out with this book, I hyped up the fact that the publisher was almost certain to get great blurbs by the student's teacher as well as others who were connected to the bestselling author.

MARGRET MCBRIDE, *Literary Agent*
McBride Literary Agency

How do you convince an editor at a publishing house to become excited?

Why does an editor *buy* a book? Think about it. An editor has a career that will be considered successful, not based on how *many* books that editor puts into the next catalog, but on how many books that editor works on that make a profit. What I like to do is offer the following: the great new big concept, the great author, and the great author's platform. My agency likes to put together an insurance package with all the reasons why the book is going to do well.

Here's how we do it. Before we send the project out, we often tell our client we are going to send his/her book or proposal to this fabulous editor and this world-class publishing house. We let them know they are going to get along famously with the editor, and the editor's skill will make the book even better. That editor is going to read our submission and say, "Okay, this proposal is terrific. I'm going to take it to the editorial board."

At the next editorial board meeting, your potential editor needs to present your work in the most effective way to the other editors at the meeting. Those editors are their colleagues yet may also be their competitors. All of these editors also have proposals from other agents that they want the house to acquire. Your potential editor must show or say something to convince a quorum that yours is going to be the no-brainer, obvious success. What is that *something* in your book that will fire up everyone in that room? A great title, a great sales hook or pitch, and a great platform. What will get the publishing house enthused about your book and you as a talent they can bank on? What is presented at that meeting is very important. The editor has my letter with proposal flagged to answer all sorts of possible questions. If people go, "Wow!" then it will move forward. If they say, "Been there, done that, nothing new," it's over at that house."

Editors depend on an agent to know their literary tastes and what types of books they're looking for at the moment. They also depend on agents to filter out the poorly written manuscripts, the books that don't have a substantial market, or the authors whose credentials aren't strong enough. As we've just heard, they contribute to the chances of a literary property being purchased by clearly articulating to the editor why it will do well in the marketplace. Good agents must be as attuned to the marketplace as the editors at the publishing houses.

EDITORS' PERSPECTIVES ON THE AGENT'S PITCH

Agent: Boy, do I have a great manuscript for you! You gotta take a look at it right now. It's gonna be snapped up quick.

Editor: [thinking] *This is only the 20th time I've heard that today.*

This is how we imagine a typical exchange between agent and editor. Let's see how it really is.

NEIL NYREN, *Senior Vice President, Publisher, and Editor-in-Chief*
G. P. Putnam & Sons

How does a literary agent go about convincing you that their client has a bestseller?

Most of the time, they can't convince me. I have to see for myself. It's much easier for them to pitch it if it's a nonfiction book with the right kind of credentials behind the book and the author. With fiction, it's entirely in the reading. The book has to do it. Most of the time, when an agent says, "This book is going to be a bestseller," you think, "I'll be the judge of that."

DANIEL HALPERN, *Editor-in-Chief*
HarperCollins

How does an agent convince you that their client has a potential bestseller?

They all have their own methods, some more effective than others. Guess what? The ones who are most effective are those whose taste I agree with. The best agents work closely with their authors on the projects they take on—before they submit something. They are careful about who they represent. So when you receive something from one of these agents, you take it very seriously. There are a quite a few good agents who represent their authors well—who also understand that we're all in this together and to bully the publisher—or for the publisher to bully the agent and author—isn't in anybody's interest. Working together makes books happen.

LEE BOUDREAUX, *Senior Editor*
Random House

Does an agent really "sell" a manuscript to an editor with their submission package?

It's always going to be about the manuscript. There are cases when I know I share a certain sensibility with an agent or I admire their list, and I'll certainly read a manuscript they send me right away, but every manuscript I receive gets a certain amount of attention. I'm going to quickly read the cover letter and go straight to page one. Then it rests on the shoulders of the writer to be persuasive, to make sure that I keep reading.

PAULA EYKELHOF, *Executive Editor*
Harlequin Books

In the case of a relatively new or untested author, how much does an agent "sell" a manuscript or author to an editor?

From my perspective, it's not about "selling" me the book; it's about the book.

Now we know: The "secret bestseller sauce" is made up of this key ingredient—*a great book.*

INCREDIBLE COMPETITION IN THE HUNT FOR AN AGENT

Every new author seeking an agent faces incredible competition—at least in numerical terms. As part of our "Editors and Agents Survey," agents were asked how many unsolicited submissions they receive per week and how many new clients they took on in the last year. Each agency, on average, received 90 unsolicited submissions per week, while each took on an average of 11 new clients a year. They agreed to represent a little more than *2 out of 1,000* authors.

Now for a *really* scary statistic.

In our survey, agents on average said they accept 2 out of 1,000 submissions. A senior editor with a top publishing house told us she accepts 1 out of 100 submissions that she receives from agents. If we combine the two, it means that there is a *1 out of 50,000* chance of a new book by an unknown author making it from the author's word processor to successfully attracting an agent, and then on to the contract stage with that publisher.

Almost unbelievably, some new authors stare down these odds without the slightest bit of flinching and capture the attention of a top-tier agent.

SCOTT MILLER, *Literary Agent*
Trident Media Group

How do you know when you have found that hidden gem of an author?

Often, I think I've found a hidden gem based on an excellent query letter. Usually, though, the manuscript doesn't live up to the pitch.

I've sold *New York Times* bestsellers that have originated from unsolicited queries, so I do think that I have a good sense of what will lead to the needle in the haystack.

I get my hopes up when I read a well-written letter that succinctly shows me a good book idea. So much of this is about the writing, and if the cover letter isn't coherent and concise, I won't go forward. The letter gets extra marks if the author is also able to tell me that they have a particularly unique marketing hook and/or their career is relevant to the novel; e.g., an ex–FBI agent writing an FBI thriller.

Once I've received the manuscript, I basically know within 50 pages if this book is going to be something special, something I can sell well. I figure that if the author can write an excellent 50 pages, coupled with the fact that I already know they have a great idea, then even if the book goes downhill from page 51, together we can work to make this book something that can sell.

Or, if you want a short answer to your question—I know that I have found a hidden gem of an author when I actually find myself reading the manuscript in bed. If it's so good that I've brought it home with me from work and actually want to read it in bed, I know that it's something special.

8

GETTING THE BOOKS ON THE SHELVES AND OUT THE DOOR

HOW BOOKSTORES SELECT TITLES

CHAIN RETAILERS

BOOK CLUBS

HOW BOOKSTORES IMPACT NEW AUTHORS' CAREERS

It has been estimated that five large publishing companies—Random House, Inc.; Penguin USA; Simon & Schuster; Time Warner; and HarperCollins—account for nearly 80 percent of all book sales in the United States. This consolidation has occurred for the same reasons as in other industries: by combining administrative or staff functions, costs can be reduced and profits increased. Publishing, relative to many other industries, has not enjoyed a high return on investment. Now, publishers are much more focused on having every single book turn a profit. This means a more risk-averse philosophy, with a preference for publishing authors with successful track records—a sound business strategy.

HOW BOOKSTORES SELECT TITLES

After the agents, editors, and the marketing departments at publishing houses have decided what will be published, in what quantities, and how the finished product will look, one final decision maker ultimately decides what books will be presented for sale to consumers: the bookseller. In the independent bookstore, this decision maker is often the owner or the owner and several employees.

Booksellers usually buy their first order of a new title from the publisher's sales rep. Subsequent orders can be placed directly with the publisher or through a wholesale distributor, which allows the bookstore to batch their orders to several different publishers and receive one invoice.

MICHAEL POWELL, Owner
Powell Books in Portland, Oregon

How does a bookstore strike a balance between carrying the most popular authors and providing customers with a wide variety of choices and categories?

I can't answer for bookstores, only for what Powell's does. We approach it from both directions, breadth and depth. Powell's has the largest independent bookstore in the country with 70,000 square feet and 4 floors of books that allow us to carry quite a few titles. We try to give our customers special interest books and literary titles as well as the bestsellers. Our smallest store has 16,000 square feet.

What retail display strategies does Powell's use to draw customers toward books?

We use a variety of methods, whatever we can: books facing out, rather than spine out, shelf talkers [brief notes attached to the shelves]; we hand sell books; we have staff pick books; tables by the front of the store; end caps displays.

Bowkers says 175,000 books are published each year. How do your buyers wade through all those titles to determine what to stock?

It's not really 175,000 books; only about 60,000 to 75,000 titles have the possibility of being stocked in a bookstore. The rest are technical books, textbooks, or books just not of interest to consumers. Some of the books are not intended for a bookstore audience and don't offer a standard discount and terms. Those books are not meant to be sold in bookstores. For the remaining titles, we talk to the sales reps, go through the catalogs, and look at what previously sold. If we already have 12 books on cats stocked, we certainly don't need a 13th.

Book buyers' decisions take into account the sales a blend of the pitches from publishers' reps, historical sales data they have collected about an author or a topic, knowledge of their customer base—and to a large extent simply what their gut instinct tells them will be popular.

JOHN BENNETT, Owner
Bennett Books in Wyckoff, New Jersey

Walk us through the process of deciding which titles to stock in your store.

A variety of factors go into deciding what books we order. Most important are the presentations, whether on the telephone or in person, from salespeople from the various publishers. Both major and minor publishers do presentations through sales reps, commissioned reps, who come in and present the catalogs from a number of publishers. Many publishers can't afford to send their own individual reps into the field but work through group reps. These reps have meetings with the publishers to discuss what the editors and publishers think will be the important books for that season. The reps then go through the entire catalog with us and say, "This title is one we anticipate getting good reviews, getting talk show attention, getting good word of mouth. It's written by a Pulitzer Prize winner, we know the writing is high quality."

The reps educate us about what is in the catalog, expanding on details that aren't in the catalog about what the publishing house's expectations are for a given book. The reps illuminate what is in the catalog; they are the biggest help in our decisions about what and how much to buy.

The second thing that helps is looking at the track record in our computerized inventory system, the track record of that author's previous books and track records of similar books. Past results are representative of what sales will be for this book. We also take into account our own experience, what our customers have been asking for or reading. We have a feel, based on 16 years in this community, for what people are interested in reading.

GAYLE SHANKS, *Owner, and Cindy Dach, Events Coordinator*
Changing Hands Book Store in Tempe, Arizona

What process do you go through to get the books on the shelves?

Gayle: The first step is, I get a catalog in from a publisher. We are always buying for the next season out. I generally review those at home. I mark up the catalogs with my choices in advance of seeing the sales reps from the publishers. Then the rep and I have a dialog. I will point out my choices, and he or she will say, "I wouldn't skip that one." Or, "You're buying two of that title. I really think you want five or ten. In your store, that would be a really popular book." We will have a back and forth dialog.

The rep might tell me a certain book has a $150,000 promotional campaign behind it. Or there's an author tour scheduled. Or the author is guaranteed to appear on *60 Minutes*. All these things, of course, can help build demand for a given book.

One author might get two full pages in the publisher's catalog. You pay attention to that, because it gives you an idea how the publishing house is thinking of the book.

How important to your overall success are bestsellers?

Cindy: For us, the Book Sense List is the bestseller list we focus on. This is different than the *New York Times* list. This is the list of books that are most popular in independent stores. How big are people like John Grisham? They are certainly good for us, too, in that they bring people into bookstores. They have the set audience. This audience will come in and pick up other books while they're here to find that top author's book.

DANIEL GOLDIN, *Buyer*
Harry W. Schwartz Bookshops in Milwaukee, Wisconsin

What influences your decision about which books to buy? Catalog copy, sales reps, reviews, customer requests, advance reading copies, promotions at the annual Book Expo America convention?

Everything that you listed plays a part in our title selection. Promotions at BEA are probably not the main source of title inspiration, as it is so removed from the actual order process, but it can certainly inspire a bigger buy on a number of key titles. Here are some additional ways that books get bought for stock at our stores.

- *Media publicity.* We pay attention to upcoming notices and when the publicity hits.
- *Bestseller or demand lists.* These are a good way to fill in gaps.
- *Special orders.* A certain number (certainly not all, but definitely not none, either) of titles are simply reordered for stock when requested by a customer.
- *Recommendations.* These come from staff, customers, Web sites, and experts.

MITCHELL KAPLAN, *Owner*
Books and Books in Coral Gables, Florida

Do reviews, customer requests, or the publishers' reps influence your decision?

All of that. You know, it's often been said that a bookseller's knowledge is like the Rio Grande, five miles wide and a half-inch deep. I think that's accurate for book buyers as well. Over the 20 years I've been buying, the way we access what is being published is primarily through reps.

Do you order while they're there or . . . ?

I order while they're there. I'm a pretty easy buyer. I sometimes review the catalogs beforehand, but typically, I'm reviewing the catalogs right then and there, with the reps. The catalogs themselves give subtle clues as to what's going to happen. I often look in the catalog to see who the editors might be, the print runs, the marketing budget, whether an author will be touring or not touring—all of those things go into my decision making. Also, I look to see if I recall a previous title the author might have had, and then I'll look it up in our system to see how it might have done. I'll even consider whether the publisher has given the title a double page spread; that gives some indication about how strongly the house feels about the book.

BARBARA MEADE, *Owner*
Politics and Prose Bookstore in Washington, D.C.

When you are selecting titles, what has the most influence on your decision?

The author and their track record. If it's a new fiction author, I'll only buy a few copies, because it's difficult to judge how a new author will perform. Customers are hesitant to spend $25 or more on a hardcover title if they're unfamiliar with the author. Publishing houses are bringing out more first-time novels as original paperbacks, and that's good because it takes some of the risk out of the customer's decision.

CHAIN RETAILERS

Bestsellers are so popular that every retailer imaginable now sells them. Popular titles are available at more locations than ever before; warehouse clubs, places like Target, and even grocery stores now carry hardcover bestsellers. This is a mixed blessing for the industry. For publishers, it means more potential sales of their blockbuster titles from the bestselling authors, but it may also translate into lost potential sales for other titles. When a customer goes into a bookstore with the intention of purchasing the latest and greatest from Mega Author, they leave with that book and usually several others they had no intention of purchasing but became intrigued by while they were in the store.

For traditional bookstores, especially independents, the availability of popular books at seemingly every other type of retail store means that a customer who was able to find that bestseller at Target didn't have to make the trip to the bookstore—and didn't purchase those other books.

DANIEL GOLDIN, *Buyer*
Harry W. Schwartz Bookshops in Milwaukee, Wisconsin

Bestselling titles can now be found at Target, Wal-Mart, even the grocery store. How has their availability affected independent bookstores?

There are several factors at work here.

- *Price.* Whether an independent bookstore discounts bestsellers (and we do) or not, the store will be hard pressed to be the low-

price option for many consumers. There is a segment of the market that will buy at the cheapest price, sacrificing time and energy to achieve this end. This is not a new phenomenon.
- *Convenience.* With four locations in the market, we are certainly more accessible than if we had one store. However, we certainly don't match the convenience of mass merchants for many potential buyers, particularly if they are buying books in addition to a vacuum cleaner or cereal.
- *Selection.* We certainly can beat mass merchandisers on book selection. Sometimes, when an unexpected title breaks out in popularity, there is a lag time with mass merchandisers discovering it, and that increases our sales.

For what it's worth, our main competition is not from mass merchandisers but from chain bookstores and Web sites.

As Mr. Goldin states, the chief competition that independent bookstores have faced in the last few decades has not been from mass merchandise retailers but from chain bookstores. Chain bookstores have sprung up all over the country in seemingly every large or medium-sized shopping mall. A number of publishing industry insiders have complained that the domination of bookselling by a few large chains has led to marketing bestselling, or proven, authors' work at the expense of titles from exciting new authors or those with a smaller audience—precisely the authors that independent stores have been so skilled at hand selling to their customers.

To take bookstore chains to task in this way is to overlook an important contribution they have made: introducing the idea of *bookstore* to millions of people who might not ever have set foot in one prior to seeing the brightly lit, beautiful chain bookstore at the mall with the attractive displays of merchandise. They wander past the front window and are irresistibly drawn in. Mall bookstores have made book browsing seem like great fun.

STUART WOODS, Author

Has publishing industry consolidation helped the careers of bestselling authors? Do publishing houses now give more emphasis to fewer authors?

It may give publishers the wherewithal to pay larger advances. The proliferation of chain bookstores has certainly helped writers. A great many more books are being written—and sold—than had been in the past. This has cost some independent bookstores their business; those without a business plan or business acumen fell by the wayside. Independents that were as smart as the chains have survived and prospered.

Borders Group, Inc.

In 1933, Larry Hoyt founded a single-book rental library in Bridgeport, Connecticut, that later became a bookstore chain, Walden Book Stores. In 1971, Tom and Louis Borders opened a small used bookshop called Borders Books and later expanded the operation. Now these two organizations are combined into Borders Group, Inc., a publicly held *Fortune* 500 company with sales of $3.7 billion. There are 1,200 Borders and Waldenbooks stores around the world with 32,000 employees.

In a conversation with an executive with Borders Group, Inc., we learned that Borders centralizes its book buying, although each store has the ability to request individual titles. Each Borders buyer focuses on one subject and is expected to become an expert in that subject. The performance data by title and author are available to the buyers to make book selections as scientific and data driven as possible.

Buyers also look to the publisher to tell them what a title is about, their expectations for the book, marketing plans, and print run. These all indicate how the publisher feels the book will perform.

For example, a first novel would be judged on who the publisher is and what the publisher's track record is in marketing, obtaining publicity, and reviews. Buyers would also consider what other, similar books have achieved. The Borders buyers try to read a portion of new books, especially fiction, but each season brings an additional 35,000 new titles to consider, so obviously they can read only a very small percentage of what's available.

Borders has its roots as a major independent bookstore chain and believes in supporting smaller new books and new authors as well as smaller publishers. At the same time, Borders was one of the leaders in the expansion of bookselling, bringing 100,000-square-foot stores to areas previously unserved.

Barnes & Noble

The first Barnes & Noble store was opened in 1917 by William Barnes and G. Clifford Noble in New York. Now the company is publicly held, with revenues of $5.9 billion in 2003, and has 40,000 employees in 800 stores in 49 states. The company operates both Barnes & Noble stores and B. Dalton stores. The Barnes & Nobles stores range from 25,000 to 67,500 square feet, while the B. Dalton stores range from 2,800 to 6,000 square feet. The selection at each is tailored to the interests of the local community it serves. Barnes & Noble is the only chain bookseller that is also a publisher. Its publishing program focuses on relatively low-profile, risk-averse titles. The company forecast that its self-published titles will generate about 10 percent of its total revenues. B&N also owns a portion of iUniverse.com, a publish-on-demand company.

Sessalee Hensley, the fiction buyer for Barnes & Noble, decides what novels will grace the megachain's bookshelves, how many will be ordered, and how they will be apportioned among the stores. Major publishing houses routinely send her galleys along with their marketing plans, book tour plans, and media placement in the hopes of convincing her to increase commitment to a title.

Books-A-Million

Books-A-Million is the third largest book retailer in the nation. It is publicly held with revenues of nearly $.5 billion. The company presently operates more than 200 stores in 18 states and the District of Columbia.

Amazon.com

Amazon.com, established in 1995, is a *Fortune* 500 publicly held company with revenues of $5.3 billion in 2003, and it is one of the landmark successes of Internet retailing. It has no bricks-and-mortar stores to compare with Borders, Barnes & Noble, or Books-A-Million. Book selling is done on the company's Web site, http://www.amazon.com.

LYN BLAKE, *Vice President of the Vendor Group*
Amazon.com

How do books get on the virtual bookshelves at Amazon.com?

We get data feeds from our largest publishers; the feeds include what books are coming, publication dates, the digital book covers, the biographic information, and the basic book description. At the same time, the publisher's national sales accounts people are preparing their sales call. When they visit us, they review the titles that they think will do the best at Amazon.com. This may not necessarily be what does well everywhere else. We do well with all the big books like everyone does, but we also do especially well with niche books that bricks-and-mortar stores may not be as comfortable carrying or don't know how to stock. The good national account reps get a sense of this. They also do their homework before they come, and that means looking up similar titles, previous editions, or other works by that author. They can answer the questions: How well did this do at Amazon in the past? What kinds of promotion programs supported those titles in the past? Quite frankly, their job is not to sell us titles but to help us create sell-through opportunities for titles. Our virtual bookshelves display every title that is made available to us. The difference is having good sales representation that helps us figure out how to make that title attractive and show up in the click stream at Amazon.

BOOK CLUBS

The classic book club has been around since the late 1920s. The Book of the Month club was developed in 1926, by Harry Scherman, a direct marketing expert. A year later, The Literary Guild was born through the efforts of Samuel W. Craig. Both clubs offered affordable books by direct mail. Both The Book of the Month Club and The Literary Guild are now part of Book Span with approximately 10 million members. Additional book clubs of Bookspan include: Quality Paperback Book Club, Doubleday Book Club, The Mystery Guild, The Science Fiction Book Club, and more than 30 others.

LAWRENCE SHAPIRO, *Vice President and Editorial Director*
The Book of the Month Club, The History Book Club, and American Compass

How is a book selected to be offered by a book club?

There are three different phases: submission, evaluation, and negotiation. The publisher submits a manuscript or a bound galley for us to consider, although sometimes we will solicit a book ourselves. The galley is read and reported on by us or a freelancer. Every week, we have an editorial meeting, and each club brings in the books they're considering. Once the decision is made to acquire a book, we negotiate with the publisher for the book club license. This license gives us the right to offer the title to our book club membership. We pay a royalty and, in most cases, an advance on that royalty.

How many books do you receive for consideration?

In 2003, it was about 18,000, and probably more than half of those titles were nonfiction. In the Book of the Month Club, fiction is the most popular category, but when you look at the number of titles and the number of clubs that we have that specialize in nonfiction, nonfiction has to be the majority of what we're considering. Not every title that is submitted gets past the first evaluation. The book has to look like it would be appropriate for one of the clubs. There are books that might do very well in the trade but happen to be specialized in a way that it doesn't fit one of our clubs.

How far in advance are the selections made?

Right now in the Book of the Month Club, we're planning the catalog that will mail out in October of this year, so we're looking at October pub dates, that's four months from now. We can act faster than that, but the biggest factor is that we're a paper-based catalog business, and that means a long lead time for preparing the catalog. We like to announce the books to our members at the same time the books are hitting the stores.

The way we put together the catalog has changed over recent years in reaction to the way publishers are publishing. They're crashing more books, rushing them to market, which forces us to react fast more frequently. There is more topical publishing, more issue-oriented publishing, and there are more publishers who are just as eager as they can be to get a book with big potential out as quickly as possible.

The time frame used to be 18 to 24 months for a publisher to get a book to market.

That was the ideal. Now there are publishers who will get a book out in six weeks. This is especially true with political books or current affairs books, because they're newsworthy and the publishers don't want to be stuck with something that looked fresh in manuscript stage and suddenly becomes irrelevant.

How has the book club process changed over the past few years?

We pay more attention to special interests and to publishing niches. We have more special interest clubs, and they are a larger part of the business. It used to be there was the Book of the Month Club and the Literary Guild, supersized interest clubs, comparable to department stores, offering one-stop shopping. These clubs still flourish and serve readers whose tastes range widely, but we also have clubs for readers who specialize in one thing like history, science fiction, crafting books, or mysteries.

HOW BOOKSTORES IMPACT
NEW AUTHORS' CAREERS

For the new author, one of the most difficult challenges is getting your book on the bookstore shelves. You have no sales track record, after all, for the bookstore buyer to use as a guide. You have no brand name yet, either. Consumers are not streaming in asking for your book. And most new authors have not created a large enough buzz within the publishing house that the house's sales reps will make a passionate case to booksellers to give your title a try. Yet, somehow, new authors succeed. They become the next generation of bestselling authors. Bookstores play an important role in the early success an author enjoys.

JOHN BENNETT, *Owner*
Bennett Books in Wyckoff, New Jersey

What does a bookstore do to promote the next generation of bestselling authors?

We are part of an independent bookstore community that is sponsored by the American Booksellers Association, called Book Sense. They produce a monthly newsletter that lists books that have been read as advance-review copies by bookstore owners around the country. It tends to focus on new and upcoming authors, or authors that haven't published for a while or haven't yet reached a large audience yet. The reviewers give their impressions of that book. We then, in turn, hand out this newsletter to customers and put displays of Book Sense books in front of the store, to show what other stores are recommending. We have a staff of eight people who are constantly reading books. So we have a Staff Pick table with their recommendations, like Book Sense, but from our store's individual perspective. These books tend to not necessarily be the latest John Grisham or Danielle Steel book but books from a younger, emerging writer or literary writer who hasn't reached bestseller status. So it is a hand selling process. We put the recommended books in front of the store. When we see a customer pick one of these up, we can tell the customer more about the book, whether it might appeal to them based on what they have bought before or their interests.

What do you think causes an author's very first bestseller to happen?

One of the very important things in making a bestseller is getting good buzz about your book going at an early stage. The best way to do this, of course, is to get an appearance on *Oprah*. No question: no other talk show competes with *Oprah* in terms of success. Other shows have been successful in helping books, such as *The Don Imus Show* and the *Today Show;* a number of venues, such as NPR (National Public Radio), help a book along. One thing that bestselling books all have in common: they get a good early buzz through a combination of talk show appearances and good reviews, whether from booksellers or trade press.

Regardless of talk show appearances and good reviews, however, there is something mysterious out there—the public buzz. People begin talking about a book, and it will take off more than you expected. And vice versa, in spite of talk show appearances and good reviews, a book will fail to sell because people talk to one another and say the book is dry, too complex, nothing new. You can get public interest in a book through media, but you can't necessarily sustain it unless people talk to each other and recommend it. This is why I think bookstores remain successful as a source of information, despite the Internet intrusion, because you can have this conversation in the store between the bookseller and the customer and, just as importantly, between customers.

When you have two people in your store, sales will not be as good as if you have five people, not just because having more people in the store gives you more chances of making a sale but because those five people will talk among themselves and say, "Have you read that book?" The bookstore is a great forum for having conversations. Those conversations in turn help books continue to sell.

GAYLE SHANKS, *Owner*
Changing Hands Bookstore in Tempe, Arizona

What effect do bookstores have on bestsellers?

Independent bookstores play a critical role in causing bestsellers to happen. *The Secret Life of Bees,* by Sue Monk Kidd, is an example. We created this phenomenon. Booksellers discovered that book before it was widely known. Their recommendations helped make that book a success. That's how bestsellers are made. I have endless stacks of galleys in my office; I pass them out to everyone who works here. We are always looking for great new books to recommend to our customers.

9

ESTABLISHING A BRAND
IMAGE WITH READERS

ARE AUTHORS "BRANDS"?
AUTHORS' VIEWS ON BRAND IMAGE
HOW TO CREATE A BRAND
CAN BRANDING BE TAKEN TOO FAR?

ARE AUTHORS "BRANDS"?

It may seem rude to describe a great author as a "brand." They are grand artists with words, after all. They have unique gifts, uncommon skill. You can't bring them down to the level of crass commerce and compare them to Budweiser beer or Lays potato chips.

Well, yes you can, because they are brand names, sometimes very powerful ones. Not only that, most popular authors fully understand this and work diligently to build their brand, recognizing branding as the key to long-term success in a highly competitive industry. They accomplish brand building in two main ways:

1. Differentiating their "product" from the work of other writers in their genre
2. Cultivating a loyal customer base, those wonderful repeat customers

The best collegiate training for aspiring authors might be to spend the morning in the liberal arts college, studying literature and creative writing, and the afternoon in business school, mastering the principles of marketing.

At the very top of the successful brand builders in the publishing industry are the authors who started with a book and created an empire. Jack Canfield and Mark Victor Hansen certainly did that with their fabulously successful Chicken Soup for the Soul series, having sold more than 85 million books in 30 countries. This duo is listed in the *Guinness Book of World Records* for having the most books on the *New York Times* bestseller list at one time.

Their first book spawned a seemingly endless series—*Chicken Soup for the Nurse's Soul, The Golfer's Soul,* etc.—all featuring motivational, uplifting stories. Oddly, we couldn't find one titled *Chicken Soup for the Lawyer's Soul.* Wonder why . . .

Then they began licensing the brand name to a wide range of products: collector plates, greeting cards, games, music CDs, wall posters, and calendars. Now there is even a Chicken Soup for the Pet Lover's Soul® brand of dog and cat foods. The authors continue to be popular speakers, conducting workshops and marketing associated training videos.

When they began marketing the first book in 1993, they got the reaction typically faced by new authors: thirty-three New York publishing houses turned them down—the first month. They received such perceptive comments as, "This book is too positive." Their big break came when they attended the American Booksellers Association Convention and found a receptive publisher, and the rest is—very profitable—history. They have even received what is capitalism's greatest honor, showing that they've reached the very pinnacle: a parody of their work. David Fisher published a book titled, *Chicken Poop for the Soul: Stories to Harden the Heart and Dampen the Spirit.*

How can you tell an author has become a brand? One tip-off is to examine the cover of the author's latest book. The author's name is usually printed in very large, very bold type, because the roving eyes of the customer browsing the new releases section of the bookstore will lock onto the author's name, not necessarily the title of the book.

AUTHORS' VIEWS ON BRAND IMAGE

Most of the popular authors we talked to had no trouble articulating their brand image with readers, although some of them believed that creating this image is a partially unconscious process that cannot be planned ahead.

SUSAN ELIZABETH PHILLIPS, *Author*

How do you go about creating a "brand image" for yourself in such a crowded genre as romance?

I didn't ever try to create a brand image. My books are pretty much who I am. I believe in the importance of all the good stuff in life: family, love, committed sex, being nice to your neighbors, going to the polls on voting day. The wonderful writer and academic, Kathleen Gilles Seidel, once said that my books take place in "SEP Land" [author's initials]. It's a fairly benevolent place, although when I compare my heroes and heroines to those in other romances, mine tend to have a bit of a subversive edge. A hero like Bobby Tom Denton, for example, in *Heaven, Texas,* has a monumental ego. Sugar Beth Carey in *Ain't She Sweet?* isn't really all that sweet. When readers think of my books, I think they know they're going to laugh, maybe cry, and that the book will be sexy. They also know they're going to be with people they want to spend time with.

DR. SPENCER JOHNSON, *Author*

Let's talk about the unique niche you've carved in the publishing industry. How would you describe your brand image as an author?

I view myself as a practical philosopher. I like what someone once observed: "Good writing is clear thinking made visible." That is my goal as a writer.

My brand as an author is creating simple, short, easy-to-read parables that don't give advice. They simply tell a story and let the reader take out of the story whatever they want. When I was a young physician, I learned that many people not only don't like advice, they don't listen to it.

All of my books have been parables. I had to smile when *USA Today* called me "The King of Parables." The brand image involves offering parables that contain useful truths that are easy to understand, and that can be used by readers almost immediately in their work and their life. The reader watches what happens to the characters in the story. Then they pull out whatever truths they want to use, the truths most applicable to their current life. This really began in 1982 with *The One-Minute Manager,* which I coauthored with Ken Blanchard.

Your books are unusual in that they can be read in one sitting.

That's how they were designed. This is an increasingly complex and fast-moving world. More and more of us seem to have less and less time. Colby, an 18th-century English writer, had some good advice for us, "Give the reader the most information, and take from him the least time." That has become my motto. This lends itself to people rereading my books easily and often. They tell me they get something a little different out of the same book each time they reread it, depending on where they are in their lives emotionally or intellectually or confidence-wise. The real power of my books is not really what I put into the books but what the readers take out of them. The smartest and most secure people realize that the best answers they've found in life are simple and sometimes embarrassingly obvious once you recognize them.

STEPHANIE LAURENS, *Author*

When people think *Stephanie Laurens, author,* what would you like them to think?

I don't want them to think about me at all. I want the words *Stephanie Laurens* to be synonymous with a fabulous romantic story excitingly well told. If readers see the Stephanie Laurens name on the front of a book, I want them to feel certain that, if they buy that book, they are guaranteed a reading experience they'll enjoy. That's the connection I want blazoned in their brains. This is a business, and Stephanie Laurens is a brand name.

SANDRA BROWN, *Author*

When people think *Sandra Brown, author,* what would you like them to think?

A storyteller. I'd like to be known as an author who always gives the reader a good story, without being identified by any specific genre. At one point in my career, not being identified with a genre was considered a disadvantage, because my books have been all over the map. I don't write "police procedural." I don't write "forensic investigation." I don't write "courtroom." But I have written about all of those topics. It was difficult, initially, for the publisher to tag me and for the booksellers to tag me. To me, not being identified with a specific genre is better, because isn't it the job of a novelist to constantly come up with something new and fresh and different and not be categorized so specifically? The people I like to read don't write the same book over and over. They don't even write in the same field over and over. Those authors go outside the box.

So I would like to be known as a storyteller that you can rely on for a great story, totally different from the last book but written in the same literary voice.

BRAD MELTZER, *Author*

This young author of legal/political thrillers has written detailed, well-researched, intriguing stories that take readers inside the Supreme Court *(The Tenth Justice)*, the White House *(The First Counsel)*, and the U.S. Congress *(The Zero Game)*. *People* magazine paid him this high compliment: "Meltzer has earned the right to belly up to the bar with the likes of John Grisham, Scott Turow, and David Baldacci." His books have a total of almost six million copies in print, have spent over eight months on the bestseller lists, and have been translated into over a dozen languages. In a delightful and unusual change of pace, Brad also writes *comic books,* including a much anticipated project titled *Identity Crisis* for DC Comics, "a murder mystery involving Superman, Batman, Wonder Woman, and the rest of the biggest characters in the comic universe."

What do you want your readers to think of when they think of Brad Meltzer?

I think my biggest fear as a writer is to be one of those authors who just churns out the books and all his readers know he's churning them out. There are guys who write a book a year and they're incredible at it—every book they write is really great. I'm not that kind of writer. I just can't do a book a year. It's tempting to do a book a year—my publisher would love me to do a book a year. I would double my salary if I did a book a year. But if I did a book a year, they'd be garbage.

So my goal would be for people to say with each book, "Wow he really did something different—he did something better."

Also, I'd hope that if you took the book jacket off the book, ripped off the cover, and took my name off the pages, that my readers would still know it's my book. I hope they would recognize my voice—and I'm proud of the fact that they think they do.

A few years back, for a charitable event, a group of legal thriller writers wrote a book. Each author wrote one chapter and then gave it to the next author, and so on. As part of the event, the chapters weren't identified by author, and there was a contest to see if readers could tell who wrote which chapter. From all the e-mails I got, people guessed my chapter dead on right. I loved that. I loved that they thought my voice was different from someone else's. It doesn't mean *better*, doesn't mean *more impressive*, it doesn't mean *more literary* or *less literary*. It just means it's mine.

BERTRICE SMALL, *Author*

When a reader thinks *Bertrice Small,* what do you hope comes to mind?

I want my readers to know that they'll get a good story and accurate history. I'm noted for writing very sexy historicals, and some books write that way, but some don't. However, I always write a good story, and I believe my readers know that or I wouldn't still be in business.

IRIS JOHANSEN, *Author*

Iris Johansen is one of several suspense writers who honed her craft and built her audience through writing category romance books. She is now firmly established in the thriller genre, with such bestselling successes as *Final Target, Body of Lies, No One to Trust, Dead Aim, Fatal Tide,* and *Firestorm.* One of her most popular recurring characters is forensic sculptor Eve Duncan, though she is equally skilled at presenting men as lead characters. Her characters face life and death situations and are pitted against realistic, contemporary villains. Iris Johansen's books involve much more than just intriguing plots and dangerous situations; her characters have great humanity and vulnerability.

When readers think of an Iris Johansen novel, what comes to mind?

What I hope and what I try for are:

1. Good storytelling
2. Fresh plots. I love to tell a story that has never been told before, or if it has been told, to tell it with fresh new twists.
3. Strong characterization. I work very hard on that.

PETER STRAUB, *Author*

What do you think your "brand image" is with readers? When a reader thinks of a *Peter Straub novel,* what do you think comes to mind?

One of the things that comes into their heads is a distinct weirdness or strangeness in the story. A kind of complexity. Good dialogue. Good characterization. And writing that isn't embarrassing.

Note in this sample of authors how very different each brand image is. No two of them expressed their image the same way, except in citing the importance of great storytelling. The author's brand starts out as an extension of the unique voice each of them brings to their work, then takes on additional strategic elements, such as Sandra Brown not wanting to be identified with just one genre or Dr. Spencer Johnson producing concisely written books that can be read in one sitting.

Stephanie Laurens's brand even comes with a "guarantee" that her fans will get a "reading experience they'll enjoy."

JONATHAN GALASSI, *President and Publisher,*
Farrar, Straus, & Giroux, LLC

Retailers have put more emphasis on "brand-name authors" in recent years. Has that impacted literary publishers?

Brands are part and parcel of the inevitable convergence factor in our mass media commercial culture. Fewer and fewer products receive more and more attention. There can be a reaction to this. In 2002, we all painfully experienced a drop of 30 percent or more in many brand-name bestsellers. There was a lot of soul searching about this shift—what caused it, whether it was to be permanent, etc. I do think readers are more fickle today than they used to be. They're looking for something fresh and new and don't so often go back to the well the way they once did. I also think that the boom of the '90s, which represented a boom in publishing as well, masked the fact of increasing fragmentation in readers' attention. More and more leisure time options, more and more hours spent in front of screens of all kinds—this has to take away from the special, quiet, uninvaded time that a reader spends with her nose in a book.

I'm not sure we'll ever get back to the good old days of the late '90s, when I, for one, felt that the potential readership for literary work was pretty much boundless. I still feel that readers are more experimental today than ever before—we're all more experimental about everything than we used to be—but the world situation, and particularly our involvement in it, is terribly distracting and worrying, and this is certainly having a deleterious impact on the reading of serious fiction.

HOW TO CREATE A BRAND

"There is no denying the fact that writers should be read but not seen. Rarely are they a winsome sight."

EDNA FERBER, *A Kind of Magic*

This opinion by the author who had the number-one bestselling fiction title in 1924, *So Big,* and again in 1930, *Cimarron,* seems rather quaint today. The goal of brand building for a contemporary author is to have that author seen as many places as possible, in as many different media as possible, as many times as possible.

PAULA EYKELHOF, *Executive Editor*
Harlequin Books

How does a publishing house go about building brand loyalty for their popular authors?

It does depend on the author. One approach is the creation of an ongoing series, usually based on place or character. Consistency of cover treatment and packaging is another. We're also making increased use of teasers, excerpts, and so on, which can create a sense of anticipation in the reader. Advertising and PR obviously have a role in this, too. And, especially these days, the author can play a part in developing reader loyalty—through Web sites and other forms of direct communication with booksellers and readers.

THERESA MEYERS, *President*
Blue Moon Communications

Theresa has been a publicist for numerous *New York Times* bestsellers, including authors such as Carly Phillips, Rachel Gibson, Vicki Lewis Thompson, Susan Andersen, Pamela Morsi, and others.

Tell us about the overall goal for your publicity and marketing efforts with a client.

One of the key elements in making a bestselling author is to create an "author brand."

It's not just about the book. You want to get your author to a point where a reader walks into the store asking for the author's name, not the title of a specific book. You want to hear the customer ask, "Can I have the next Carly Phillips book?" If you hear that often enough, you know then that you have created an author brand that will have longevity. That is my goal as the publicist.

What are some of the benefits of a strong author brand?

Strong brands bring in dollars. A strong brand will influence buyers to consider purchasing an author when they have only limited money to buy their books. It will create a loyal readership that will bring an author bigger contracts from publishers. It helps authors win awards, because they stand out clearly against other brands in the same market space.

How do you build an author brand or create one?

First off, let me give you a concept to wrap your brain around. The word *brand* is used to refer to a product or company name or anything unique that identifies something using a logo or trademark. The marketing term or concept grew out of a need to identify products and developed into a serious approach to explain why consumers were attracted to a specific product and how they made their purchasing choices. Author branding is an extension of that effort.

Today, when we talk about an author brand, we are talking about building an image, perception, or identity that is used to create:

1. "Emotional Velcro"
2. A perception of higher quality
3. That little something special that no one else can offer

In publicity, perception is everything. It's the same with your brand. Even if you develop a strong brand and build a great awareness for it, if you don't manage it correctly, it can flop. To manage your brand, you have to decide how you want people to perceive you. You can use publicity and message points to shape and manage how your multiple publics perceive your brand to keep it healthy. At this point, an author might be scratching their head and asking, "Why do I need an author brand anyway? I'm small right now."

The point is, you want to grow big, right?

You can take a long, painful, expensive trip to get to from point A to point B without a road map, or make it there for far less expense, time, and effort with a map. All I am trying to do in creating their brand is build the map first.

How do these three branding steps work for an author?

Step one (emotional Velcro) is achieved because readers love certain stories and are moved by them. This, in turn, leads readers to believe that they have formed a relationship of some type with that author and understand him or her. Because of this emotional attachment, they are willing to purchase a book written by this author simply because her name is on it.

Step two (perception of higher quality) is achieved because this author brand has received accolades from every sector of the industry in the form of awards and top placement on the *New York Times* list. The author has garnered numerous industry or writing awards and is usually considered synonymous with a genre. All of this contributes to the consumer's perception of higher quality of this material. If the writer wasn't good, she wouldn't be getting all this attention, right? (Not necessarily folks, but that's how the perception works.)

Step three (a little something special or distinction) is achieved via the author's voice. Now this is unique to fiction as a product, because in other product fields, certain attributes of your product can be ripped off or copied by rivals. In fiction, it's a totally different ball game. No one is going to write exactly the way you do. It's what's called an author's voice. It's the thing that will make a reader read to the end of your book in the middle of the night, even though they know they have to get up early the next morning for an important meeting.

Wrapped altogether, a brand is an implied promise to the consumer that they'll receive a particular thing consistently from an author. That's part of the reason that publishers don't like authors to change their writing style too much or hop from one subgenre to the next, because it might upset the consumer who feels that the brand hasn't delivered.

But isn't building an author brand and building awareness about a book the same thing?

Not necessarily. Here's the problem. Even if you run out there and create a great buzz and get all kinds of brand awareness, unless you can define what makes your brand unique and different from others in the same product field (books here), you're doomed to failure. That's part of the reason that advertising isn't enough to build a strong brand. Branding is more than a logo, color scheme, tagline, or message points. These are just tools to help you create a solid brand that you can then build and make people aware of.

Because branding at its roots is based first on establishing an emotional connection, publicity often works better than advertising to get your foot in the door. It is used to help you make a connection with people—create word of mouth through reviews, interviews, chats, and workshops at conferences. If you can communicate your brand clearly and consistently, you will go a long way toward developing that emotional

Velcro with your consumer. It's about creating distinction in the market-place.

How does a strong author brand impact book sales?

Strong brands are created by word of mouth. The process is modeled on the same methods used by the largest corporate manufacturers of consumer goods in the world. By having your brand pop up all over the place—in the case of authors online, at conferences, etc.—you are getting people talking. This is also where media interviews and using your message points come into play. Ask yourself this: what good is it going to do if I see a commercial about a brand new soap that I've never heard of? There's very little chance I'm going to go race out and buy it, especially if I like my old soap just fine, thank you very much.

Now, rewind yourself to before sitting down and seeing that commercial. What if I've heard about it from some of my friends? What if I'd just seen the name of the soap in an article in a women's magazine about great new products? What if I got a sample and liked the smell? Now imagine that I see that commercial again for the first time with all of this experience behind me. I am far more motivated to find out what all the fuss is about and possibly take a chance on the new soap, even if I'm still attached to my old soap. Does this make more sense?

Now you understand why, although advertising is one of the main tools publishers use to help create brand awareness, it isn't the foundation piece for building a brand. You need to create the emotional drive and connection first, then the perception of higher quality, and finally make your point for why an author is unique.

CAN BRANDING BE TAKEN TOO FAR?

The family of V.C. Andrews, author of the bestsellers *Flowers in the Attic, Petals on the Wind, If There Be Thorns,* and *Seeds of Yesterday,* among others, hired a ghostwriter to continue writing under her name after her death in 1982. It seems they found papers that detailed the plots for 63 further novels. The ghostwriter was recently unveiled as Andrew Neiderman, who has written quite a few novels under his own name as well.

Several bestselling authors of today now write with coauthors; the most well known is James Patterson. His coauthors include Howard Roughan, Andrew Gross, and Peter de Jonge. Why does he do this? In marketing terms it is called brand extension. He is able to multiply the number of "products" with his brand name on them and occupy more shelf space in the bookstores. Patterson's method here is also interesting, because many authors have more good ideas for novels than they can possibly write. He is able to get more of his good ideas onto paper.

Clive Cussler is considering writing the Dirk Pitt series with a coauthor as well, to keep the series going and to take advantage of retirement at the same time.

The question is whether the author's unique voice can be maintained adequately in collaborative efforts, because the unique voice was one of the attributes that turned the author's work into a distinctive brand. Readers would be disappointed with a watered down version of the author's voice.

Then there is fan fiction, an activity that is growing in popularity, where fans of the author take favorite characters or plot lines from their novels and continue the story in the voice of that author. The bestselling author and his or her publisher take a dim view of this activity, because it violates the copyright to the characters. But it does point out how readers pick up on the subtle differences in pitch and timbre of a bestselling author's voice.

It is difficult to overstate the value to an author of having a widely recognized brand name.

"Almost anyone can be an author; the business is to collect money and fame from this state of being."

A.A. MILNE, *Not That It Matters*

10

PROMOTION

Publishers' and Publicists' Efforts and, of Course, Bookstores

PUBLISHERS PACK A PROMOTIONAL PUNCH

PROMOTING ON AND OFF THE INTERNET

THE TV BOOK CLUB FACTOR—THE WILD CARD OF BOOK PROMOTION

THE AUTHOR AS PRODUCT SPOKESPERSON

THE BOOKSELLERS

For all those aspirants to the bestseller list, it isn't enough to be confident that you can write better than currently popular authors. The real question is, "Can I sell more copies than those guys, and if so, why and how?" That becomes the key issue, being able to convince publishers that there is a large, addressable market for your work.

But defining a market and reaching a market are two separate challenges. The promotion of a book turns out to be the result of a partnership among a host of parties—the publishing house's promotion department and sales reps and, sometimes, the author's public relations firm; the bookstores that are enthusiastic about a book and make sure their customers know about it; the author who is determined to tell the media and the booksellers about the book; the cooperation of those annoyingly independent individuals, Luck and Timing; and, most importantly, the Readers Themselves.

PUBLISHERS PACK A PROMOTIONAL PUNCH

JANICE GOLDKLANG, *Publishing Director*
Pantheon and Shocken

What does a publishing director do?

I'm responsible for everything that's noneditorial. The books are acquired by the editors and edited by the editors, obviously, but once the books go into production, I have to oversee everything. I become involved in shaping the list, deciding publication dates, determining how a book is going to be published and what kind of efforts will be put into it, deciding who the readers are and what kind of potential the book has. I work with the sales and marketing department, our publicity people, and advertising. All of that comes under my position. I make all the decisions about *how* something gets published.

Can you tell us about the marketing efforts for a recent release?

We have a first novel that will be coming out this September. The author is the kind of writer that other writers recognize: she teaches at the University of Michigan. The editor asked me to read the book because it was going to go to auction and we had to determine how strongly we felt about its potential. The book had been sent to at least a dozen other publishers, and every one wanted it. We were not the high bidder, but the agent had faith that we could do a good job with it.

That book created an early buzz within our house. We brought the author in from Michigan and had a lunch for all our national account salespeople. When we invited them, we gave them a bound galley of the manuscript. At that lunch, everyone was talking about the book.

We took those bound galleys and sent them out to key people. I sent them out, the agent sent them out, the editor sent them out, and we got these amazing quotes back. At BookExpo America, we gave out advance reading copies (ARC) with these wonderful quotes from these extraordinary people on the cover instead of the jacket of the book. The first thing you saw was these testimonials to the power of the book.

The author was brought in to BookExpo America, and we hosted a dinner for booksellers. We are doing a mailing of the ARCs to booksellers, and we've planned a reading tour. Advertising is planned. We've done an aggressive push to get the book noticed. We have decided that this will be a "make" fiction book for us. We've done it before with *Three*

Junes, which started with very similar in-house enthusiasm. It's gone on to sell over 600,000 copies.

We try to do a lot for each and every book and do what is appropriate for each and every book. Not every book gets the same treatment. Each of our books is different, and that's the challenge and beauty of publishing.

Sending out galleys, which are bound, copyedited manuscripts, and advance reading copies are the traditional methods publishers use to introduce new titles to independent bookstores, chain stores, reviewers, the media, and tradeshows such as BookExpo America prior to publication.

For some titles, distributing these is no small project. Three thousand ARCs of Alice Sebold's *The Lovely Bones* were distributed by Little, Brown. Random House sent out 4,000 galleys of Sarah Durant's *The Birth of Venus*. Five thousand copies of Jodi's Picoult's *My Sister's Keeper* were printed by Atria, and 10,000 ARCs of Dan Brown's *The Da Vinci Code* were distributed. Keep in mind that many, many books don't *sell* as many as 10,000 copies.

Most publishers look for a hook in either the author's background or in the book itself to design a promotional strategy around. Authors such as Linda Fairstein, who was a legal prosecutor before she was an author, have a built-in hook, especially because the protagonist of her legal thrillers is a female prosecutor.

Promotional tactics can be quite imaginative. When Hyperion was planning the publication of Linda Greenlaw's *The Lobster Chronicles*, it printed 36,000 disposable lobster bibs advertising the title. These were given to seafood restaurants who agreed to promote the book through readings and posters.

Morrow, who published Marian Keyes's *The Other Side of the Story*, organized a reading for Keyes in conjunction with Club Monaco, a trendy New York clothing chain store. Attendees sat in the middle of the fashion aisles and could peruse the latest designs while sipping seltzer and listening to Keyes read.

The first 10,000 customers who preordered Michael Connelly's *Lost Light* received a free CD of his protagonist's favorite music.

Time Warner sent a cheese plate to each of their top booksellers to promote Sara-Kate Lynch's first novel, *Blessed Are the Cheesemakers*.

The noted literary house of Farrar, Straus, & Giroux sent the author of the lead title in their spring 2004 catalog, David Bezmozgis, and his editor and publicist on a promotional blitz. They wined and dined independent booksellers and select members of the media in Washington, D.C., Chicago, Los Angeles, and San Francisco.

Publishers determine what kind of advertising will be utilized, whether there will be a book tour and in what cities. They send out the prepublication galleys/ARCs for book reviews and media placement and the book itself afterwards. Each program is developed specifically for that title.

DANIEL HALPERN, *Editor-in-Chief*
HarperCollins

Can you go through the process of deciding what kind of marketing resources will be used to promote a certain title?

I think everybody does it differently in publishing. Sometimes, how much you pay for the book determines how marketing funds will be given over to that title. Other times, there are books that will respond to marketing in a way that makes it worthwhile to put in more money. Take a first book of short stories for example; you can send an author out to 100 bookstores, and they're going to get crowds of three to ten people if they're not known. That's a serious waste of money, not to mention the ego strain. You can do more through prepublication efforts—sending out more galleys, getting it into the hands of independent booksellers who will, in turn, get it to readers—that is, establish some excitement.

We certainly did that for Nell Freudenberger, and that started with a *New Yorker* story. Then came the story of how we bought Nell's book. She wanted to be at Ecco, an imprint of ours, which made me very happy. She benefited from having an enlightened agent in Amanda Urban of ICM. Then she produced a great book of short stories. We (all three of us!) worked very hard together on that book. We got the right package for it, and it spoke to what we imagined the audience would be, which was a younger audience, although as it turned out, the book cut across many age groups. It sold incredibly well, which also made me happy. The marketing was done primarily before the book came out, because it seemed to me—and to my marketing guru Carrie Kania—that was the best way to spend the money.

PROMOTING ON AND OFF THE INTERNET

In the last ten years, a powerful new book promotion tool has become widely available, the Internet. This tool can be used by bestselling and brand-new authors alike. It has brought authors and readers closer together, into a "community," and created in effect a global independent bookstore, where readers can exchange information and recommendations about new titles.

FAUZIA BURKE, *Founder and President*
FSB Associates

What's the difference between Internet marketing and publicity and traditional marketing and publicity?

The most profound difference is that the Internet provides authors with an unprecedented opportunity to market their books directly to their audience and fans—at a surprisingly reasonable cost. The term *Internet marketing* represents a wide array of tools for connecting readers and writers. A well-designed Web site functions as a home base for established fans and a gathering point for new ones. E-mail can announce bookstore or TV appearances or keep fans informed with a newsletter. Newsgroups, discussion lists, reading group sites, author chat sessions, and the descriptions and reader reviews on bookseller sites—all these are part of the online buzz that can help to break a book out of the pack and send it up the bestseller lists.

These tools can be harnessed to wage highly effective Internet book publicity campaigns that are cheaper and less labor intensive than traditional methods.

Another key difference is that a traditional book campaign has a limited life span. No matter how big the budget, the ads run their course, the press releases lose immediacy, and the author tour comes to an end.

But Internet marketing and publicity have staying power. Articles, reviews, and features that go online stay online for years, often with links to booksellers and the author's Web site. Type *Sue Grafton* in any search engine, for example, and the top results will include the site we created for Sue. Whether you've just discovered *A Is for Alibi* or you're eagerly awaiting the July 2004 release of *R Is for Ricochet,* there is something at this site for every fan.

Simply put, authors cannot afford to ignore the cost efficiency, ease, and effectiveness of this powerful resource. Every imaginable interest group—both personal and professional—is represented on the Internet and is eager to receive relevant information.

Amazon.com is the number-one spot on the Internet for books, escalating from just offering books and CDs when it first started in 1995 to selling a myriad of consumer products. Their virtual bookstore has two formidable competitive advantages over a brick-and-mortar bookstore: an astounding selection of available titles and substantial discounts from retail price.

LYN BLAKE, *Vice President of the vendor group*
Amazon.com

Does Amazon try to replace the hand selling that goes on in brick-and-mortar bookstores?

I don't think I would use the term *replace*. Everything Amazon does is all about selling one to one. All the technology we build is dedicated to finding out what the shopper is looking for in that visit, and what the shopper has looked for and purchased in the past, and coming up with a million different ways to make it easy to find the product they're looking for now. No one person in a bookstore could orient all those data points on any individual, no matter how long they've known that person. Amazon, in many ways, is more successful in hand-to-hand selling than a bookstore.

The Internet is becoming increasingly important in book promotion, but the traditional publicity tools still provide most of the impetus that drives sales. Without the correct blend of media and message, though, a publicity campaign can sometimes seem like that Search for Extra-Terrestrial Intelligence project (SETI) that constantly listens to radio signals from outer space in the hopes that somewhere, sometime, an intelligible message will be heard. How does a PR professional know if the message that was sent out about a book will actually reach the readers' eyes and ears?

RICK FRISHMAN, *Founder of Planned TV Arts, Coauthor*
Guerrilla Marketing for Writers and Guerrilla Publicity

How do you go about creating a hook for a PR campaign?

We aren't promoting a book per se; we're promoting a person. In teaching people about publicity and hooks, for nonfiction books I recommend they pay close attention to what's in the news affecting people's lifestyle, their kids, and their pocketbook. What is keeping people up at night with worry? What do people care about? That's your PR hook. Then look at today's headlines. Hooks change day by day depending on what's in the news. Producers and editors don't care about your book. They care about whether you can come on a talk show or be interviewed and teach us about what's going today that their listeners, viewers, readers care about.

THE TV BOOK CLUB FACTOR—
THE WILD CARD OF BOOK PROMOTION

Oprah Winfrey now devotes the book recommendation segment on her program to stoking the fires for "classic" books, but for nearly six years between 1996 and 2002, she had a book club segment on her program that was devoted to current authors. Over that time, she recommended 44 adult titles and 3 children's titles. The results were nothing short of amazing; 43 of her recommendations ended up on the bestseller lists for at least 10 weeks. So what, you are thinking. She just recommended already popular authors. That is what is so striking about the power of Oprah's recommendations: only ten of the authors whose books she picked had ever been on any bestseller list before.

Getting recommended on TV can have a lottery windfall impact on a book's sales, but of course, the odds of a book being the one chosen are about the same. Authors and their PR people have to devise clever means to get their books noticed by the TV show's producers. Vicki Lewis Thompson and her publicist, Theresa Meyers, got her romance novel, *Nerd in Shining Armor,* noticed by the *Regis and Kelly* producers by sending Kelly the book in a Hawaiian floral basket. *Nerd in Shining Armor* was recommended by Kelly Ripa, and the recommendation gave a jet propulsion boost to the book's sales, sending it from a first printing of 28,000 copies to more than 228,000 copies within three days, and rocketed the book's Amazon.com standing to number seven in less than 24 hours.

A particularly literate visitor from another planet in a distant galaxy might have the temerity to inquire, "Why do you earthlings care what Kelly Ripa says you should read?"

Book recommendations from television stars have such tremendous power, much more than reviews in even the most widely read print media, for two reasons.

1. Viewers look at the star as a trusted friend who comes into their homes each day, so in effect, the recommendation is a kind of electronic word of mouth.
2. The audience for these daytime shows is extremely large and extremely loyal.

MATT BIALER, *literary agent*
Sanford J. Greenburger & Associates

Does the agent advise the author about the realities of the publishing industry?

All the time. You always read about the music industry, how it is consolidating, how they just care about the bottom line. It's true about publishing as well. It can be a very impersonal business. Editors come and go. They don't edit as much as they once did. That isn't their fault; it's just that their time and skills are stretched so thin that they just don't have the time as much anymore to hold the author's hand, or to make sure that a particular book gets very customized publicity.

Suppose an author has written a Civil War novel. You might hear them say, "Why didn't the publisher send it to all the Civil War magazines to get attention? Publishers aren't built that way. Their publicity department works on a book for a month, and it is one of many they are working on. They'll send it to certain places, maybe some specialized places.

As an agent, you have to get the author to realize that you can't wait around for your publisher to do things all the time. You should start your own Web site—don't wait for them to do it for you. You may need to hire your own freelance publicist. It's your career. You need to be proactive, especially in the beginning. The competition is fierce, and you're not a proven success to the publisher. They probably aren't going to spend a lot of money on you. You need to create whatever advantage you can.

Eventually, the publisher takes over most of these tasks and really puts their marketing resources behind the author's books. Publishing most beginning authors to them could be described as throwing it up on the wall and seeing if it will stick. The author has to do everything they can to make sure it does stick.

THE AUTHOR AS PRODUCT SPOKESPERSON

The promotion strategy executed by a publishing house or by a PR firm requires the author's input and participation to be successful. What's a show without a star?

From the author's standpoint, the book promotion process can seem like a strange new world. You go from the quiet, reflective world of crafting prose by yourself to the rushed, brightly lit, crowded, split-second timing atmosphere of the media. The other issue is one of message. Consumers are used to being bombarded with messages about how a given product is the best, most magnificent, amazing thing to come around in decades. We discount most of it, so the advertisers become even more brazen with their claims. When they first start out, authors generally aren't comfortable with pitching a product on TV, but they can learn this skill.

GENE TAFT, *Vice President and Director of Publicity*
PublicAffairs

How does a publicity campaign contribute to a book's success?

Publicity is one of the key elements for promoting a book. One of the reasons publishers rely on it so much is that, though it isn't free, it is relatively free. The house has publicists on staff who receive a salary, but there aren't many other significant departmental costs. That's why the book industry is not a huge consumer of advertising. With publicity, you get the same kind of visibility for your book for free, from reviews and articles about the book. Publicity might even be relied on disproportionately. These days, you don't even need to have the authors travel that much, except for appearances on national media such as *The Today*

Show. Radio and TV studios are everywhere. Authors can do interviews from almost any city, without leaving their hometown.

One drawback is that book publishing is, sadly, somewhat the bottom rung of the media. Let's say you have an author booked on a major network morning show. The first segment to get bumped off if they run behind schedule is not the interview with Jennifer Lopez; it's the book segment.

The other piece of good news about publicity, besides that it is relatively inexpensive, is the fact that every newspaper, every magazine, every radio station, and every TV show is a possible candidate for having author interviews. Any book with general interest is of interest to the media.

How do you get a new author ready to appear on TV?

It is somewhat difficult to coach someone. I remind authors that there is lots of competition for the entertainment dollar—their book is not the only choice consumers have. With TV interviews, they have to learn to talk in sound bites—and most of us do not do that in normal conversation. And the average author segment is usually four to six minutes, not a lot of time to convey a message. The author has to strike a delicate balance between showing knowledge of a subject, providing information, and also promoting the title. Ideally, you want the interviewer to mention the book. You don't want to keep having to say, "In my book titled . . . ."

THE BOOKSELLERS

We've already seen how bookstores go about selecting which new titles they will order, and in what quantities, from the mind-boggling number of choices available. But what happens when the books get in the stores? What role do booksellers play in promoting or recommending a given title to their customers? How much impact do bookstores actually have?

CAROL B. CHITTENDEN, *Owner*
Eight Cousins Bookstore in Falmouth, Massachusetts

My own rule of thumb is always: write great stories, edit them carefully, illustrate them with beauty and originality (which is not to say prettily or weirdly), and we'll make sure our customers know about them. They'll tell the world.

Some bookstores believe they have a huge impact. We asked an owner of a genre-specific bookstore if she would like to be included in the book, and she replied, "I'm too busy *making* bestsellers to have time to talk to you about it."

Changing Hands bookstore in Tempe, Arizona, came up with a unique event for first-time novelists dubbed "First Fiction." Five authors, Nell Freudenbergr (*Lucky Girls*), Julie Orringer (*How to Breathe Underwater*), Ryan Hartly (*Bring Me Your Saddest Arizona*), Nick Kelm (*Girls*), and Audrey Niffenegger (*The Time Traveler's Wife*) were invited to a joint reading given, not at the bookstore but at a nearby restaurant, which agreed to serve five-cent first drinks and free food to attendees. The event was a rousing success.

GAYLE SHANKS, *Owner*
Changing Hands in Tempe, Arizona

Why are events so important for authors and bookstores? An author can only sign X number of books in two hours.

It's not just about the event they're doing in your store; it's the publicity around the event. Publicity is a cumulative thing. Readers enjoy sitting down with an author and hearing parts of the book being read aloud. The top authors typically make a limited number of stops. It could be as few as five, scheduled through their publisher. Then there is the case of a new author who gets in his car on his own initiative and drives to 60 places across the country to do book signings and generate interest in the book.

An author's willingness to promote a book matters more and more. Agents will even tell you that it helps to discuss your willingness in the cover letters they send to publishers on the author's behalf, saying, "By the way, this author loves promoting, loves reading excerpts of his book." There are a lot of books out there today. Success depends on promotion.

Anything you want to add about what makes bestsellers?

The timing of a book's debut is critical. Each publishing house has a limited promotional budget and has a difficult task allocating those dollars among all the new titles. As an author, you don't want to come out the same season as a huge blockbuster book that is getting all the promotional dollars and attention from your publisher.

I would also mention that we have much more information about new books and book reviews delivered to us much faster, thanks to e-mail and online book review sites such as Salon.com and Bookbrowse.com. Bookstores can communicate so much more quickly with one another and spread the word about a great new book. Back when we began, 30 years ago, we had to make photocopies of reviews and send them to our friends. Now, the communication is instant.

SUSAN ELIZABETH PHILLIPS, *Author*

Why does word-of-mouth buzz occur for some books and not others?

For *It Had to Be You,* a lot of the buzz happened in the new/used bookstores. These tend to be stores where readers gather and talk about books, where there's a lot of one-on-one interaction. The booksellers really pushed *It Had to Be You.* They read it, they loved it, and started hand selling it. These stores were really critical to the book's success. Shortly after the book came out, I remember getting an e-mail from a store owner in Costa Mesa, California, telling me she had already sold 157 copies of *It Had to Be You.* Now this was a relatively small new/used bookstore. Right then I knew something very positive was going on.

But it is not just through the independent bookstores that this occurs. I can tell you about a number of chain stores as well where there's an individual bookseller who happens to love romance novels, and that bookseller will hand sell like crazy. Some of this is just luck; they have a bookseller on site who really knows a specific genre.

DANIEL GOLDIN, Buyer
Harry W. Schwartz Bookshops in Milwaukee, Wisconsin

How can an author help you sell their books?

Do the following:

- Promote their book at an author event. It makes a big difference.
- Go the extra mile before the event to help with advance publicity.
- Buy books from us. Why not?
- Mention the store in interviews. (This, of course, takes sales away from other stores, but you asked.)
- Be available for book club interviews.
- Make sure their book is not ugly, overpriced, or hard to obtain.
- Be nice to the owner, the buyer, the marketing person, and the booksellers.

We try harder for our friends.

BARBARA MEADE, Owner
Politics and Prose Bookstore in Washington, D.C.

How is buzz created around certain books? How do booksellers help?

The publishers try to start the buzz by handing out a lot of galleys, particularly at BEA. For example, Little Brown was handing out hundreds of galleys of Malcom Gladwell's new *Blink*. The publishers are very high on that book, and they've created a buzz for him, probably more buzz than the book deserves. Gladwell is a bestselling author. *The Tipping Point* still sells about a dozen copies a week in our store. He has postponed writing another book for so long—it's been about six years since *The Tipping Point* came out—a lot of anticipation has built up.

Another way publishers create buzz is scheduling authors on media tours and getting their name into the press, but the biggest way is sending out galleys. Publishers depend on a number of people reading a book and creating a lot of noise about it.

Our store helps create buzz through our newsletter, a monthly calendar, and a weekly e-mail. The books we're interested in, we put in one or all of those. We have an author event every night, and on the weekends we usually have two events, one in the afternoon and one in the evening both Saturday and Sunday.

11

CLIMBING THE MARKETING MOUNTAIN

THE AUTHOR'S EFFORTS
CREATING WORD-OF-MOUTH BUZZ

THE AUTHOR'S EFFORTS

One of the great things about being an author is that your success very much depends on how much effort you are willing to expend—first, in writing the best possible book you can; then, in your tireless devotion to telling potential buyers about your book, using every means and medium possible. Your work actually has the potential to change peoples' lives, to be so memorable that your readers will take the time to tell other people they should buy the book. In a sense, every reader is a potential sales rep for your book.

The publisher cannot do all the promotion by itself, even one of the megapublishers with enormous financial resources and clout with booksellers. Random House was said to have a budget of $100 million for the marketing and promotion of their 2003 list. They publish roughly 3,000 titles. That works out to an average promotional expenditure of $33,000 per book. We know that the relatively small number of front-list titles get the most marketing support, so not every book gets as much as $33,000 behind it. In those cases, the author must be out front, leading the promotional campaign and devising and implementing tactics to make sure people know about the book.

Clearly, most of the top-selling authors have a very good handle on the importance of promoting their books and on how to go about it. Nicholas Sparks is an example of an author whose willingness to put in extra promotional effort, right at the outset, launched his career as a bestselling author.

NICHOLAS SPARKS, *Author*

One of the stars of the romance genre, Nicholas achieved great success with his first published novel, *The Notebook,* in 1996, and he followed that with *Message in a Bottle, A Walk to Remember, The Rescue, A Bend in the Road, Nights in Rodanthe, The Guardian, The Wedding,* and *Three Weeks with My Brother,* all with Warner Books. All were domestic and international bestsellers and were translated into more than 35 languages. Nicholas has the distinction of being only the second contemporary author to have a novel spend more than a year on both the *New York Times* hardcover and paperback bestseller lists. (The other is J.K. Rowling.)

How did you promote *The Notebook?*

When I received information about my first book tour, in April of 1996, I learned that it was scheduled for just five cities. Even then, I realized I would need to visit more cities for the book to be a success. I needed to get out and promote, but the publishing house wasn't willing to commit to more. Thankfully, fate intervened. It turns out that the head of one of the foreign agencies was having a housewarming party out in Phoenix. My agent suggested I go, because the head of Warner Books was going to be there. She was hoping that if I met him, he would be impressed enough to send me on the road more. So I went out, at my own expense, to Phoenix. Sure enough, my tour was upped from 5 to 25 cities. It eventually grew to 50 cities, and the buzz helped to build interest in the book.

Despite not having much review attention, *The Notebook* hit the bestseller list the first week out, tied for the tenth position. It became a word-of-mouth book, a book that readers enjoyed, so they told someone else about it. In time, *48 Hours* did a show on the book, but it wasn't responsible for launching the book—by then, *The Notebook* had been on the list for over two months.

In the publishing industry, there are really only three ways to make it big. One: you can have incredible reviews in major news media, and by that I mean *Time, Newsweek, U.S. News and World Report,* the *New York Times,* the *Chicago Tribune,* and the *Washington Post.* All of those wrote about *Cold Mountain,* by Charles Frazier, describing it as one of the best books written in the last 20 years. It's been said that *Cold Mountain* was launched by the independent bookstores, but the truth is that reviews appeared in the major media before it was even published, so there was a lot of pent-up interest in it before it reached the bookstores. *Cold Mountain,* in fact, debuted on the list its first week out. Reviews essentially launched the book.

The second way is to be picked up by a major media source that recommends books. That would be Oprah, Kelly Ripa, or the *Good Morning America* reading club. All the books chosen by hosts on these shows become bestsellers.

The third and final way is to become a word-of-mouth book. *The Secret Life of Bees, The Notebook,* and *The Bridges of Madison County* are examples.

One bestselling author who was willing to do whatever it took to promote his book is Christopher Paolini. Not only was he willing, but he enlisted his entire family to assist with the promotion, creating an ongoing roadshow of appearances and selling the book themselves for many months. He built his fan base literally one individual at a time.

CHRISTOPHER PAOLINI, *Author*

Christopher's first book, an extremely imaginative fantasy novel titled *Eragon,* was initially self-published, then picked up by major publisher Knopf, and soon became a bestseller. What is especially remarkable is that he began writing *Eragon* when he was just 15. *Eragon,* planned to be part of an Inheritance Trilogy, is about a young man who meets his destiny armed with a mythic red sword and aided by a beautiful dragon named Saphira. The second volume of the series is titled *Eldest.* Christopher has been hailed as a fresh new voice in the fantasy genre.

What were some of the things you did to promote the self-published version of your fantasy book, *Eragon,* prior to its being published by Knopf?

Dressed in medieval costume, I did over 135 events across the country at bookstores, schools, and festivals. Promoting *Eragon* became the family business: books sold meant food on the table, so we were incredibly determined.

We started by doing book signings in bookstores but quickly learned that no one shows up for an author they have never heard of. I was very determined and would stay for eight hours straight and talk to every person who came in the store and try to sell them a book. On a good day, I might sell 40 books. That's not bad for a signing, but it's a lot of work.

I then learned that if I went into a school and did a presentation, in one day we could sell 300 books or more, and inspire students to read and write, so I concentrated on that. We also started charging a fee for the presentation, to help cover travel expenses.

My dad and I made two trips to Houston, where my grandmother lives. I called numerous school librarians and spoke to them about my book and presentation. They didn't know who I was, so it took a bit of persuading, but I managed to arrange to visit several schools, along with a few bookstores, that first trip. One of the librarians posted an enthusiastic recommendation of my presentation to an online teachers' forum, so by the time we returned home to Montana, my mom already had a second trip to Texas planned, and I didn't have to do any cold calls. That second trip was a solid month long, with three or four hour-long presentations every single day.

You will notice in this next series of interviews that there is considerable disagreement among publicists, agents, and authors about what type of author-based promotional efforts work best and how much time—and money—the author should expend on them. Publicist Rick Frishman and author Brad Meltzer stress that the author's demonstrated willingness to promote a book creates a favorable buzz for the book throughout the publishing house. It is all part of being a team player, recognizing that an author's eventual success is due to the thoughtful and dedicated work of many individuals.

RICK FRISHMAN, *Founder*

Planned TV Arts and Coauthor of Networking Magic: Find the Best—from Doctors, Lawyers, and Accountants to Homes, Schools, and Jobs

How does an author's attitude toward promotion contribute to their success?

It is all-important. One hundred percent important. Mega-important. The author must communicate a passion toward the marketing of the book. A buzz starts to happen very early in a publishing house about a new book. It starts with the agent, with the editor, with the first meeting with marketing and publicity people. The buzz is about you, the author. You are a mover, shaker, doer, and reliable and ethical; you'll do what you say you're going to do. You are someone a publisher wants to work with. The opposite, unfortunately, can also occur. The buzz is that the author is a pain in the ass.

The impression you make contributes to how you are positioned in the publisher's catalog and what is being said about you to the sales reps who are getting ready to go out and talk to the buyers.

BRAD MELTZER, *Author*

How important do you feel an author's efforts toward promotion are to the success of their books?

On some level, it's probably more psychologically rewarding to the author than actually effective in gaining more readers. If I sat home and did nothing, I'd be chewing the curtains; my wife would kill me. I would be so nervous I wasn't doing anything and thinking, "How can I possibly sit here when there are books to be sold?" But by my going out and doing something—does it actually sell more than maybe a couple hundred or a thousand books? I have no idea, but it lets me sleep at night, and it lets me feel like I gave it my all.

I think that you owe it to all the people in your publishing house to try. I'm the one whose name is on the book, but only a fool would think it's a one-person show. An entire fleet of people at Warner Books is counting on me, and it's not just to write the book. It's to go out and promote the book. It's not just good business; it's common courtesy. There are people killing themselves to put that book in the stores. There's a sales force working to put the book in every retail store that sells anything with pages and a cover on it. They're working hard for me, and you know what? I'm going to work hard for them and do whatever they need me to do. There are booksellers out there who push my book. And you know what? *That's* the only reason I get to do what I do today. So I don't think about it as, "Did I sell five books today by going out and doing an interview?" I just think it's the right thing to do because people are working hard for you.

Sometimes an author doesn't need to leave home to be active in promoting their books. A content-rich Web site with lots of author involvement helps build a loyal readership.

FAUZIA BURKE, *Founder and President*
FSB Associates

How important is the author's attitude toward promotion to the success of a book?

The author's attitude and availability can make a big difference, especially with Internet marketing. The Internet lets authors interact with the audience in a much more intimate way, strengthening the bonds of reader loyalty. We've had authors who posted regularly to the discussion boards on their Web sites, keeping in touch with readers, reporting on their own book tours—it can be thrilling to witness.

Research shows that Web exposure leads to traditional media coverage. Journalists and media producers use the Internet more than ever for e-mail, research, to find expert commentators and for finding story ideas. This really came home for us when Don Imus interviewed Douglas Stanton on his radio show and praised the Web site we created for Doug's bestseller, *In Harm's Way*. The strength of an author's online presence can influence the television producer or magazine editor's decision to feature a particular book or author.

Authors Stuart Woods, Mark Bowden, Barbara Delinsky, and Stephanie Laurens stress that the publisher's promotional strategies and efforts are still the most important and that the author's most important contribution is to put the best effort into the writing process itself.

STUART WOODS, *Author*

Are the most successful authors more marketing and media savvy than typical authors?

James Patterson, I've read, takes a keen interest in the marketing of his books. He was in advertising earlier in his career, as I was. Most writers, though, don't know about those things. I had some knowledge because I spent time in advertising. Most writers are just writers, they don't have marketing backgrounds.

Does it get easier to build the sales of your books as you have achieved more success?

My role is simply to write the book. The writing process has gotten easier over the years, because I've gained confidence. Confidence gives you a great boost. All the rest takes place in the publishing house. I'm pretty much cut off from that. I've taken a greater interest in the marketing side at times in my career. My current publisher does a good job, and they would rather do the marketing function themselves, so I don't meddle in the marketing too much.

MARK BOWDEN, *Author*

Is part of the reason certain authors attain bestselling status because they are more skilled or savvy at marketing and promotion?

For some people, that is definitely true. I know authors who make a study of this side of the industry and are greatly responsible for their own commercial success. In my case, it's not true. I owe the commercial success of my books to my publisher.

BARBARA DELINSKY, *Author*

How important are a new author's promotional efforts for the success of their book?

If a new author has the physical strength, the time, and enough money to do enough promotion for long enough, and *then* repeat it all for several years running, it can be a huge help vis-á-vis the success of a book. Unfortunately, few authors, new or otherwise, have the strength, time, and resources to do that.

Taking out one $10,000 ad in a magazine won't do much. Moreover, most writers don't have $10,000 to spare, which means making sacrifices, with very little to show for it.

Some publicity firms suggest putting the entire advance into promoting the book.

Those firms forget the fact that one needs money to live on. The advance was originally designed to give the author money to live on while they wrote the book. For a new author, those advances aren't often big—and money that isn't big can't buy much promotion. Only large-scale promotion makes a real difference.

That said, there are cases where the bottom line isn't all that counts. For instance, I don't know how many books my Web site sells, though the site is costly, what with redesigning, adding pages, general upkeep, and Web promo. Does the money correlate into a larger audience? I don't know. But the Web site does make me feel good.

So. If printing bookmarks—or taking out an ad, or making a TV appearance, or doing a book signing—makes a new author feel that they are doing something, I say *do it.*

Unfortunately, promotional efforts take time away from writing the next book. Now, there are some people who only *want* to write one book and, therefore, do have time for promo. Me, I'm a continuous producer of books. If I were to spend one month a year doing promotion, even if I had the money and the emotional wherewithal and no family, I would lose that month from writing. That month is precious. If I'm going to produce a book a year, I need it.

STEPHANIE LAURENS, *Author*

How important to the success of a book is the willingness of the author to promote it?

I believe this varies hugely, depending on the type of book. In genre fiction, you need to build an audience—beyond having a decent Web site, author-driven promotion is in my opinion useless and a waste of time. Publisher-generated, targeted promotion, yes, and being available for that is a contracted obligation, but you only need to do the math to see it's pretty impossible for an individual to reach and influence the thousands it takes to affect your sales. In genre fiction, generating another excellent book and getting it out there is a better bet for increasing your sales figures. In genre fiction, success is not about personal promotion but about readers' reaction to the story. It's the story they buy, not the author.

I'm going to add a catch-22 here that relates to promotion and reviews. In genre fiction, a large part of the reason neither of these is of any great value in initially building your audience, even when they are good, is because the distribution of your book is already set. Accounts buy based on previous sales of your books, and their orders come in from five months to one month ahead of release. So, unless you are already a bestseller and can be assured your book is going to be on the racks across America, readily accessible to every potential reader, then any promotion or review can only have an affect when it influences someone who can actually find your book to buy. This greatly limits the effectiveness of author-driven promotion and reviews.

The authors we have just heard from, of course, are enjoying hugely successful careers and sell books in the hundreds of thousands and even millions of copies. What about the midlist author or the author just launching a career?

GENE TAFT, *Vice President and Director Publicity*
PublicAffairs

Is book promotion increasingly on the shoulders of the author?

Certainly for the smaller authors whose books have print runs of 5,000 to 20,000 copies. They need to be out there promoting. I tell authors, the more you can do, the more I can do. There are only so many hours in the day. If the author is working in cooperation with the publisher, in partnership, we cover twice as much ground. There is still this misconception that the relationship is, "I wrote the book. Now you (publisher) go sell it." I don't think that was ever the case, but it is even less the case now. There is so much competition. We don't just wave a magic wand and make books sell. If we could do that, we'd do it for every book.

RICK FRISHMAN, *Founder*
Planned TV Arts

How can an author's promotional efforts enhance a book's chances of success?

Dr. Wayne Dyer was one of the first authors to realize the importance of creating publicity, in the 1970s. He realized that you can't simply rely on your publisher to do the publicity for you. The author has to have his own PR people, his own PR program. He was famous for putting his books in the trunk of his car and driving around the country, talking to newspapers and appearing on TV shows to promote them. He changed the way authors thought about publicity. Wayne is really the granddaddy of it all.

Most authors should take a good portion of their advance, whether it's $20,000 or $200,000, and use it for marketing and publicity, because by and large, the publisher isn't going to do much in that regard. The major reason the publisher might do a lot is if they gave you a huge advance and they have to make sure they earn that back from book sales. Or sometimes it is in an author's publishing contract they will spend money on publicity. They may notice a book is starting to take off right away when it is published, so then they do more. Most of the time, though, they just do a galley mailing. Maybe do some publicity in the author's hometown. Perhaps send the author to a couple of cities for book signings and publicity. Many times, they don't even do that, though. They just piggyback on what the author is doing. If you are going to a city anyway, they will do some PR for you prior to your arrival.

Bestselling author Sandra Brown advises that new authors should spend time making friends with booksellers, and she puts this issue in perspective by showing that successful authors have widely varying approaches to promotion.

SANDRA BROWN, *Author*

How important to the success of a book is the willingness of the author to promote it?

I know so many successful authors who never do any kind of personal appearance. If you want to take it the ultimate extreme, J. D. Salinger is a recluse, and still *Catcher in the Rye* sells hundreds of thousands of copies a year.

When an author is first starting out, one of the best promotions they can do is meet with booksellers, to try and meet the people who order the books, who stock the books, who drive the trucks loaded with books, because then you become more than just another name. There is some value in cultivating relationships with owners of independent bookstores.

You know, there are writers who never go on tour, who never do TV or radio, who don't do print interviews—and they are enormously successful. Danielle Steele—very, very rarely does she ever grant an interview. But then Mary Higgins Clark goes on tour with every single book.

A lot of it is the author's personality. I don't think it would work well for someone who is absolutely terrified of crowds or who isn't a people person. They may do themselves more harm than good. Other authors are very gregarious and comfortable in that situation, so when they go, they make an impact.

It's not a black-and-white answer.

Literary agent Margret McBride points out that, even with a great deal of author involvement in the promotional campaign, it can still be a dismal failure if it is not properly planned out. Authors are not all born to be effective media advocates for their work. Training in what to say and how to say it is absolutely vital.

MARGRET MCBRIDE, Literary Agent
McBride Literary Agency

How can a book's promotion be improved?

The one very important ingredient that gets left out of effective publicity and promotion of the book is the *author*.

The author knows why they wrote the book; they've spent a year or two writing. What was the thing that kept them up nights working on it? Sometimes the question of why is the *reason* for the book. It can become the *theme* for the advertising, the publicity *hook*, and the catalog copy and ultimately determine the success of the book.

Another current publishing rule: "We as publishers don't send authors on tours anymore—we'll do national television shows, and then we'll go from there." A big reason most authors don't sell a warehouse full of inventory, even if they get media coverage, is because they are *untrained*—untrained for national or local media exposure.

Every author should set aside a portion of their advance to hire a speech/media coach to train them for radio, television, and call-in shows. Each category has an entirely different dynamic. Imagine being on the *Today Show* and thinking you're going to have 3 minutes and suddenly being told that you're down to 60 seconds. You have to think fast— and pull a few bullet points from the dozen you've prepared and *own*— that get your message across clearly, powerfully, and succinctly. It's really frightening if you've merely memorized but don't own your own points.

This is what I used to tell my authors.

You're on *Oprah,* or *Montel*—you've got to tell exactly what your book is about. There is a lady or a man at home. They have a bad cold; they're feeling miserable. You come on, and Oprah asks you a question about your book. You give an answer. Their computer is down because of the storm outside, so Amazon .com is out of the question. They immediately call their favorite local bookstore. The sick person throws on a trench coat, grabs a box of tissue, and drives through the pouring rain to the bookstore. What did you say on that show that made them do that?

What compelled them to get your book as soon as possible? Unless your pitch has that ASAP factor—it won't have the rate of sale necessary to make it to a bestseller list.

What's currently happening is that the publishers send these nice but *untrained* (for media) authors onto national television. This nice author has been locked up in a room for two or more years, working on this book, and is scared out of their mind when the red light of the camera turns on in front of their face. The author does an OK job—gives the nice, polite author answer—and *nothing* happens to the book. Everyone is shocked! She was on *Oprah* or he was on *Today,* but nothing happened.

An author has to be coached, for at least a full day. Better give them a few weeks on local TV and radio in their own town, then hit the nationals. There is a big difference between giving information about your book and promoting your book. The author, I think, is the best promotion for the book. When the audience can react to *the author's passion* about their subject—it's a *beautiful* thing!

So you feel publicity is important?

It's not merely important—it's *critical* to a book's success. Publicity can make or break the success of the book.

Word of mouth starts at the grass roots and swells.

CREATING WORD-OF-MOUTH BUZZ

Word of mouth is the best kind of publicity—it is absolutely free; it proceeds silently, efficiently, and exponentially; and it can run 24/7. First, there has to be a catalyst to get the book into the hands of a certain number of readers who love the book. Then, word of mouth can take the book all the way to the top of the bestseller list. The question is: what qualities make a book the fortunate beneficiary of word-of-mouth, reader-to-reader selling?

SUSAN ELIZABETH PHILLIPS, Author

What about creating buzz among readers? Let's say a book is recommended in stores and people buy it. Why does it become a book we all recommend to our friends?

I think it comes down to this whole issue of an author's voice. It's such a hard thing to talk about. Sometimes a writer is just given a voice that appeals to readers. A God-given gift. I'm not sure it is something you can develop. You either have it or you don't. Every writer has a voice, but some voices appeal to a broader group of readers.

People were not writing funny romances when *It Had to Be You* came out. It's hard to believe now with all the romantic comedy fiction out there. I was pretty much the founding mother of that genre. The idea that you could have a sexy romance and be laughing through it was revolutionary. That helped spread word of mouth for me.

Another thing that helped was the annual convention of Romance Writers of America. My publisher came up with the idea of giving away 1,000 copies of *It Had to Be You* to the members attending the convention. This was 1994–95. Now it seems everyone does these giveaways, but this was about the first time it had been done. It was a big factor in generating word of mouth for the book.

Why one writer kicks in with the audience and another doesn't has to do with the book being a compelling read, one the reader doesn't want to put down. When I find a book like that, the first thing I want to do is tell my friends about it. Now, of course, the Internet is a huge factor. There are genre message boards and chat rooms where large numbers of readers can get together and recommend books to each other.

DR. SPENCER JOHNSON, Author

What have been some factors that boosted sales of your books?

Most of my books have reached the bestseller list by word of mouth. There was hardly any promotion of *Who Moved My Cheese*, but in retrospect, people think it was a "brilliantly" marketed book, which it wasn't. Word of mouth is by far the most important factor in creating a megabestseller.

The individual reader who tells five people about a book is the unsung hero of the publishing industry.

Great point. They are the unsung heroes of the bestseller list, the people who spread the word. And that's why you realize you are a very fortunate author when that happens. Again, it is humbling, because you realize how lucky you are when that happens.

NICHOLAS SPARKS, *Author*

What is it about those books that become word-of-mouth sensations? Are they easy to describe in one or two sentences, so one person can easily tell another what the book is about?

No. It comes down to two factors. The story touches a nerve, and it ends in a memorable fashion. Upon closing the book, the reader's response is, "I have to tell someone about this." If you take *The Secret Life of Bees*, it really appeals to the power of friendship and love, the goodness of people, the strength of women, childhood. It struck many universal chords and ended well, so people loved it and wanted to recommend it to others.

So you arrived on the bestseller list with your first book, which must have been quite a thrill, although it sounds like you did a lot of advance planning to improve your chances of success.

That's all just hope, though. You can do everything right in this industry, and it never guarantees anything. Picking the right story is only half the battle. The other half is writing a book that makes people want to talk about it. These types of novels come in all forms, in every genre. *The Secret Life of Bees* is very different than *The Da Vinci Code*, but both were very successful. Both are unique in the way they move the reader, and each one ends in such a way as to compel the reader to tell someone else about it.

Perhaps there should be a Word-of-Mouth Bestseller list on the Internet, where readers could vote for the books they are recommending most often to their friends. One wonders how that list would compare to the *New York Times* bestseller list. Many authors would not even have careers if it weren't for these people who take the time to make a word-of-mouth recommendation of books to their friends, starting an exponential growth in sales for the authors. Perhaps they should be commemorated with a statue outside the high-rise offices of one of the major publishers—the Unsung Heroes of Publishing, the readers who take the time to recommend a book to their friends. They certainly deserve some kind of formal honor.

12

BUILDING A CAREER

A TALE OF TWO AUTHORS

GETTING STARTED

MIDLIST, FRONTLIST, OR BACKLIST

HOW AUTHORS MANUFACTURE THEIR OWN LUCK

COMING BACK FOR SECONDS

A TALE OF TWO AUTHORS

It is mid-December; the holiday shopping rush is accelerating toward a typically frantic climax. At this large chain bookstore in an upscale mall, the aisles are so crammed with merchandise that it is difficult for the huge throng of customers to navigate from one end of the store to another. These are the wisest of all holiday shoppers, because as we all know, books make the most wonderful presents. In the high traffic areas, you notice that a select few titles are prominently displayed in their own racks, others in three-foot high pyramidal stacks. You wonder: can the store really sell 50 or 100 copies or more of this one single book during the holiday season, given that more than 150,000 books are available in the store?

The answer is, certainly. These are the latest books from the bestselling authors, the publishing industry elite. Those writers' names are as powerful and magnetic a brand to the book-buying public as the golden arches are to those tired, hungry shoppers seeking respite in the form of a hamburger and fries in another part of the mall.

In one of these busy bookstore aisles, you notice someone who doesn't appear to be shopping. This person is just staring at one of the bestselling titles featured in its own display: *Murder in the Foul Mist*, by

Charlene Charttopper. There is unmistakable joy on this person's face, mixed with great satisfaction. This is the author of the book, and it is her first bestseller, the first big success after two, five, ten—or more— years of dedicated effort and perhaps gritty financial struggle. Think about the thrill you would feel to see your name on a book in the front window of the store, on display to the thousands who stroll by. Consider the even greater thrill of walking inside the store and seeing shoppers pick up *your book* and head for the checkout stand.

So, going back to our author in the store, let's lift a mental glass of champagne and toast her triumph. What this author did is an astounding achievement.

Now, through the front door of the bookstore comes another author. He followed exactly the same path as Charlene: he studied, honed his craft, sweat blood onto blank pages, faced rejection after rejection until that unforgettable day when the letter arrived from the publisher— "We are proud to be publishing your book." He made it through the painful months of editing that followed, before the book went to the printer. Our second author looks excited, expectant. He knows his title, *Foul Murder in the Mist,* has been shipped to retailers and is available for sale this holiday season. His heart is beating wildly as he looks for the aisle where his title should be on the shelves of mystery novels. He bumps into you as he rushes toward it; he doesn't mean to be rude, he's just manic. Dreams that come true are sometimes the most dangerous.

But his hopes are quickly crushed. He finds his book there, but the store has ordered just one copy. It sits on the shelf like a lonesome puppy at the pound, with little hope of adoption. Even motivated readers would have to go on a virtual scavenger hunt in the store to find it, particularly when there are blinding, colorful stacks of the bestselling authors' titles enticing them at the edge of every aisle.

Our dejected author doesn't realize it, but he has just entered the author's twilight zone, from which there is little chance of escape. What's especially frightening is that he is most likely going to spend his entire career there: the midlist.

GETTING STARTED

The road to bestsellerdom isn't straight and smooth; there are detours, construction barricades, and wrong turns. Many authors who start out never complete the journey. Others, however, seem to be permanently in the fast lane.

Jackie Collins, superstar Hollywood novelist, wrote her first book while still in school and went on to sell 400 million copies in 40 countries. Mary Higgins Clark was a secretary and then a stewardess for Pan American, married, had children, and wrote radio scripts before she wrote her first book. Her second book became a bestseller as has each of her subsequent novels. Jeffery Deaver, thriller author, wrote his first book at the age of 11. When he became a practicing attorney, he decided to write the kind of books he liked to read during the long commutes to work. Joy Fielding wrote her first story at eight, submitted it to *Jack and Jill* magazine, and received her first rejection as well. Undiscouraged, she wrote her first TV script at 12, which was also rejected.

NICHOLAS SPARKS, *Author*

Tell us how you got started with your career as a novelist.

I may be somewhat different from other authors, because I've focused on the business side of publishing ever since I first began writing. Even before I'd written a single page, I knew that I wanted to write a book that would reach a large audience, but we all know that's easier said than done. But in the hopes of raising the odds of success, so to speak, I began studying the publishing market, to see if I could discern any patterns that might be beneficial.

I used the *USA Today* Top 50 bestseller list—because it lumps all types of books together on a single list—and I quickly learned that the most important prerequisite for making the list was the author's name. If John Grisham or Stephen King comes out with a new book, the book will hit the bestseller list. While this might strike people as obvious, I also saw another, less obvious pattern, one that helped to launch my career.

Essentially, I came to understand that genres could be broken down into subgenres—for instance, thrillers could be legal thrillers, techno-thrillers, etc.—and each subgenre could support three major authors. If you looked at techno-thrillers, you had Tom Clancy, Dale Brown, and Dale Ellis. In horror, you had Stephen King, Ann Rice, and Dean Koontz. In legal thrillers, you had John Grisham, Scott Turrow, and Richard North Patterson. In political thrillers, you had David Baldacci, Robert Ludlum, and John Le Carré. There were, of course, other successful authors in the subgenres, but not quite at the level of the Big Three.

Once I realized this simple fact, I set about finding a subgenre that, at the time, didn't have three major authors. I came upon love stories. In 1994, only Robert James Waller was writing them, and I decided to give that subgenre a try. From there, I drew upon the lives of my wife's grandparents and told their story, one that I hoped readers would enjoy. That book became *The Notebook*.

Once it was completed, it sold for $1 million up front.

MIDLIST, FRONTLIST, OR BACKLIST

What exactly is a midlist, frontlist, or backlist book? Publishers list all their season's new titles in a catalog that sales reps use to entice booksellers to purchase books. The front of the catalog is devoted to those books the publishers think will do well, and those titles will receive most of the publisher's marketing efforts and dollars. The titles in the front of the catalog have a full-page description, sometimes two pages, including the advertising money, promotional programs such as radio tours, and the initial print run. If there is a book tour planned, that will be noted, also. Frontlist titles receive their name because they are in the front of the catalog.

Midlist titles share their listing in the catalog with several other books on the same page. The description is briefer, and little advertising is noted. The titles are in the middle of the catalog, hence the name *midlist*. The publisher believes the title will perform reasonably but not at the same level as the frontlist titles. Midlist authors are caught in a paradox; their books probably won't sell as well as frontlist titles, because they don't have the marketing resources behind them. But those titles don't have the resources allocated to them precisely because the publisher doesn't think they will sell at a great rate.

Backlist titles are those that were published in previous seasons, are still in print, are still being sold in bookstores, and continue to be ordered by the booksellers. Publishing houses love having backlist titles that sell year after year. They bring in revenues with few marketing dollars required to promote them. Reaching the bestseller pinnacle can result in a revival of interest in an author's backlist titles, because readers specifically look for that author's name in the bookstore.

This revival can be a financial windfall for the author, who might earn a large advance for their next hardcover book, a large advance for the paperback rights for their previous book, and steadily increasing royalties for long-ago books that they thought were dry financial wells. Hence the author's axiom: *happiness is multiple revenue streams.*

HOW AUTHORS MANUFACTURE THEIR OWN LUCK

Authors who find their career progress stalled have to be skillful at identifying what they've been doing wrong and correct it; or, put another way, they have to solve the puzzle of what the reading public really wants—the same puzzle that confounds publishers who come out with hundreds of titles each year. For the authors, cracking the code of readers' interests is absolutely critical. The future of their careers hangs in the balance.

Successfully solving the puzzle can give an author's career amazing velocity, as Susan Elizabeth Phillips has enjoyed.

SUSAN ELIZABETH PHILLIPS, *Author*

You had written a number of novels before you hit the bestseller list.

I first hit the *New York Times* bestseller list relatively early in my career, 1989, and then not again for almost ten years. The breakout book was *Fancy Pants,* published by Pocket Books. Then the next two books pretty much sank, and I ended up having to reinvent my career. Since then, it's been a fairly steady upward trend. But having had such an early success, then having things go flat, definitely makes me appreciate what I have now even more.

How did you go about reinventing your career?

I'd like to say that I sat down and made a set of goals or plans, but actually it was serendipitous. I'd had an idea for a long time that I wanted to write about a woman who knows nothing about football and inherits a professional team. At that time, my career had kind of tanked with Pocket Books, despite a good faith effort on their part. I left them and started working on *It Had to Be You,* not knowing it was going to jumpstart my career. This was the first of what became The Chicago Stars books. That book, more than my previous books, let this comic voice that I didn't know I had, come out.

The publisher [Avon] only printed 100,000 copies initially, but the book got a huge amount of buzz and set me up for the future. It still took a few books after that for me to get where I am now. The slow and steady build that started with *It Had to Be You* reenergized my career. The key was coming up with an idea that really tapped into my comic voice.

BERTRICE SMALL, Author

How did you build such a successful career?

I wrote a book. I never considered back in the 1970s that I was starting/building a career. I loved writing and thought I could write, so I did. It was a lot simpler in those days than it is now. But then I grew as the industry grew, learning how to work with the publisher to promote and insisting on the best cover artists of the day, among them Robert McGinnis and Elaine Duillo. I did what needed to be done according to the time; e.g., distributing bookmarks and paying for my own ads in *Romantic Times,* the fanzine of the genre, when my publishers would not.

I also have the reputation of being on time with the manuscript, the line/copy editing, and the galley proofs. It's very important to be professional in any business. I'm *reliable,* which I know isn't a romantic word, but I've lasted 26 years in this industry writing for Avon (HarperCollins), The Ballantine Book Group (Random House), Kensington Books, NAL (Penguin-Putnam), and now Harlequin.

BARBARA DELINSKY, Author

For My Daughters was your 60th book and your first hardcover. What was the reasoning behind going hardcover?

It was a business decision, which is what so much of publishing is about. I had written many, many books in paperback. I had hit the *New York Times* bestseller list in each of the previous two years with my two most recent ones. I didn't know when I wrote it that *For My Daughters* was going to be a hardcover, but the publisher decided that the sales figures had been high enough with those two previous books to merit going into hardcover with *For My Daughters.*

Were you excited about it?

Of course. It was my dream. I was *totally* excited, but I also knew I was advancing into a whole different level of publishing, and that the competition would be even more fierce. The hardcover market is tough.

It's interesting how things have changed. It used to be that an author was published in hardcover first, then reprinted in paperback. Now, authors like me start in a genre in paperback and build the numbers until they are high enough for the publisher to risk the greater costs of hardcover publication. It's a profit-and-loss decision.

CARLY PHILLIPS, *Author*

A *New York Times* bestselling author, Carly Phillips is an attorney who has tossed away legal briefs in favor of writing sizzling romances. Her first single-title (that is, not part of a series) contemporary romance, *The Bachelor,* landed her on the number-five spot of the *New York Times* bestseller list. She has written *The Playboy, The Heartbreaker,* and *Under the Boardwalk.*

You are an example of an author who kept persevering, writing a number of novels before making it to the *New York Times* bestseller list.

I think it's so nice that you say it that way. So many people view my career as an overnight success.

That took how many books before you hit the bestseller list—13?

Thirteen, if you don't count the ten unpublished ones that came before.

Many bestselling authors we have talked to say the same thing: it took a long time and a lot of books to get there.

I know one or two people that made it with their first book. I know many, many more people who faced years and years of trying and writing many books before success came. I remember reading that, on average, an author had to write seven books before making the first sale to a publisher. That was what I used to hang onto when I was unpublished. Then when I hit book eight, nine, then it was ten . . . . [laughs].

The Bachelor's big break came when it was recommended by Kelly Ripa on the Regis and Kelly television program, and it immediately shot up to the bestseller list. How did that all come about?

One day I was home, working and reading. I began watching Regis and Kelly, and they were talking about Oprah giving up her book club. Kelly started talking about having her own book club. They weren't entirely serious about it at that point. It just clicked inside my head, and I called Theresa Meyers at Blue Moon and said, "Don't laugh, but I think we have to send *The Bachelor* to Kelly Ripa."

We sent the book to her right away. At that point, her show really didn't have the book club set up yet. But Theresa kept calling and following up. They did a segment on best summer reads; it was still pre-book club. I watched it and thought, "What can we do to make me stand out?" We came up with the cookie basket idea. We had a place called Clever Cookie make a basket that was tailored to the book cover. We sent Clever Cookie a copy of the book to wrap up and deliver to Regis and Kelly, with another copy of the book. The Regis and Kelly show called Warner and let them know that *The Bachelor* had made the list under consideration. There was then a two-week wait until the decision was made. Warner didn't want to tell me until the book definitely made it, because they knew I might not last the two weeks.

Bestselling authors recognize that, although writing may be a solitary effort, success in the publishing world is a collaborative effort. A solid team effort and a relationship of trust between an author and the editor contribute greatly to a book's success.

PAULA EYKELHOF, *Executive Editor*
Harlequin Books

How does an editor help with strategic planning for a successful author's career?

It's important for the editor to have faith in the author's ability and continuing potential—and to demonstrate that faith. Mutual trust is key; the author needs to know and believe that the editor has her best interests at heart and will give her good guidance and advice (on *every* level, from issues of language and story revision to those of overall career direction). At the same time, the editor needs to know that the author is honestly committed to her career, to the publishing house, to her readership, and to the quality of her work.

The editor has to recognize the successful author's strengths and encourage her to capitalize on them. The editor also needs to develop a sense of who the author's readership is—and so does the author! Writing might be a solitary profession, but it does not take place in a vacuum.

Both editor and author should have a feel (based on instinct as well as analysis) of *when* it's appropriate to take editorial risks. This would reflect the author's own progress and development and desire to try something new *and* an awareness that the readership might be willing to see something new and different from her.

A good example of this is an author's successful series—of mysteries, for instance—that have garnered her a steady and perhaps growing audience. But a series of this kind can become stale for the writer, and she may feel a need to expand. That decision needs to be carefully made. One approach is to alternate a series title with something else, as *New York Times* bestselling author Debbie Macomber is currently doing with her *Cedar Cove* series and her hardcover novels. Another approach is to use a different name when publishing a different type of book, as many authors have done.

How is the editor's role different when working with a veteran, popular author versus an author early in a career?

In the case of a new author, the editor is helping to *establish and build* her career; with a veteran author, the editor helps *maintain and build* the career.

When we're working with newer authors, though, many of the same things still apply—recognizing the author's writing and storytelling strengths, providing guidance to focus on and improve those strengths, determining who that author's readers are (or could be), and striving to communicate with these readers effectively. Strategic planning is equally important for the brand-new and the veteran author. They both have a place in the publishing program, whether that's a romance series or a single-title imprint.

A book from a newer author can catch readers' interest as they come across an unusual voice or an exciting kind of story. With a book from a veteran author, there are undeniably expectations on the reader's part. Those *specific* expectations don't exist for new authors, which can definitely be a plus.

JENNIFER ENDERLIN, *Publisher*
St. Martin's Press

What role does the editor play in helping a popular author further develop that author's career?

I constantly try to make sure an author is giving me their best work. There have been times when I've said to an author, "You know, this part of the book really didn't work for me." The author will say, "Oh, I knew it! But I thought I might be able to get away with it." I make sure they don't get away with glossing over something or being lazy, or with taking the easy way out.

Are you referring to the plotting or the characterization?

Both.

How much friction does this cause between the author and the editor?

Most of the biggest authors are surprising amenable to taking my suggestions. They understand that a lot is expected of them: they have to be delivering their best work. I do find that a lot of authors tend to have, after you give them the suggestions, a visceral reaction. They want to explain why they did it that certain way and why it can't be done another way. Then they get that out of their system and listen to you. They get their feathers ruffled, then they agree.

Are the changes typically minor, or are they wholesale revisions that take a long time to complete?

This varies. Sometimes you can talk to an author about changing one single line in the book, and they might get their feathers ruffled. In another case, I worked with a suspense author whom I had to convince to change the identity of the killer in the story. I told her that I completely guessed who the killer was right in the beginning, and we can't have a suspense novel with your name on it going out like that. That was a huge change, but she said that if I guessed it, other people would, also, and the book wouldn't be a satisfying read. So she went back to the drawing board.

LEE BOUDREAUX, *Senior Editor*
Random House

How do you help an author who has been modestly successful, but not a bestseller, really amp up the next book so it takes off? Is it a matter of tweaking the concept so it is more exciting?

With nonfiction you can tweak the concept more, because there's a way to quantify it: this is the *only* book out there on this concept, or this is the only one written by such a well-known authority. You can zero in on what makes it unique, and you can get more off-the-book-page coverage for nonfiction. With fiction, your efforts are geared more toward making it the best book you can, but that often happens on a line-by-line basis rather than on a more conceptual level. Either way, the key to amping it up is to get people to read it early. Once they start telling each other it's a great book, you've gotten their attention. This year, we published Sarah Dunant's *The Birth of Venus,* and we took her to an extraordinary new level. But the book was very different from her other books, which hadn't done as well, and the editor articulated that immediately and got everyone in-house to read the book. With my author Peter Straub, it's enormously helpful to have him writing a book a year for us. We're going to capture a much bigger audience for him if he's writing excellent books (and *Lost Boy, Lost Girl* just won the Bram Stoker Award for best novel) every year instead of every five years.

Getting the author out there to the marketplace is important. You are always trying to book them on radio and TV, which is very, very, difficult for fiction, but one National Public Radio interview can sell a lot of books.

Success can stem from being the right author with the right credentials in the right place at the right time with the right book.

LINDA FAIRSTEIN, *Author*

Linda Fairstein has had not one, but two celebrated careers. First, she was a prosecutor for the New York County district attorney's office for two decades, where she earned a reputation for toughness and determination for solving many high-profile cases. In 1993, Fairstein was named Woman of the Year by *New Woman* and *Glamour* magazines. Since 1994, she has been writing mysteries featuring tough, savvy, unstoppable assistant district attorney Alexandra ("Alex") Cooper, starting with *Final Jeopardy* and then *Likely to Die, Cold Hit, The Deadhouse, The Bone Vault,* and *The Kills.* Her knowledge of the courtroom and police procedures—and New York—lends a great realism to her stories, and critics also applaud her storytelling skill.

What factors do you think caused your first big success?

My breakout book, *Final Jeopardy,* was the first book in a series. I think two things happened for me. Because I had a high-profile career, not only in New York but in criminal justice nationally, I was able to get attention for the book and publicity that a first fiction author would not normally get. That was a gift, because it meant reviews you wouldn't normally expect, getting articles in journals and magazines about a real-life prosecutor turning crime writer. Clearly, I broke out, not because my book was a better mystery than others that came out that year, but because I had real-life experience that got me attention.

The second thing is that *Final Jeopardy* was published in 1996, and that was still early in the cresting popularity of women writers of crime fiction. There were several bestselling women out there—Grafton, Cornwell, and Paretsky—but not nearly as many as now. I was hitting the wave at just the right moment.

A good agent is crucial to an author's career, and the agent's job isn't over once the contract has been negotiated.

SCOTT MILLER, *Literary Agent*
Trident Media Group

What role does the agent play in developing an author's career?

In this day and age, the agent plays the major role in developing an author's career. Unfortunately, it is hard for editors to be the Max Perkins type, because they are under so much pressure to acquire books that are already suitable for publication. Because of this, most editors are reluctant to take on new novelists, unless their books do not require much in the way of editing. And, with regards to career shaping, many editors move around from house to house, so often an author is left with a different editor than the one they started with.

A good agent is someone who will find the diamond in the rough, work with the novelist to hone their work until it is the best it can be, and then will stay on top of the publishing house to assure that the book and author are given as much attention as possible. A good agent doesn't just get an author the most money they can but edits the material to make sure it is ready to go to the publisher. Also, an agent is there to advise the author about career decisions such as: do I stay with my current publisher, do I accept this film offer, should I write a novel that is more attractive to the market?

In general, I think the agent plays the major role in developing an author's career.

MATT BIALER, *Literary Agent*
Sanford J. Greenburger & Associates

Does the agent serve in an advisory role in helping an author build a career?

No question about it. Agents have to, because publishers don't do it, particularly in the beginning of an author's career. Once there is some success going on, then it is a larger group effort. In the beginning, it is the agent and the client doing the planning.

I had a client who wrote a "woman in jeopardy" novel. She had decided to write something that was commercial; she was tired of writing literary novels that, if they sell, they sell to a small publisher and go nowhere in the marketplace. At first, my antenna went up, because usually if someone wants to write a novel for the sake of being commercial, it doesn't work. The writing does not sound genuine enough; they aren't being true to their own story and their own talents. However, in this case, she had an idea for a novel based in Cape Cod, where she lives, based on her own fears.

She worked on it really hard; there was a lot of talent there already, obviously. I gave her a lot of feedback. I read four or five different versions of the story. That doesn't always happen, but I took an interest in this story. She was so driven; I thought she could pull it off.

So she finished the novel, and we went out to publishers. We got two kinds of offers. One was for hardcover/softcover, and the other publisher wanted to have it be a mass market paperback original and do lots of copies, hopefully blow them out. If you do the hardcover, you'll be lucky to get out 10,000–12,000 copies, and you net 7,000 after returns. This other publisher had the idea: this is a very commercial story, let's try to get more copies out. They are going out with 180,000 copies.

So I thought this idea was exciting. We're skipping the hardcover and going to paperback. A lot of authors find it doesn't have as much prestige as saying, "I'm going to be in hardcover." But I told the client, the goal these days is to be in hardcover eventually. That's where the money is, that's where the reviews and attention are. This is another way of getting there, perhaps at a higher level, sooner.

That's where an agent can make a difference. Perhaps if she didn't have an agent, even if she made it to the point where she received offers from publishers, she might have chosen the other route, going with the hardcover. Perhaps that would have worked. Who knows? All an agent can do is bring their experience to the table and let the author benefit from it.

COMING BACK FOR SECONDS

Authors who have a fabulously successful first book often face a difficult challenge in writing the second book. If book number one was based on an unusual premise or concept, the challenge is even more difficult. How can their second book possibly live up to the reputation of the first one?

Then, if the first book, especially if it was a novel, doesn't do as expected, publishers are hesitant to bring out the second book. Expectations are strange, troublesome little creatures. A book that has a first printing of 10,000 but sells 20,000 exceeds expectations, but a book that has a printing of 50,000 of which 20,000 sells fails to meet expectations, yet both books sold the same number of copies.

DANIEL HALPERN, *Editor-in-Chief*
HarperCollins

Some editors have said that getting the first novel published isn't the challenge; it's getting that second book out that's the challenge.

That's absolutely true. I'll tell you why—it's no mystery. With a first novel, there's no track record, and anything's possible. As soon as you have a track record, booksellers can look up the sales, then order accordingly. Any normal person would agree that the second book should not be penalized based on the sales of the first book. We need to believe that an author may have learned something between the first book and second. If this weren't the case, would anyone remarry?

NEIL NYREN, *Senior Vice President, Publisher, and Editor-in-Chief*
G. P. Putnam & Sons

What about authors who have a unique concept for the first book but whose second book doesn't live up to the performance of that first title?

If the writer is a real writer, then they will have another idea. If the person just has the one idea, that's fine; it happens, and you adjust accordingly. Sometimes you know going in that that's going to be the case—but what you're always looking for, of course, is the writer fizzing with new ideas, who just keeps getting stronger.

13

FROM THE BOOKSHELF
TO THE SILVER SCREEN

THE SYNERGIES OF BOOKS AND MOVIES

"That story was much better as a book," laments the disappointed filmgoer exiting the theater.

"I loved that movie. The credits said it was based on a novel. I think I'd like to read that book," says a second, much happier filmgoer at the same theater that night.

Books and motion pictures have been inextricably twined since the first theaters began showing flickering silent films to the mass public. Books are, and always have been, the most popular source material for films, whether big budget movies or less costly independent movies.

This is not to say the relationship between the two mediums has always been smooth. Screenwriters and novelists are, to borrow the old joke about Americans and the British, two peoples separated by a common language. Later in this chapter, screenwriter Kirk Ellis outlines the challenges of adapting a novel or nonfiction book to film.

From the novelist's standpoint, there are pluses and minuses to having one of their works made into a movie. Here's a big plus: added Fame.

Mystery writer Elmore Leonard, a veteran of the bestseller lists, has said that the number of people who recognize him increased dramatically after the release of *Get Shorty*, starring John Travolta and Danny De

Vito, in 1995. This example is a particularly effective endorsement of how having a film based on your work can enlarge your audience: Leonard's first novel was published in 1953, and he'd had dozens of extremely popular novels published since.

A movie has broader reach than books. Attendance at a theatrical feature film can be—is expected to be—in the millions, and the movie gets video and DVD sales, broadcasts on network and cable TV, and international box office.

This mass film-going audience now becomes a vast new pool of potential customers for the author's current or past works.

MARK BOWDEN, *Author*

Writing a book is an individual process. Screenwriting is more of a collaboration—with other writers, the director, sometimes even the actors. How do you work successfully in both arenas?

I really enjoy both. My creative product is the book. I have complete control over it. If it's good, it's because I made it so. If it's bad, it's my fault, and I like that. A movie, ultimately, is the director's creative product. Everyone else who works on the movie serves the director, in one way or another. Because I have no ambition to direct, I am very content to work for a director and help them realize their vision.

Suppose they had made an atrocious movie out of *Black Hawk Down*. It would still have sold a million more copies of my book. I think having a film made out of your story is a wonderful commercial for your book. Whether the movie is good or bad, it exposes your work to countless more people than would know about it otherwise.

Does it impact your subsequent books?

It does. It gives you an automatic audience for your work. I have a book out now called *Finders Keepers* that is not a bestseller but is selling better than any of my books prior to *Black Hawk Down*. It's very much worthwhile for the publisher to put out almost anything I want to write.

Hollywood snaps up literary properties, because it is always looking for great stories. Hollywood may be hoping as well that, in the case of a bestselling novel, the movie adapted from the story has a built-in audience. A filmmaker's second challenge after choosing a story is to arrange financing for the film. Because investing in movies is one of the riskiest ventures imaginable, being able to say that a built-in audience exists may help the producer sway investors. How much bang do the producers really get for the bucks they pay authors for film rights?

KIRK ELLIS, *Screenwriter*

Screenwriter Kirk Ellis received the 2001 Writers Guild of America Award for the two-part ABC miniseries *Anne Frank*. He has won the Humanitas Prize and an Emmy nomination for best writing. He has also written other popular biographical films, such as *Life with Judy Garland: Me and My Shadows*, *The Beach Boys* (on which he served as coexecutive producer), and *The Three Stooges*. He adapted James Ellroy's novels *American Tabloid* and *The Cold Six Thousand* for HBO and Bruce Willis, and he is working on adapting David McCullough's *John Adams* as a 13-part miniseries for Tom Hanks's Playtone Company. Ellis is also a sought-after lecturer at screenwriting conferences and seminars.

How does being able to say, "From the novel by (Bestselling Author)," impact the box office prospects for a film?

I think there are very few authors today that have so much name recognition that their name above the title of a film will guarantee major results. Even those top-tier authors' films don't necessarily become hits. Calling the film *John Grisham's Rain Maker* still didn't help it become a hit at the box office. Not every Stephen King movie adaptation has been a hit. I would suspect that more have not hit than have.

Are we talking about two different audiences, those for books and those for movies?

If Miramax thought that *Cold Mountain* could stand entirely on being based on a huge bestseller by Charles Frazier, they wouldn't have felt the need to spend all those many millions of dollars to cast Nicole Kidman, Renee Zellweger, and Jude Law in the film. That shows you a kind of lack of confidence that a reading public will translate into a viewing public. I think that has always been true.

Authors may look at this opportunity in reverse: the movie comes out and is a big hit, and now you have a large new audience for your next novel.

That's a very astute assessment. The benefit is often to the author of the book, after the movie comes out.

To take advantage of a movie's popularity, publishers often issue a new version of the novel from which the movie was adapted with the art from the movie poster, usually involving the film's star, on the cover. This is called a *movie tie-in edition*. One example of a book and a movie having marketing synergies was 2003's *Master and Commander,* starring Russell Crowe, based on two books in Patrick O'Brian's 20-volume *Master and Commander* series. The film was a risky one to make, carrying a *Titanic*-sized $150 million budget. But more than five million copies of the series' books were in print—a huge built-in audience for the producers to target with their marketing campaign. The movie generated such renewed interest in the books that the publisher brought out more than 600,000 copies of the movie tie-in editions—a tremendous revival for books that first were published more than a decade ago.

Authors also like to have their books adapted to film, because the remuneration from selling film rights can be fantastic. Here are a few examples from http://www.publishersmarketplace.com.

- Film rights to G.P. Taylor's *Shadowmancer* were optioned in a major deal for almost $1 million against a pick-up, an additional payment if the film is made, of up to $6.2 million.
- Film rights to Jennifer Weiner's forthcoming *Little Earthquakes* were optioned to Universal Pictures for high five figures, against a middle six-figure pick-up.
- Film rights to Alex Kershaw's forthcoming *The Few* were optioned to Paramount in a major deal for high six figures.

Film rights sales can certainly provide authors and publishers a nice chunk of cash. And remember, the author is being paid for work that has already been completed. This is not an advance; the author usually has no further obligation except perhaps to review the script(s) as they are being written and perhaps make comments.

Hollywood agents are constantly scouting for books that can be adapted to film, just as they look for the next hot screenwriters. More than 50,000 original motion picture scripts are registered with the

Writer's Guild (WGA) each year. Add to that the more than 15,000 novels published each year, and the chances of any one book being made into a movie are extremely slim, even if the author has sold in the millions.

Producers and agents are always on the lookout for the novel or short story that has that almost ineffable quality: movie potential.

JOEL GOTLER, Agent
Intellectual Property Group in Los Angeles

What characteristics must a book have to be an attractive film/ TV acquisition?

I look for uniqueness of style and voice, plotting, characterization. The material has to be fresh or, at least, a new approach to an old idea. Nonfiction is appealing to Hollywood.

Has the market for film and TV rights sales changed over the last ten years?

Yes, fiction is harder to sell, the prices have come down, the number of studio movies has decreased.

Do already established, bestselling authors find a new audience for their books as a result of a film being made from one of their novels?

Authors will find a new audience as a result of a film being made from one of their novels. It's inevitable.

When a movie adapted from a novel bombs, does it have any impact on the author's popularity with readers?

The author may have a popularity decline, but more often, only the emotions of the author are bruised.

Do you ever encounter authors who are opposed to having their stories turned into films?

There are some authors who don't want their books adapted. I know some.

How does an author go about getting Hollywood's attention?

Buzz, recommendations . . . rarely the slush pile.

KIRK ELLIS, Screenwriter

What qualities in a novel make it a good candidate for adaptation to film?

The criteria for choosing a piece to adapt are virtually the same as choosing a piece from your own imagination to turn into a screenplay. It's all about story, knowing what will make a good movie story. There are things that make a movie story different from a novelistic story. Film is a very direct medium, very visceral, not introspective the way many novels are. Even when you are dealing with difficult prose and complex books and narratives, you are always looking for what can be extracted that will lead to a compelling visual story.

Why are novels currently so popular as source material for motion pictures?

I would argue that novels have always been the most popular source material for films. I think there is a myth that so-called original scripts have always represented the majority of film stories. I don't think that is true. When you look at films from the Golden Era especially, almost all of those films came from novels, short stories, or magazines. There's nothing new in that trend. Producers and studios are always looking for previously successful material.

How do the novels make their way to the producers' hands?

These days, novels are often read in galley form by large agencies like CAA and the William Morris Agency, both of which have very strong literary departments. They forward these to their stable of producers and filmmakers so they can be snatched up, essentially before they come on the market. I can't tell you how many times I've read about a book in the *New York Times,* and I've made inquiries because I thought it was a book I could really nail as an adaptation, only to find that book had never even entered the market. It was taken off the market prior to publication by a preemptive sale. That's true of magazine articles as well.

Given the potential financial rewards and the possibility of adding moviegoers to your fan base, why would a top novelist resist having one of their novels adapted by Hollywood? Imagine the fun of attending a movie premiere or the thrill of seeing your name in ten-foot letters on the big screen.

SUSAN ELIZABETH PHILLIPS, *Author*

You seem reluctant to pursue having your books made into movies. Why is that?

Every romance novel I've seen that's been turned into a movie has been terrible. I'm not exactly sure why Hollywood can't get it right, but they can't, and I don't want to watch one of my babies get destroyed.

Every one of my romance author friends who has had a book turned into a film has had awful results. Some of it is the casting. Maybe because so much of a romance is internal, and that doesn't translate well to film. I can't stand the idea of watching one of my books turned into something totally different than what I've imagined. The only way I'd consider it is if they threw so much money at me it numbed the pain! I don't think that is going to happen.

But doesn't it get your name mentioned on TV for weeks in advance of the TV broadcast or the premiere of the movie? That's pretty great publicity.

Often they don't mention the author at all in the promos. The only time you see the name is in the opening credits. The movie might help your book sales a little, but it's not worth the emotional strain of watching your baby being mutilated. I'm very protective of my work and of my readers. I know how my readers feel about the characters in my books, and I'm those characters' caretaker.

KIRK ELLIS, *Screenwriter*

You hear so frequently about authors' dissatisfaction with a film based on their work. Is it the casting—an author knows the characters backwards and forwards and doesn't think the actors chosen are appropriate?

A novelist needs to understand that adaptation is a process of translating from one medium to another. Screenwriters pass their work on to a producer and director who will execute the screenplay. If the dissatisfaction is with the casting or look of the film, those are out of the hands of the screenwriter unless they are also a producer of the film. As a screenwriter, you can only hope to remain true to the spirit of the original material.

I'm not sure there is a correlation between the original author's dissatisfaction with the film and the work of the screenwriter.

LINDA FAIRSTEIN, *Author*

What's your view on having one of your books developed into a movie or TV show?

There is no question with movies that you can develop an entire new audience.

Many of us were told: don't ever sell because a bad movie can hurt books, which is the Sara Paretsky story. Paretsky wrote the Chicago private-eye V.I. Warshawski novels. The movie starred Kathleen Turner at the top of her game, but the movie was a flop. People in the book business claimed that Paretsky books didn't sell for a while. Well, she's a bestseller again. I suppose a very bad movie could hurt a book.

Movies have a much greater scope, reach, and audience than TV. I made the decision to sell my first novel, *Final Jeopardy,* to ABC to be a movie of the week, because if they did make a mess of it and people didn't want to buy the book, there was far less chance of its ruining the book series than with a wide-screen flop. Fewer people are going to watch or hear about a TV movie than a theatrical movie released nationwide. I consider myself lucky—the TV movie of *Final Jeopardy* was well done, had a good cast and director, and was pretty faithful to the story, when you consider it was a 400-page book that became a 98 page screenplay. You have to tell yourself that you may be losing a lot of your favorite descriptions and scenes.

I know because of the mail I received that there were people who started reading my books because they saw the movie.

HARLAN COBEN, Author

Does having a story turned into a movie or TV show help an author develop a new audience for their books?

I don't know if it helps develop a new audience or not. I've known many authors who have great Hollywood success who still can't sell a book in the stores—and, of course, vice versa. I don't worry about that much. I think it was James Cain, who, when asked if he was upset about what Hollywood had done to his books, pointed to the shelf behind him and said, "Hollywood hasn't done anything to my books. They're right there." Books and movies are two different mediums. If you sell to Hollywood, you have to accept that.

One romance author who has had a positive experience with Hollywood is Nicholas Sparks. In June 2004, the film based on his first novel, *The Notebook,* opened to terrific reviews and great box office. Prior to that, several of his other novels were successfully adapted to films that were well received by moviegoers.

NICHOLAS SPARKS, Author

Your stories have a strong internal aspect. Why do you think they translate so well into movies, given that films tend to emphasize external conflict?

My stories deal with internal conflict, but I make sure to set them in an interesting and original external situation.

If writing novels with external conflict, the best authors also have internal conflict within the characters. In other words, the main character is getting through something. For example, while solving a crime, the detective is struggling with his marriage. The best writers balance both the internal and external conflicts. Mine are just more weighted to internal conflict rather than external.

Other genres, by the requirement of the genre, require more emphasis on the external, which is why in many thrillers you have characters fall in love but you won't necessarily feel it.

And I've been fortunate with movies. My books are more attuned to the big screen than TV.

Do you get involved with the production of the films?

I read the script and toss in my two cents worth. Of course, they don't have to take my two cents worth.

KIRK ELLIS, *Screenwriter*

Nicholas Sparks's novels have been successfully adapted to film, though they deal with internal conflict, considered more difficult to translate onto the screen.

In the case of Sparks, the stories he deals with are romantic stories, and romance is a very external emotion, because you are interacting with another individual. The difficulty with certain novels is that there is psychological complexity—page after page of a character's interior monologue—and interior monologues simply don't translate into film. I've never been one to believe that you can't suggest some of that on screen, because to say that does a tremendous disservice to actors, many of whom are immensely capable of projecting a variety of moods.

One of the first things you're told in writing classes—which is one of the reasons I abhor them—is that you should never indicate "significant looks," because they never work on camera. Think about how many "significant looks" you can remember from films, virtually from the invention of the medium. *Casablanca* is an obvious example of that. I don't agree with the tenet that psychological complexity is impossible in a film, but it has to be manifested in more physical ways than in a good novel. The advantage a novelist has that a screenwriter and dramatist does not is that, in reading a novel, you can take your time, you can process information at your own pace, you can always return to a passage earlier in the book. You don't have that opportunity with viewing a film. Film moves forward 24 frames a second.

THE PROCESS OF ADAPTATION

Pick a favorite novel off your bookshelf, and imagine that a major film studio has just hired you to turn that novel into a movie. The first question that pops into your head is, "Where on earth do I begin?" You may just sit there and stare at the book cover for a long, long time. Award-winning screenwriter and bestselling novelist William Goldman said, in his marvelous book about his career, *Which Lie Do I Tell?*, that when offered an assignment to adapt a book to a film, he asks himself two questions: "Do I love it?" followed hard upon by, "Can I make it play?"

We all have a sense that a novelist employs different means of storytelling than a film producer or director. The skilled screenwriter knows what aspects of a novel work well on screen and which don't.

KIRK ELLIS, *Screenwriter*

A novelist creates his or her own little world. How does a screenwriter gain access and enter that world?

The task of an adaptation is not fidelity but essence of story; it is being true to the spirit, if not always to the letter, of the material you are adapting. When we speak of a novelist's voice, we are talking about the way that writer uses prose to express a worldview. Screenwriters don't have that option, because we write a text that is never meant to be read; it is meant to be seen. The task of an adaptation is what I call cracking the spine, finding the underlying theme of the story and its most salient points. We must decide how we convey in action—some of it taken from the source material, some of it invented freely—the essence of that particular story in a cinematic medium.

In adding new material to a novelist's story, how does a screenwriter know it's not being changed too much?

I would be hard pressed to name a film taken from a literary source that did not step away significantly from that source material. One of the criticisms frequently leveled at the first *Harry Potter* film was that it was, in fact, too faithful to the original books. That has been dealt with in the course of making the succeeding films. I've heard that the third film does incorporate a lot of original thinking, many of the ideas endorsed by the author of the novel, J.K. Rowling.

How much you change or add is a function of each story individually. I've had adaptations of books such as James Ellroy's *American Tabloid* and its sequel, *The Cold Six Thousand,* which I'm doing as a miniseries for HBO, where you have an incredibly intricate narrative, and to make radical wholesale changes in that narrative would be to essentially tell a different story. By the same token, you can't include everything that Ellroy does in those books, because he has 1,300 pages of text to work with as opposed to eight one-hour screenplays. So you have to make choices about what threads of narrative you are going to pick up for your script. You will always find, in making those choices, that you are leaving things out that are important linkage material in the original book. Therefore, you have to create that connective material from whole cloth.

One writer who has successfully made the transition from book author to screenwriter is Mark Bowden. Not only that, he seems very much at home in the Hollywood culture. This is not always the case. Novelist F. Scott Fitzgerald's accounts of working on scripts in Hollywood in the '30s sound like he experienced long years of highly paid torture.

Screenform, the rules of how a screenplay is set down on paper, including peculiar abbreviations such as *INT., EXT., O.S.,* and *V.O.,* and the collaborative nature of filmmaking have not been a problem for Mark Bowden. He even seems to be having fun.

MARK BOWDEN, Author

Talk about how you felt when you attended the movie premiere of
Black Hawk Down.

It was a tremendous thrill. I actually went to dozens of premieres, because it was premiered in Los Angeles, New York, London, Madrid, and military bases. I could have gone on with them to more, but I eventually stopped. At a certain point, I had to get back to work. It was tremendous fun. Wonderfully fulfilling and exciting, to see that much attention and interest generated. I was interviewed 5,000 times it seemed and asked every conceivable question. But every single time, I enjoyed it.

I can see where this could become like an addiction, that level of attention. For me, it became a little exhausting, and I was anxious to get back to the work I love to do. But it was a great experience.

The success I've had in Hollywood has given me the opportunity to write films. So now, if I see a story that I think would make a great movie, I'll just write a screenplay. Before, the only chance I had of having something made into a movie was to have a successful book.

Many writers, though, find it sheer torture to sit in those movie production meetings where they have to listen to people telling them, "I think you ought to lose that scene, change that character, the ending doesn't work for me . . ."

I probably won't find that particularly torturous. Because I think the film is primarily the director's medium, I'm there as sort of a hired hand, in a way that I'm not when writing a book. If I had to go to an editor's meeting about a book that I was writing and the editors were all saying, "Well, you should change the ending, or you should to this, do that," it would begin to drive me crazy. For a movie project, I view it differently. It makes a nice contrast, a change of pace, from the solitary process of book writing to working with a group of other really fun people. I think it is a really nice balance to have.

KIRK ELLIS, *Screenwriter*

Can novelists successfully adapt their own work?

Sure. Often, Hollywood will hire a writer of a book to do the screenplay, and that experience will allow them to go on to other script assignments. It's a frequent occurrence. David Benioff whose novel *25th Hour* was made into a film, got the assignment to write the film *Troy*. Sometimes the scripts that novelists write are used, sometimes not. Sometimes the experience for the novelist is such that they will never, ever attempt a screenplay again.

The key is to understand the differences between the two mediums?

Novelists who succeed as screenwriters have looked at movies that they like and analyzed how and why these movies worked. The trick in adapting your own novel is ruthlessness. You have to let go of things. There's no room on film for a 16-page dialog sequence. What is enjoyable about reading a novel is that the writer has time for long descriptive paragraphs and to go into great detail about each character. You're starting to see in some popular fiction these very short chapters and one-sentence paragraphs. Those are just screenplays in hiding. That's going too far in the other direction.

Despite the brave souls like Mark Bowden who cheerfully work in both worlds, a degree of separation will always exist between the publishing houses and the movie studios.

When you talk to editors at the major publishing houses, you get the clear feeling they can envision many of their authors' works on screen. Hollywood has one giant hurdle to overcome before green-lighting any film project: money. It can take incredible amounts of money to bring a novel to the screen in a manner that will do the story justice and satisfy the somewhat jaded audience. Budgetary constraints are one reason some of our favorite books have not yet made it to the theaters.

LEE BOUDREAUX, *Senior Editor*
Random House

Why does Hollywood turn so many novels into movies?

I don't know that side of the business very well, but I can only assume they're looking for compelling stories and books are a natural place to look. I'd love to see one of my books make it to the big screen, and I think both Adriana Trigiani's *Big Stone Gap* and Elinor Lipman's *The Ladies' Man* are getting there. And, of course, I think that Peter Straub's books would all make excellent films. As would Arthur Phillips's *The Egyptologist*. Here's hoping.

14

WHERE DOES THE IDEA COME FROM?

THE MAGICAL PROCESS OF INSPIRATION: EMERIL OR EDGAR?

A VISIT TO THE IDEA FACTORY

**SO MANY IDEAS, ONLY ONE LIFETIME:
GIVING AN IDEA THE GREEN LIGHT**

Novels are propelled to the top of the bestseller lists by several factors: the strength of the idea, the power of the story, the quality of the writing, and the reputation—or what in marketing is called *brand-name recognition*—of the author. One of these factors must exist in abundance for the novel to make it to the top. The author, of course, hopes all four factors work together. If so, the combination is virtually unbeatable. As an author's career progresses, the importance of brand-name recognition grows and may even overwhelm the other three. But bestselling authors will argue that, if they weren't able to come up with superior ideas and weave brilliantly crafted stories, they wouldn't have earned any sort of reputation in the first place.

Authors who make it to the bestseller list seldom say they set out to write a bestseller, although that delightful goal may exist in the back of their mind. The real emphasis is on producing the best quality book possible. First, you have to satisfy yourself, they all say. At the outset of a book project, they are by no means certain the idea is strong enough to be a bestseller.

KAREN KOSZTOLNYIK, *Senior Editor*
Warner Books

When a bestselling author is at the idea stage of a new book, how much do you get involved in planning it?

Some authors don't want to talk about a new idea until they have something on paper to show me. Some want to call me and brainstorm. I do find, overall, that authors like to talk the concept out when they are planning it. Some wait until they have a few chapters to show me before they continue. They bounce ideas off me. That's what I love about my job. I'm part of the process.

A unique, great idea can certainly be a catalyst to eventual success. Think about Michael Crichton's *Jurassic Park,* one of the greatest ideas to have come along in many years. It ended up creating a money-making machine for Hollywood that continues churning out dollars more than ten years after the book came out. The core concept, bringing the dinosaurs back from extinction, was immediately accessible and powerful to many different demographic groups of readers. It appealed equally to children's and adults' imaginations, and Crichton wisely made two children central characters who became endangered when the dinosaurs got loose. Also, it benefited from its amazing simplicity: readers could recommend that book to their friends without going through a half-hour explanation of what the book was about or why they liked it.

Jurassic Park had another advantage: it was clearly written to be a motion picture. You read that book and right away thought, "That would make a great movie!" *Jurassic Park* was among the highest of the "high concepts," as they say on Avenue of the Stars in Los Angeles, and, as you read the book, you may even have let your imagination create the movie scenarios in your mind.

Peter Benchley's *Jaws,* published in 1974, is another prime example of a phenomenal idea being the basis for a phenomenally successful novel. It certainly didn't sell based on the brand-strength of Benchley's name at the time. It was his very first novel. The great idea here played up a primal fear of being eaten by sharks. Popular novelists for centuries have dealt with the fear of what lurks beneath the waves. But instead of a ship at sea being menaced, Benchley brought the fear very close to home, right offshore, where most of us have gone swimming. This was a terror we all could possibly experience.

THE MAGICAL PROCESS OF INSPIRATION: EMERIL OR EDGAR?

"I suppose I am a born novelist, for the things
I imagine are more vital and vivid to me
than the things I remember."

ELLEN GLASGOW, from *Letters to Ellen Glasgow*
(Ellen Glasgow appeared on the bestseller list in 1916.)

An archaic definition of the word *inspire* is, "to breathe life into." That's a wonderful way to think about what a successful author does: make ideas come to life. Such authors can make characters that seem real, more real than even the people you work with in your daily life. Certainly more real than your boss.

Bestselling authors clearly have a superior gift of imagination. It does seem like a magical process, the ability to sit down, pull a concept out of the air, and develop it into a book-length work. Many of these authors do this year after year for 20, 30, or 40 years. Some authors can, almost routinely it seems, craft two or more books each year. They are also superb technicians, who know how to organize a seeming jumble of ideas, plot twists, characters, and scenarios into prose that flows like honey. Consider how many ideas populate a book with memorable characters and labyrinthine plot twists. Then multiply that by a 10, 20, 30, or 40-book career.

Where, exactly, do these great ideas for books come from? Is it an event or a process? Perhaps it comes to the author like a lightning bolt in the middle of the night, and they have to get up in a fever, hurry downstairs, and write it down. Maybe the old light bulb analogy is more accurate: the mind seems to be a blank slate as the author sits with a pad and pen at their desk; then the idea just appears. Perhaps the idea announces itself with a loud *BAM!*, like TV chef Emeril Lagasse seasoning a pork roast.

Perhaps the process is less picturesque; it's just plain work, 100 push-ups for the brain. The author sits at the word processor for a long time, turning concepts over in his or her head, painfully rejecting one after the other until, "Aha! That's the one!" Edgar Allan Poe may have been describing his own process of idea creation in the famous poem, *The Raven.* There Poe was, up past midnight, tired but still pondering, "Over many a quaint and curious volume of forgotten lore." So here is the author, deep in late-night, exhaustive research, when he hears that tapping, "As of someone gently rapping, rapping at my chamber door." The Raven's quiet arrival may have been the way new ideas came to this great writer, who lived in an era where bestselling authors' compensation was, unfortunately, not nearly as generous as today. On the other hand, he didn't have to have to sit through the bad movies that have been based on his imaginative, suspenseful work.

Suppose you were in the United Kingdom one afternoon, sitting on a train that had stopped due to mechanical trouble. You were trying to pass the time. Perhaps you were too tired to read or do any work, so you just began staring at the lovely green countryside, dotted with grazing cattle. It was an idyllic, uniquely British scene: no mad cow disease in sight. Then it just flashed in your head: Harry Potter and his wizard school! That's the tale J.K. Rowling tells about how her literary empire began. But even magic takes time to become powerful; Rowling required most of the next five years to complete the first Harry Potter novel and develop plot lines for subsequent books.

A VISIT TO THE IDEA FACTORY

One writer who never seems to run out of fascinating ideas is Catherine Coulter. She has so many great plot ideas, sometimes she treats her readers to two independent plot lines that run in parallel for most of the book, almost like giving the readers two books for one.

CATHERINE COULTER, Author

How do you start your next book?

I always start with a what-if idea. For example, before I started writing *The Target*, all I knew was that there was a guy in an isolated cabin in the Rockies in Colorado. I didn't know who he was or why he was there, just that he had to be there. One day he finds a little girl physically and sexually abused in the forest. What happens? That's how most books begin. It's usually a big surprise to me what happens next, because I never have a clue."

How many ideas do you go through before you decide this is the one?

Not many, maybe two or three at the most. And it's not really a matter of dismissing them. It's a matter of thinking, "Okay, would that idea be good for a secondary plot?" Or I'll come up with a brand-new idea in the book that never even occurred to me before I started writing. This happens very frequently. The Ghouls in *Hemlock Bay* were a real shocker. No clue where they and the Tuttles came from.

How did you come up with the idea for Savich and Sherlock, the FBI couple? How did you decide they were a couple?

It was happenstance. When I wrote *The Cove,* I had not a single series thought. As it turns out, there was a secondary character in *The Cove,* Dillon Savich, an FBI computer nerd with a laptop named MAX. When I was wondering what to write next, Savich said in my ear, "What about me?" And then I got the what-if idea. We have a 19-year-old girl who lives in San Francisco. She's an excellent pianist and plans to go to Julliard. Then her half-sister is murdered by a serial killer. What happens to her? And that's how Sherlock came into being. It wasn't planned; everything just came about, by serendipity—a lovely thought.

Bestselling authors seem to get asked the question, "Where do you get your ideas?" more frequently than any other except perhaps, "Which of your books is your favorite?" Some have even begun posting the answer to the question on their own Web sites, to perhaps stem the tide of inquiries at book signings and via e-mail.

Stephen King, on his site (http://www.stephenking.com) has a simple answer: "He has a very active imagination."

Stephen King got the idea for Carrie from his experiences as a part-time janitor at a high school when he was 19 or 20 years old. One of his responsibilities was to clean the boys' and the girls' locker rooms. As he describes it in his book *On Writing:*

> This memory came back to me one day while I was working at the laundry, and I started seeing the opening scene of a story: girls showering in a locker room where there were no U-rings, pink plastic curtains, or privacy. And this one girl starts to have her period. Only she doesn't know what it is, and the other

girls—grossed out, horrified, amused—start pelting her with sanitary napkins . . . The girl begins to scream. All that blood! She thinks she's dying, that the other girls are making fun of her even while she's bleeding to death . . . she reacts . . . fights back . . . but how?"

David Baldicci was a young lawyer living in Washington, D.C., when he wrote his first novel, *Executive Power*. He sold the book and film rights to the novel for the tidy sum of $5 million; the movie was retitled *Absolute Power*, starring Clint Eastwood. Baldacci has since gone on to more great success with books such as *Last Man Standing* and *The Christmas Train*.

Baldacci, at http://www.davidbaldacci.com, says:

I am always thinking about and seeking story ideas. As a writer, you can never "turn off" your passion for the written word and love of a great story. So I watch life, listen intently, and basically drive everyone around me a bit crazy as I absorb every environment in which I find myself. And, believe me, being naturally curious uncovers many possible storylines. Writers have to see the world exactly as it is, and then go a step further and realize the potential of what could be there.

SO MANY IDEAS, ONLY ONE LIFETIME: GIVING AN IDEA THE GREEN LIGHT

Think of what a critical step this is, the leap to committing months or even years of your life to the research and writing of a book. One editor at a major publishing house even told us that she thinks the truly great novels take up to five years to develop and write.

Even if you don't agree with that editor's point of view, because it would mean that some of today's most popular writers must be 225 years old, you have to respect the amount of effort that goes into a bestselling author's career. Bestselling authors do not have the luxury of sitting at the word processor, staring out the window, going to lunch, and coming back and staring some more. They have publishing contracts in place that require meeting rigorous deadlines and maintaining a relentless pace of productivity.

STUART WOODS, *Author*

You mentioned on your Web site that you have more ideas for books than you can use.

That's probably true. I've never failed to come up with one when I've needed it.

When starting a new book, do you seek input from agents, editors, or friends about it, or do you just proceed with the writing?

I give the editor and my agent half a dozen chapters and a brief synopsis, just to give them some sort of idea what the book will be about. Unless I get some objection from them at that point, I just continue on.

Prolific authors have trained their minds to constantly generate new ideas. All the sensory input from the world—what they see, hear, touch, taste, even smell—can become elements in the idea.

PETER STRAUB, *Author*

Many authors have more ideas for books than they could possibly write in a lifetime. Let's say you woke up one morning with a terrific idea for a romance novel, something that might compete in Nora Roberts's territory. Would your publisher be enthusiastic about that project?

The publisher would probably be a little surprised. But, because they knew I would be doing the writing, the publisher would probably be pleased in the end. It would turn out much darker than a Nora Roberts novel.

By the way, I do not have a mind filled with ideas. I generally have to work up the ideas from other little things that occur to me. Situations in my novels very rarely come to me fully formed. I have to work my way through many layers of error before I find what the book is really supposed to be. That's all part of the process. Also, when I get an idea that seems familiar, or that I really understand all the way through to the end, I don't want to do that book or that story. I want to do things that work toward some sort of mystery, some area I really don't understand, and force myself to find my way through that mystery. Otherwise, the writing would become really tedious.

For a novelist, the idea, the basic concept for a story, may actually be the easiest part. Many would-be novelists have file drawers full of ideas for stories they have sketched out. More often than not, the ideas stay in the drawer and never become books. What bestselling authors have learned is how to sustain the drive to complete the story, for however long it takes. They have the ability to envision the project as a whole, completed work. Years of practice have enabled them to develop the mental tools to build a story framework that will stand up. Most importantly, they have the confidence to know that, no matter how fragmented the story seems now, it will all come together in the end. It always has before.

The challenge is no different for nonfiction authors, though they face an additional test as well: choosing a topic with the quality of immediacy. Nonfiction authors must seize the moment; novelists' concepts often have a timeless quality.

DR. SPENCER JOHNSON, *Author*

How do you go about selecting a new topic or theme?

I do a lot of listening. If you write the book you want to write, as I suspect most authors do, instead of the book readers want to read, where you are almost serving yourself more than you're serving your readers, then I don't think you can be as successful.

I choose my subjects by listening and watching, looking at what's going on. And catching the trend at a very early phase, so by the time the book is written, it is well timed for the market. I have kept books inside me for as long as 15 years. I created the idea for *Who Moved My Cheese* in 1979, but in 1979, not enough people were conscious of change and its impact on our lives. By 1998, they certainly were. If I had come out with the book when I first thought of it, it would not have been nearly as successful.

Authors universally say that they get their ideas by being observant, by paying closer attention to the world around them than the average person does. They also rely on that venerable axiom: *Write about what you know.* In 2004, Melanie Craft came out with her third romance novel, *Man Trouble,* whose plot centers around a romance author who is trying to tame a billionaire playboy whose career is facing choppy waters. The author just so happens to be married to Larry Ellison, founder of the world's second-largest software maker, Oracle, and 25 years her senior—who, it just so happens, in early 2004 gave up his chairmanship of the company to a man who had been his chief financial officer.

Perhaps Bill Gates is lucky his spouse does not have literary aspirations. Or maybe she does . . .

Some authors turn to their readers for ideas, as does true-crime writer and bestselling author Ann Rules, whose latest book is *Heart Full of Lies.* Ann says on her Web site:

> My last six books have come from readers' ideas. I get suggestions from readers, detectives, victims, even the families of killers. I probably go through 500 cases for every case I select for a book. My books are over 800 pages long in manuscript form, so I have to choose a very intricate, convoluted, case. I never want to "pad;" I look for true stories where, just when you think nothing else bizarre can happen, it *does.* I have written fiction in the past, but what real people do is far more compelling than anything a novelist can think up!

"It is a fact that few novelists enjoy the creative labor, though most enjoy thinking about the creative labor."

ARNOLD BENNETT

15

THE PROCESS OF WRITING

CHOOSING A GENRE

RESEARCH

PLANNING AND PLOTTING

THE DISCIPLINE OF WRITING

EVOLUTION OF AN AUTHOR'S STYLE

CHOOSING A GENRE

The genre of a book is that neat little label by which it finds a home on the bookseller's shelf. Science fiction, fantasy, horror, mystery, romance, thriller—all are distinct genres, and that's just the beginning. Subgenres include chick lit, lad lit, political thrillers, cozy mysteries, crime novels, English mysteries, erotic romance, paranormal romance, legal thrillers—the list goes on and on.

Genre provides a welcome and necessary degree of organization for publishing industry professionals as well as readers. Booksellers know where to stock the book by its genre, customers know where to find it, and publishers know how to sell it. Publishers also look at what genres are selling well to decide which new titles to purchase.

Romance is the largest genre. According to Romance Writers of America, the official definition of a romance is: "a book wherein the love story is the main focus of the novel and the end of the book is emotionally satisfying."

At the present time, nearly 36 percent of all fiction published in mass market, trade, and hardcover are categorized as romance, followed in popularity by mystery and general fiction. More than 50 million people read romance novels. Total sales of romance novels are a little over $1 billion a year. (Data courtesy of Romance Writers of America)

A genre for an author is like a friendly port for a ship. It's a wonderful place to stop, but you don't have to spend your whole career there. Authors often are beckoned by new, equally interesting ports as they transition from one genre to another.

Other authors do spend their whole careers writing in a single genre, focusing on the never-ending challenge of achieving a mastery of, say, crime fiction.

IRIS JOHANSEN, Author

Why did you decide to transition from category romance to romantic suspense, and then to suspense/thriller-type novels? Was it a difficult transition to make, given that the readership base of those genres is so different?

It evolved very naturally. I had an idea for a story that started out as a romance, and it just evolved into romantic suspense. I had a lot of fun with it. Then I had an idea for another story and just proceeded from there. I always put some romance in my books.

I just tell the story that comes to me. No matter what genre I'm in, I try to tell a good story. The different genres require changes in emphasis. In a romance, the emphasis is on the love story. In a thriller, you emphasize suspense.

The Ugly Duckling was your first hardcover title. When the book was coming out, were you apprehensive, or were you confident that it would be successful?

The Ugly Duckling was a dream book. I had it in mind for some time. I loved it so much that I couldn't imagine my romance readers not liking it. When it seemed to appeal to everyone else as well, I was very happy.

While many authors deliberately begin writing in a specific genre, others just write the strongest story they can and let it land where it may.

STUART WOODS, *Author*

When you first started writing, how did you decide what genre to focus on?

I wasn't concerned with genre. My first novel I'd been thinking about since I was a child. I just wanted to get it finished. I was very surprised when it won an Edgar award [from the Mystery Writers of America], because I didn't think of it as a mystery. I thought it was a book about how small towns work.

So you didn't concern yourself with the size of the potential market for the book?

I've just written the books I wanted to write. I thought of myself as writing mainstream fiction, and the size of the market was limited only by how well I wrote the book.

Why did you choose to write two series characters, Stone Barrington and Holly Barker?

The books didn't start out to be a series. At the beginning of my career, a publisher suggested that I should write a continuing character so my readers would know what to expect from me. I told them that the last thing I wanted my readers to know was what to expect, and I took pride in making every book as different as possible from the others. But the opportunity came along to use previous characters in new books. I took these opportunities as they came, and that's the way the series developed. It happened almost by accident.

The fiction genres of the past could be thought of as buckets of paint in primary colors. There's red over there; that must be romance; and green—that could be horror. Blue perhaps is suspense. These days, the color codes aren't so simple. Authors and publishers are blending colors into a bold new palette of subtle, wonderful (and sometimes weird) shades. The romance genre, especially, is cross-pollinating. Now there are paranormal romances, romantic comedies, sci-fi romances, romantic suspense, steamy romance, contemporary Christian romance, hip-hop romance. Yes, hip-hop.

The artful marketing strategy behind this blending is to draw new readers into the romance genre. Fans of suspense stories, for example, are attracted to the category by the wonderfully talented romantic suspense authors such as Iris Johansen or Linda Howard. The covers of these authors' books reflect the readers' tastes; they have a sense of mystery, danger, sometimes even an eerie feel to them. Nora Roberts had an incredibly successful trilogy of paranormal romance stories, starting with *Key of Light*, which bridged the gap between romance readers and fantasy fans.

The horror genre, sometimes referred to as "dark fantastic" or "macabre," is undergoing a renaissance of reader interest. It also has gone through a number of mutations. Authors are now including horror elements in historical fiction, romance, science fiction, mystery/thrillers, and erotic tales.

The combinations are virtually endless.

Consider Eric Garcia's innovative mystery novel series, begun with *Anonymous Rex*, featuring protagonist Vincent Rubio, a private detective who is a Velociraptor posing as a human.

This genre-bending has freed authors to let their imaginations run wild. The narrow constraints under which authors have sometimes labored have been replaced with wide creative latitude. (Sir Arthur Conan Doyle was so desperate to escape writing Sherlock Holmes stories, he threw his beloved detective off Reichenbach Falls.)

Who knows what interesting new subgenres we will see in the future? We could invent a variation right now. Let's title the story, *The Howling Detective*. A werewolf with paranormal abilities turns into a gorgeous, blonde attorney by day. She uses her powers to solve crimes before they happen and takes grisly revenge on corporate evildoers by night—while, of course, finding time to romance her boyfriend, the handsome, crusading district attorney who's running for the U.S. Senate.

Wow, you're thinking. I've been waiting for a sexy werewolf/detective legal thriller. When is it coming out?

Well, the concept might need a little tweaking.

PETER STRAUB, *Author*

Your stories are difficult to categorize into the neat little genres that publishers talk about—they have elements of mystery, horror, suspense, and the supernatural. How did you decide to blend the genres in that way?

It was just an expression of what I wanted to do with my writing. It was innate. I didn't consciously break any rules. But that I did so was a result of my goal of writing novels first, and genre novels only secondarily. After I got tired of writing supernatural material, I just adapted the same technique toward crime fiction.

HARLAN COBEN, *Author*

Early in your career, how did you decide to write in the suspense/ thriller genre?

I don't look at it as a genre as much as a form. To me, saying *suspense/ thriller* is like saying *haiku* or *sonata*. Within that form, I can do (and have done) pretty much whatever I want. What the suspense/thriller form does, however, is force me to tell a story, to keep the pages flying, to not get caught up in the brilliance of my own prose or ideas. You need that narrative drive, I think.

ANNA JACOBS, *Author*

Australian author Anna Jacobs writes historical romances, historical sagas, modern novels, and even occasionally a science fiction tale. She has gained large numbers of fans in her home country but also in the United Kingdom and, increasingly, in the United States. Her recent titles include *Marrying Miss Martha, Our Lizzie,* and *Mistress of Marymoor.*

Your titles cover an enormous breadth of subject matter—historical romance, science fiction, fantasy, and how-to books for writers. Was this part of your strategy for building your career and fan base, or did you just follow your own interests?

Neither of those. I wrote all sorts of things when I was trying to get published, partly because I knew it all added experience and also to see where I fit. I was very determined to get published. But I only wrote in genres I enjoyed reading. By sheer chance, my first saga was accepted five weeks before my first fantasy novel. I received contracts for six novels that year, the saga and fantasy novel, their half-written sequels, and a science fiction thriller/romance that I'd written to improve my management of pacing/tension, plus a to-be-written part three of the saga. So you might say it's a result of my seeking experience and writing, writing, writing.

RESEARCH

"Poets need not go to Niagara to write
about the force of falling water."

ROBERT FROST

Writing both fiction and nonfiction involves substantial research. Bestselling authors, such as Linda Fairstein, are acclaimed for the realism they bring to their stories; readers feel as though they are actually in the courtroom, listening to real people. Crime fiction is another area where meticulous attention to detail is required to pull off a story that readers will accept as "real." Some of our most popular fiction authors today had earlier careers as cops, reporters, forensic investigators, and lawyers. Having encountered, at least to some extent, the situations faced by characters in a novel can give an author a tremendous advantage over the author who is trying to imagine what it is like to address those situations—conduct an investigation, solve a crime, or win a court case.

It may come as a surprise, but even fantasy writers often conduct detailed research.

LAURELL K. HAMILTON, Author

Can you give me an example of something that you had to specifically research?

Guns. I had only shot two guns in my entire life when I started the Anita books, and she uses guns on an everyday basis. She's not a police officer; she's an executioner. Her job is to take lives, not protect them. So guns are in use a lot more than in police work. I started the research on guns by reading gun magazines, and then when I felt like I knew enough that I wouldn't ask stupid questions, I found a gun expert. I went to gun stores and looked at guns and finally went to the shooting range. I try to shoot everything Anita shoots but not everything that is in the books. One of my characters, Edward, uses a flamethrower. I've had people offer to show me how to use a flamethrower. I just don't find it appealing to strap an incendiary device on my back with fuel in it. I know it's perfectly safe, but I just don't need to do that.

I try to have an expert for each book that has had real police experience or combat experience. People who are into guns, who really know guns, have only found one mistake, and that was because my expert at the time hadn't had active combat experience.

What was that mistake?

You cannot cut a person in half with the clip of a small machine gun, you would have to have a J clip or a mushroom clip to have enough ammunition to literally cut a person in half.

And one of your readers caught that?

Yes they did—you better believe they did. There is always an expert out there, say on 14th-century armament, and if you get it wrong, the book is ruined for them. For most people, if you get that detail wrong, it spoils the rest of the book.

I write fiction, yes, but . . .

It has to be grounded in reality?

Yes. Many people think that in writing fantasy, you can write anything—there are no rules. But to write the fantastic and make it really work, you need to make the readers feel they could step into that world and live in it—that's what you need for readers to come to your books and love them. You have to make sure your reality is every bit as real as you can make it. You want to make them feel that they can walk in and rub their hand along the wood grain of a table and it would be soft under their hand.

I have been told by people in New York that I do more research for my fiction books than some writers do for their nonfiction books.

I have a degree in biology and in English literature, and I'm only three classes away from a major in history. I've always been a generalist. I think my biology degree solidified how I approach research. That's a different way of looking at things.

MARK BOWDEN, *Author*

It looked like *Black Hawk Down* took a tremendous amount of research to complete. How do you stay motivated to plow through a project of that scope?

I've always found that my interest grows as I learn more about a subject. This is kind of an affliction for a newspaper reporter, because for years I would go to work on a story and begin reporting and feel like, "Aha, I'm just beginning to understand what happened here. Now I can really get to work." But it would be time to write, and you would only get to write what you considered a hasty, incomplete little summary of the story. So I was always looking for opportunities to do stories the way I wanted to do them and to really be able to follow up on all the alleyways and avenues that would present themselves over the course of reporting.

I was very lucky to work for a newspaper, the *Philadelphia Enquirer,* that encouraged that kind of work, where it was not at all unusual for reporters to spend weeks or months, or even years, on stories. So I was the beneficiary of a wonderful newspaper that allowed me to develop those skills.

With *Black Hawk Down,* I got more and more excited as I worked on it, because as I learned more, I saw how much better the story was going to be. I think if that's how you're built, that kind of research never becomes tedious. It's a thrill.

I know writers who don't share that approach. Some of the best writers I know have no desire to write books. They prefer to work in a shorter form, to work for a more limited amount of time on a story. In some cases, those short stories turn out better than books.

Does your background as a journalist help you in producing book-length works?

For me, writing books is just a straight evolution from writing newspaper articles. From the very beginning as a reporter, I was always more interested in story telling than straight reporting. So I began writing short narratives for newspapers years ago. The books I write today are just longer, more complicated versions of the process I was going through 20 years ago. It hasn't changed at all.

PLANNING AND PLOTTING

The question, how much of your book should you outline before you begin writing, is impossible to answer. There appears to be a happy medium between having so much in outline form that your imagination feels constrained, and having so little on paper that your story has no direction. Between those two extremes, though, fiction authors' approaches vary widely.

"Unlike the architect, an author often discards his blueprint in the process of erecting his edifice. To the writer, a book is something to be lived through, an experience, not a plan to be executed in accordance with laws and specifications."

HENRY MILLER, The Books in My Life

PETER STRAUB, *Author*

Some of your novels are incredibly complex in their structure. Do you begin with a detailed outline, or do you sort of build in layers of complexity as you go?

I usually start with a kind of outline, a fast-forward summary that goes through the first 200 pages. Sometimes, I have almost no material outlined when I begin, and it just generates itself as I go along.

All that complexity is a way of keeping myself entertained. I enjoy reading books like that. John le Carré was a kind of model for me for a long time. I appreciated his use of different characters at different times and how you aren't always sure what their relationship is to the underlying story.

LINDA FAIRSTEIN, *Author*

Do you plan all the turns and twists in your plots ahead of time?

When I begin the book, I always know who the killer is and why the crime occurred. I think that is fairer to the readers when laying in clues—hopefully subtle ones—and creating the twists and turns. When the reader gets to the end, there is some reflection in recognizing the clues that were laid in along the way. Some other writers, very successful ones, say, "Well, the police get there, and they don't know who the killer is, so I don't need to know when I start." I disagree with that.

I need to know who the killer is, but I don't do a tight outline; I find tight outlining too confining. I lay out some of the suspects, and that helps decide what directions—what twists might take place. I find that once I get about a third of the way into a story, as I develop the characters and know where I want to take the plot, twists and turns begin to find their way into the story. Once I've picked the killer, I need logical suspects, and as I'm writing those suspects and developing them, they take me in directions that I had not planned at the outset.

How do you balance the need for intricate plots and strong characters?

I've always been interested in intricate plotting. I dislike books where it's painfully obvious from an early chapter who did it and why. I admire intricate plotting; it's what I set out to do. When I first started, I wanted a strong women protagonist in a nontraditional field—at least, it was nontraditional when I started prosecutorial work 30 years ago. One advantage I have in writing this kind of fiction is that I had the same job my character has. I do know what her professional life would be like. I hate books and movies where the "big case" happens and everything else gets swept out of the way. I try to show that the big case happens, but everything else that she has been working on is still there. Those other victims are still calling about their cases; you're still getting lab results that can change the outcome of another matter sitting on your desk. That's the intricacy and crossed plot lines that come easily to me, because I know how my character would work in real life.

CATHERINE COULTER, *Author*

Do you work from an outline, or do you plot the story ahead of time?

There is no story ahead of time, because I haven't written it. I'm not the kind of writer who can figure out what everybody is going to do from scene to scene and make it happen, because I don't work that way.

HARLAN COBEN, *Author*

Your readers love all the twists and turns your plots take. Do you plan those out ahead of time, like a blueprint, or does the writing process itself have its own twists and turns?

I know the beginning and the end. I know very little of what will happen in the middle.

After a number of extremely popular novels, how do you keep coming up with fresh twists or surprises for your readers?

It doesn't get easier, that I can tell you. I don't know how the ideas come. Most of them spring out of desperation and boredom, sitting on the couch and gazing up in the air, asking, "What if?" a whole lot.

How do you decide a concept is strong enough to turn into a novel?

If it compels me, I figure it will compel readers. I'm a tough critic and audience. I'm harder on myself than any editor.

How do you balance the need for intricate plots and strong characters?

I do it by not worrying about stuff like balance. I tell a story. If you stop every few pages and say, "Ooh, wait, I need some more character development here," you're in trouble. One should be a natural extension of the other. It's a car and gas. You can have a great car, but without the gas, you're not going anywhere.

What are some of the keys to writing thrillers that are so absorbing, readers stay up all night to finish them?

I'll give you the single best piece of writing advice I've ever heard. It comes from Elmore Leonard: "I cut out all the parts you'd normally skip." Do this on every page, every paragraph, every sentence, if you can. That doesn't mean you can't have descriptions or themes or even throw in personal philosophy. What it does mean, however, is that it must propel the story forward, not stop it in its tracks.

As you go from one novel to five or ten or more, does the writing become easier or more difficult?

Depends on the day you ask me. But mostly I think it gets tougher.

KIRK ELLIS, *Screenwriter*

Planning is an underrated aspect of writing, it seems.

Particularly in screenwriting. I spend at least twice as much time planning the script as I do writing it. I don't want the writing to be torturous. The way I ensure that is to spend a lot of time thinking about the story and writing detailed outlines.

James Ellroy told me that for *American Tabloid,* which ended up being a 600-page novel, his outline was 250 pages. He had everything thought out beforehand. That doesn't mean the writing was somehow automatic. The outline freed him to deal with things like voice and style, because he wasn't having to worry about, "I don't know what's going on the next page."

THE DISCIPLINE OF WRITING

"They can't yank novelist like they can pitcher.
Novelist has to go the full nine, even if it kills him."

ERNEST HEMINGWAY, quoted in *Portrait of Hemingway,* by Lillian Ross

Many first-time authors fear that they will not be able to finish a book. This fear can be chased away quite simply by observing how the bestselling authors do it: they stay at their word processor, day after day, sometimes even not taking a break on weekends. It is similar to the difference between the marathon runner and the person who has just purchased their jogging shoes with the goal of completing a marathon someday. Top athletes go through a rigorous step-by-step training process to build up their strength and stamina. Similarly, bestselling authors have trained their minds to produce content at will, whenever they turn the light on in the office and sit down. They can shut out all distractions. They don't wait to be in the perfect writing "mood" and don't depend on being kissed by a muse. The bestselling author knows to fear nothing when encountering the blank page. The human mind is capable of doing amazing things, day after day, book after book.

BARBARA TAYLOR BRADFORD, Author

Internationally renowned, bestselling romance author Barbara Taylor Bradford has written over 20 novels since her first, *A Woman of Substance*, was published in 1976. Her heroines show an irrepressible strength of character while overcoming formidable obstacles to love and success. Her books have been published in 40 languages and sold more than 70 million copies. Her books include *Unexpected Blessings, Emma's Secret, Three Weeks in Paris*, and *The Triumph of Katie Byrne*.

What part of your life as a bestselling author might surprise your fans?

I'm really a down-to-earth woman who keeps a rigorous schedule and leads a normal life. Though my publicity photos portray me in glamorous clothes, jewelry, etc., my existence most of the time is very unglamorous. I usually wake up around 5:00 AM, and I'm at my typewriter by a quarter to six. I use a typewriter, not a computer, though I do use the computer for research and e-mail. I start my day by reviewing the last chapter from the day before. After some editing, I go to work on a fresh page and keep on going until around noon. I don't get dressed up to write. I generally wear a comfortable pair of sweatpants and sweatshirt, or a T-shirt depending on the weather. After a lunch break, I return to the typewriter around 1:30 PM and go at it until 5:30 PM, or later. I don't generally like to write late at night, though I occasionally will do so when my husband Bob is away on business.

When I'm not writing or researching, I love to cook favorite recipes in the kitchen. Though we do dine out often, my favorite meals are the ones I prepare with my own hands.

My weekends are spent reading the work of my favorite writers. I love books by Patricia Cornwell, and I love historical books, especially those on Winston Churchill.

Bob and I do like to travel, though we spend most of our time in our New York apartment. The one luxury I will splurge on is car service. Neither of us drive, and we don't own a car, so we take taxis or car services frequently around the New York area.

The most surprising fact is perhaps that I do still work around the clock on deadlines, even though I honestly don't need to knock myself out. Surely, I could happily sit back and enjoy my success of the past 25 years, but writing is my life. So I press on and keep to a tight schedule in an effort to complete at least one book every year.

ANNA JACOBS, *Author*

How are some authors able to be so prolific and produce 28 titles, as you have?

Sheer hard work. I start at about 6:00 AM and work through until 5:00 or 6:00 PM, usually six days a week. You can write a lot in that time, even allowing for other writing activities like answering readers' letters and e-mails, editing, proofreading, etc.

SUSAN ELIZABETH PHILLIPS, *Author*

How does a popular author strike a balance between spending time promoting their books and doing the actual writing?

I fight this every day. My oft-quoted motto is "Protect the work." Everybody has to figure out what that means for themselves. For me, it frequently means moving to a computer that has no Internet access and screening calls.

EVOLUTION OF AN AUTHOR'S STYLE

Bestselling authors seldom allow themselves the luxury of being totally satisfied with their work. They constantly challenge themselves to bring new, exciting, even groundbreaking books to their readers. They make subtle changes to their writing style as well. Obviously , they don't want to depart too far from what is already successful, but they definitely strive to improve, and in this way, the process of writing remains fresh to them as well. It continues to be the eventful journey of self-discovery it was when they began their very first book and does not become a repetitive "job." If you follow a popular author's work for, let's say, five or ten years, you can see their skills evolve.

BARBARA DELINSKY, *Author*

Has your writing changed much over the years?

I hope so. I certainly try to grow—struggle to make each book more streamlined in terms of both language and plot. I try to write a tighter story, while preserving the emotional impact—try to improve with each book. I've always been acutely aware of the importance of making each book different from the one before it and keeping my work fresh.

My readers are my *raison d'etre*. I can't write a lousy book and pass it off to them, knowing that they'll buy it just because it has my name on it. I don't sell books that way. I like to give it my all. Honestly, I can't imagine spending nine months working on a book that I didn't like, that I didn't think was good.

I have worked hard on style, teaching myself, and there, editors do help. My writing has become cleaner, more sophisticated, and streamlined.

IRIS JOHANSEN, *Author*

Your books appeal to both men and women—not many authors can say that. Why do you think that is, and is it something you deliberately tried to achieve?

I have both male and female protagonists. I try to portray both as strongly as I can. Hopefully, it is characterization that carries the day.

How did you go about developing your tremendous skill at creating suspense, even terror, coming from a romance-writing background?

Again, it comes down to good storytelling. Instinct has a lot to do with it. When I put terror elements in a story, I probably portray my own fears to some extent. It usually works.

You were quoted as saying that your ideas about plot structure have changed over the years. How so?

When I first started, I was doing category romance, which has very simple plots, relying principally on emotion. As I wrote book after book, the plot structure became much more complicated, having much more to do with storytelling than emotion. One of the reasons I dipped into suspense was that the plotting is much more intricate. I don't do it intentionally, but I find the more books I write, the more intricate the plots become.

Do suspense writers employ classic elements of fear, or do they try to make the books reflect what's happening in today's world by weaving in what people currently fear?

I have written about very current fears, like anthrax and dirty bombs, though I don't consciously try to make a story current. But I live in this world like everyone else, and what I write reflects that.

What gave you the idea of having secondary characters appear in more than one novel, sometimes having a secondary character in one novel become the protagonist of the next one?

I started doing that years ago, when I was doing category romance. It was because a secondary character intrigued me, came alive for me. When a secondary character comes alive, you want to keep them around. I almost always end up giving them their own story. They become so strong, they can't be a secondary character anymore. I've had some books where the secondary characters become so strong, I had to send them out of the book for a while, because they were starting to dominate it.

Even after one book's completed and on the bookstore shelves, a few characters are burning quietly like embers, ready to go on the next adventure?

Absolutely.

SABRINA JEFFRIES, *Author*

Have the expectations of romance readers changed over the last five to ten years?

Reader expectation is always changing. The world has grown more fast paced, and books have had to keep up. No one has the time anymore to sink into a description-heavy tale these days. (Being a little ADD—Attention Deficit Disorder—myself, I never did like those books, so I'm right at home in the new world.) There's more emphasis on dialog and action than on long, lyrical passages, which suits my writing style. Readers also want a hipper sensibility, even in their historicals. Smart-alecky heroines are more of the norm, I think, along with heroes who don't know everything. The dialog has to be snappier and the characters more compelling. It really keeps a writer on her toes, believe me.

BARBARA TAYLOR BRADFORD, *Author*

How has your writing style evolved over the years?

I began as a journalist, so I guess you could say that I learned to write against tight deadlines, while on the run. It was crucial to get all the facts straight, though this required exhaustive research. This process undoubtedly helped me to become a better researcher as a novelist.

My second writing career was for newspapers and magazines in the area of women's interests, fashion, and decorating. In the United States, I wrote and had published several books on decorating for apartments and homes. This was a great joy for me, as I still love to decorate. More importantly, in writing features on design, I learned to pay attention to detail when it came to clothing, fashion, furniture, and antiques. Dedicated readers of my books will tell you that I've made great use of this knowledge in setting the scene for locations in my 20 bestselling novels.

My career as a novelist began humbly. I started, but did not complete, three novels. I simply didn't like them after 50 or 100 pages, so I tucked them away and have never revisited them. I didn't give up, however. Instead, I went around seeking advice from writers whom I respected, trying to figure out the magic formula to unlock the creativity of my imagination. The best advice was from an interview with Graham Greene, who told *Time Magazine*, "Character is plot." Up to that point,

I'd been trying to fit characters into my stories. With this advice, I realized that I first needed strong characters to build the story around. Once I took on this strategy, I was able to create Emma Harte, enabling me to write *A Woman of Substance.*

My writing style hasn't changed drastically since my earliest novels, though I always look for different, interesting locations and professions for my stories and protagonists. What has changed is the speed with which research can now be conducted. I used to spend weeks in the library, researching reference books on locations and periods of history. Now I can pull things up on the Internet in a matter of minutes.

16

THE BESTSELLING AUTHOR'S LIFE

CHANGES TO THEIR LIVES

MONEY, MONEY, MONEY
COULD BESTSELLING
AUTHORS BECOME EVEN MORE FAMOUS?

FAME, RECOGNITION, AND LET'S NOT FORGET MONEY—
BUT THAT'S NOT ALL

CHANGES TO THEIR LIVES

Early in their careers, authors feel as though they are in a footrace that never ends, chasing after an elusive literary marketplace and never quite catching up. Then, that first big success comes, bringing about an exciting reversal: now the marketplace is chasing them. They no longer hear, "Well, I'm not sure there's a market for your book." They hear, "What an intriguing concept!" All the formerly closed doors swing open, and once the author passes through those doors, they find this new world is very different from the old one.

PETER STRAUB, *Author*

What did *Ghost Story*'s success mean to you?

It was immensely satisfying to me. A layer of worry had been removed from both my life and my consciousness. From that point, I was clearly going to be able to keep on getting published and to live well on the basis of what I earned from my books. Early on, I did fear poverty, and when I had no money, I got tired of it. It's hard on the soul to be always worried about cash. Suddenly, all that worry was gone, and I could relax a bit.

MARK BOWDEN, Author

How does it change your life and career once you have the term *bestselling author* attached to your name?

One of the things it does, it gives you a heck of a lot more money than you had before. The value in that, apart from the obvious ones, is the freedom it gives me to do what I want and not really have to chase around for a paycheck every week.

Magazines and publishers who wouldn't give you the time of day once upon a time are now really interested in everything you're writing. You go very quickly from being the person who is always trying to promote an idea or get somebody to buy an idea to a position where you are having to turn away proposals for things that, otherwise, you would really love to do. Magazine editors and publishers will present you with ideas that you would love to do, but you realize there are only so many hours in the day. The idea is to take pride in everything you do and not produce mediocre work just to get the money.

You have to realize you don't have to take every opportunity that comes along, because you're not climbing the ladder anymore. In a commercial sense, you've already had a level of success, and it sticks with you to some extent. So you concentrate on climbing the quality ladder.

CATHERINE COULTER, Author

How did your life change?

When you hit the *New York Times,* you're "made"—until you stop making that list. In my case, I wasn't an overnight success. My sales just kept building higher and higher. When *Moonspun Magic* hit the *Times,* I learned that the world is a very different place. The publishers treat you like you're a very different animal than you were before. You make more money. Other authors admire and hate you. And almost immediately, there starts the expectation that your next book has to perform better than the last one. Not only do you expect it, but so does the publisher.

Making the *New York Times* is very exciting; you can never downplay that. And no, you never get tired of making it; you never stop worrying about making it. I've been on the *Times* list 45 times, and believe me, every single time is extraordinarily important.

RACHEL GIBSON, *Author*

How did your life change as a result of making the *USA Today* bestseller list the first time?

At the time, I really didn't know what it meant. I'd just been trying to hit above 50 on *USA Today*, because I like each of my books to do better than the last. Now that I do know, I've noticed that I get more respect within the publishing industry. There is also *a lot* more pressure to have each book outsell the last.

MONEY, MONEY, MONEY

The financial rewards for publishing success are almost breathtaking. One screenwriter has said that when he sold his first script, it felt like winning the lottery. With some of the deals that bestselling authors get, it's more like winning the multistate Powerball drawing. Notice in the examples below how big money is going to veterans of the bestseller list, and new authors, and fiction and nonfiction authors, and to what could be described as midlevel media celebrities. Authors from all genres, including children's, are receiving fantastic book contracts. And let's not forget the added bonus of selling movie rights to a book.

MICHAEL CADER, Publisher
PublishersMarketPlace.com and Cader Books

It appears that the deals bestselling authors receive are escalating in dollar value. Is that true, and if so, why?

Like almost all products of popular culture, the big hits get bigger and bigger, as most everything else gets smaller. And the ability of the biggest producers to extract top dollar from their corporate partners also tends to increase. In publishing in particular, the rapid rise of the mass merchandisers in selling large quantities of deeply discounted hardcovers in a short period of time has the most to do with the kind of numbers being reaped.

In 2001, Michael Crichton received a $40 million advance for his next two books, joining HarperCollins after years at another publisher. *Prey* was the first book produced under that contract. The book received a record 1.5 million copy first printing. That seems like an outlandish amount of money. Why do publishing houses do this? One reason is to trumpet to the marketplace that they have the (most likely) top-selling book of that publishing season. Their sales reps can charge into battle with the confidence that their catalog contains "the hot book." This kind of buzz helps with generating interest in other titles from the publisher.

In the case of *Prey,* there's a certain irony that a book about infinitesimal machines could end up being such a huge money-making machine.

The Web site http://www.publishersmarketplace.com provides an excellent source of information about deals being made in the publishing world. Here are some examples. A major deal means it is valued in excess of $500,000. Remember, too, that "eight figures" can mean anywhere from $10 to $99 million, seven figures from $1 to $9 million.

- *Publishing Legends Get BIG, BIG, BIG BUCKS.* Three books by Dean Koontz, to Bantam, in a major deal, for eight figures
- *The Movies Pay BIG BUCKS for Strong New Voices.* Film rights to Lolly Winston's first novel, *Good Grief,* optioned to producer Marc Platt *(Legally Blonde* and *Wicked)* for Universal Studios, in a major deal

- *Romance Authors Get BIG BUCKS.* Susan Elizabeth Phillips's two additional Chicago Stars books (in the first, a matchmaker desperately needs to find a wife for her sports agent client), to William Morrow, in a major deal
- *Hard-Nosed Businessmen Get BIG BUCKS.* Former GE chief Jack Welch and former Harvard Business Review editor-in-chief Suzy Wetlaufer's *Winning,* called "the ultimate business how-to book," to Harper Business, in a major deal for seven figures
- *The Right Wing Gets BIG BUCKS.* MSNBC television host and former Republican congressman Joe Scarborough's "definitive book on how Washington wastes our tax dollars," to Harper, in a major deal for a reported $600,000
- *The Left Wing Gets BIG BUCKS.* The next two books by Molly Ivins, author of the bestseller *Bushwhacked,* the first a currently untitled collection, the second presenting new material on the Bill of Rights, in a major deal
- *Children's Authors Get BIG BUCKS.* Stephanie Meyer's debut, *Twilight,* a teenage vampire love story, to Little, Brown Children's, in a major three-book deal—"the most Little, Brown Children's has ever offered a first-time author"
- *Western Authors Get BIG BUCKS.* Romance author Linda Lael Miller's three books, featuring bigger, richer, Western stories dubbed "female versions of Larry McMurtry," in a major deal
- *Trendy Fiction Authors Get BIG BUCKS. Devil Wears Prada* author Lauren Weisberger's *Doors Open at Eleven,* called "an inside look at the city's yuppies of the new millennium," in a ten-page proposal, to Simon & Schuster, in a major deal for at least $1 million reportedly
- *Nothing Comical about Getting One Million BUCKS.* Universal Pictures has paid $1 million to preemptively option Doug TenNapel's graphic novel, *Tommysaurus Rex*

For the gods and goddesses of publishing, all those years of work don't culminate in a pot of gold at the end of the rainbow: it's more like being given a deed to the entire platinum mine.

It wasn't always true, say 50 years ago, but now becoming a popular author leads to wealth. Several sources have reported that James Patterson's annual earnings are in the tens of millions of dollars. To show how different this world is from that of the typical author, consider that most first-time novels earn an advance in the $5,000 to $10,000 range, and most of the time, the sales do not earn out the advance. In other words, they get no further royalties. Bestselling authors have no more relation to the typical writer than NBA stars have to teenagers dribbling a basketball on a crumbling inner-city playground.

It is not uncommon these days for the hardcover sales of a bestseller to crest above one million copies. Suppose the author earned a 15 percent royalty off the wholesale price of a book that retails for $25. The royalty would total nearly $1,875,000. Subsequent sales of the movie rights can be several hundred thousand dollars or more. We also can't forget the paperback rights. It is possible for the paperback sales of a novel to approach and even exceed 10,000,000 copies, as *The Godfather* did.

"I'm opposed to millionaires, but it would be dangerous to offer me the position."

MARK TWAIN from *Mark Twain at Your Fingertips*

COULD BESTSELLING AUTHORS BECOME EVEN MORE FAMOUS?

The Bestselling Author as Celebrity is a relatively new phenomenon, brought on partially by the pervasiveness of the media. It makes you wonder, would Edgar Allan Poe have enjoyed going to a book signing? Suppose he meets a young admirer named Bobby who says, "Yo, Ed, just sign that, ah, 'to your greatest fan.' By the way, in that one story, it was so cool when that creepy Usher chick got stuck behind that wall." Giants of literature in the past cast intimidating figures, at least in our minds. You can't easily conjure up an image of a tourist from Sheboygan chatting up Hemingway at the Barnes & Noble in Key West. "C'mon, guy, did you really run with the bulls?" Or how about talking to some of the more dissolute 19th-century writers:

"Where do you get the inspiration for your stories?"

"Generally after a glass of absinthe, sir," comes the reply.

The apex of celebrity status comes, as we know, only from being invited to appear on reality TV. How would bestselling authors fare on:

- *Fear Factor: Commercial versus Literary.* Authors are chained to their chairs and forced to read as much of the other's work as they can before throwing up or passing out. It's Danielle Steel versus Donna Tartt in the semifinals. The winner squares off against the victor of the hotly contested James Patterson versus Susan Sontag match. If they survive that round, in the finals they are forced to watch TV movie adaptations of their books. "Oh, no! It's James Brolin playing my lead character! I imagined him as Brad Pitt. Turn it off, turn it off! Please!"

- *Temptation Island.* Your favorite romance authors read spicy sections of their novels to supposedly engaged but hopelessly confused females, right before a boatload of hunky guy models lands on shore. On the other side of the island, their boyfriends are immersed in the classics that boys so enjoy: Dickens, Hawthorne, Steinbeck, Melville. Yeah, right.
- *Survivor "Book Tour."* We see 10 top authors traveling for 3 months on a 30-city book tour, trying not to lose their minds. Starting with only three changes of clothes, unlimited credit at Starbucks, and a box of felt-tip pens, they set off on a perilous journey, endeavoring to look perky and sound fascinating while taping a local TV show in Des Moines at 5:00 AM in February, being asked for the millionth time, "Where do you get your ideas?" The crankiest author gets voted off the book tour first. (Tom Clancy's paramilitary training won't do him any good here.) Tension mounts as the authors scramble for clues on how to find the Borders Books stores in busy metro areas during rush hour without the aid of a publicist.

FAME, RECOGNITION, AND LET'S NOT FORGET MONEY—BUT THAT'S NOT ALL

Celebrities are different from us; they have more fun. This rule must, of course, apply to famous authors. They get to meet other celebrities, perhaps people they have admired for years. They get the invitations to the bright summer parties in the Hamptons and the winter soirees in Palm Beach. They attend premieres of films based on their books and awards banquets where their books are nominated. They are fawned over at writers' conferences and genre conventions. It sounds like nonstop excitement. Well, maybe . . .

BRAD MELTZER, Author

What aspects of a bestselling author's life might surprise their fans?

It's just not that *thrilling* day to day. It's not like there's a literary roundtable where I call up Grisham and Stephen King and discuss current events as we light our pipes and put on our bathrobes.

It's a very solitary lifestyle. When *The Tenth Justice* was about to come out, I called up all the top thriller writers in the country. Every single one called me back. And at that moment in time, I remember thinking, "Why are you calling me back? Aren't you busy going to movie premieres and literary lunches?"

No. They were all sitting at home. That's all we do—that's our job. We sit and write. There's no going to red carpet premieres. There's no premiere for your book. You're sitting there and writing. Alone. And that's okay—that's what I like. I like having the time to myself to be creative and to come up with things. I get paid to talk to my imaginary friends. How could I possibly complain?

SUSAN ELIZABETH PHILLIPS, Author

You don't seem to take yourself quite as seriously as some authors do. Has your sense of humor helped you cope with the difficulties and challenges of sustaining a successful career as a novelist?

I have a husband and two grown sons. If I took myself too seriously, they'd laugh their a**** off. I think my attitude goes back to my initial motivations in writing. I just wanted a little something to do part-time (!) while I raised my kids. Someplace in my mind, I guess I still think of this as a part-time gig. My family is at the center of my life, and that keeps everything else in perspective. At first, I started writing to keep the "alpha" part of me entertained.

Do successful authors look at other bestselling authors as competitors to some extent and keep an eye on how those authors' books are selling?

Years ago, I was talking to Sandra Brown. She was expressing her delight over another author's success, and I still remember what she said: "A high tide floats all ships." That has never been more true than in the romance genre. Women readers are voracious. Other writers' successes have led readers to my books. My success leads readers to other writer's books. The romance community is tight-knit. We're constantly on the phone with each other, sharing information, and that cooperation has made us extremely powerful and wealthy women. Other industries would be wise to look at our dynamic.

What aspects of a bestselling author's life might surprise their fans?

How hard the work is. How much we whine (and whine, and whine) when a book isn't going well, which, for most of us, seems like most of the time. How really cool it is when you realize how much your book has touched someone. How badly dressed we are while we're working.

IRIS JOHANSEN, *Author*

Would anything about the life of a bestselling author surprise your fans?

They would definitely be surprised. Most of the bestselling authors I know lead relatively boring lives. We work very hard. I write two books a year. Not because I have to do it but because I can't *not* do it. Writing is a passion for me. When we go on the TV interview circuit, our lives appear very glamorous. But that is only for a few weeks a year. Then we're right back at our computers.

LEE BOUDREAUX, *Senior Editor*
Random House

What about the life of a bestselling author might surprise readers and fans?

How infrequently "overnight success" occurs. A lot of people write and write and write and never see their work published. Some people publish in paperback for years until they finally break out in hardcover. Some people publish books that don't get noticed, don't get reviewed, don't get read, and they sit right back down the next day and start the next one. I think being a writer is such a hard job, and the rewards are often few and far between. I have the utmost respect for both the talent and hard work it takes.

17

THE UPS AND DOWNS

THE PRESSURE TO STAY ON TOP
FAMOUS WRITERS' TIME IS NOT THEIR OWN
THE GLORIOUS FIRST SUCCESS
A PERSPECTIVE ON LONG-TERM SUCCESS

THE PRESSURE TO STAY ON TOP

The problem with any kind of fame, whether in sports, movies, or publishing, is that when you fall, lots of people are there to cheer as you hit the pavement. Authors who have initial success are often beset with insecurities instead of exhilaration, because it is very difficult to pinpoint what you did with the first book that resonated with readers to such an astounding degree. Some of the marketing factors that led to success seem to have an element of luck—the great review in major media just at the right time or the timeliness of a topic. Quite a number of authors have said that the second book after an initial "hit" is the most difficult to write.

LEE BOUDREAUX, *Senior Editor*
Random House

There seems to be pressure on fiction authors to build sales with each successive book. Is that realistic, given the competition in the industry?

I think you can build the audience with each book. With a new hardcover, you generate as much review coverage as you can. You hope booksellers pay attention to it and start hand selling it. You might send the author out on tour. You might advertise. The paperback comes out a year later, and a whole lot more people are going to buy it at $12 than at $24. When the next hardcover comes out, there should be much more awareness of this author's work, and you hope those hardcover and paperback readers will buy the new book, and that the new raft of reviews and publicity appearances and ads will attract even more readers. Of course, so many books are published each year, it's always hard to get people to buy a relatively unknown author, and you really don't know what's going to become a runaway bestseller like *The Lovely Bones*. Sometimes the stars align. Editors are, by and large, a wackily optimistic group. We always think, "This one could be the one."

Seabiscuit was like that. No one would necessarily expect it to be a *New York Times* bestseller or the bestselling sports book of all time. But at sales conference that year, they showed a news clip of Seabsicuit's famous race against War Admiral. Remember, that race was 70 years ago, and everybody knew who won. Yet, when Seabiscuit crossed the finish line, the entire room broke into applause. I remember thinking, "This has to be what a bestseller looks like!"

PAULA EYKELHOF, Executive Editor
Harlequin Books

In such a competitive publishing world, is it realistic to expect an author's sales to keep building with each successive book?

Obviously, the attempt to keep building sales is inevitable. I do think that, by and large, publishers are realistic: expectations are determined by circumstances. Not that every editor and publisher isn't hoping to defy those circumstances and put out a massive bestseller!

Publishing decisions, of course, are also determined by circumstances—by sales, retail climate, and so on. This might mean that fewer copies are printed and distributed or fewer titles published.

In the case of a first-time author whose book meets with success or acclaim, how does an editor keep the author grounded and make sure the second book is just as good?

For one thing, the editor should not lower their expectations when it comes to the quality of the second work. The author should be held to the same standards. Granted, authors sometimes have difficulty with the second book, particularly if they spent years on the first one, polishing and perfecting. "Second-book syndrome" isn't exactly uncommon! But, once the first book is published, the author becomes part of a system, and the publisher then hopes and expects to release a second book within a particular period of time (say, a year, for instance). So, I think the process of writing the second book can be a somewhat humbling experience, and yet a necessary one that teaches authors about their own goals and limitations—and about the realities of this business.

In the end, it comes down to story (it really does): the love of story and how to tell each individual one.

Bestselling authors have the most difficult challenge of all to stay on top, because the publishing house makes such a huge financial investment in each of their books. Their books are in all the stores. If they don't sell, there is nowhere to hide. It's great fun to be that fresh, up-and-coming face in the literary world. Staying on top requires tremendous focus and tenacity.

SABRINA JEFFRIES, Author

What is the most difficult challenge you face as a writer?

To write the exceptional book. I strive to write books that resonate with readers on a deep emotional level while remaining fresh and original. Editors always say they want books that are "the same but different," but that's because readers want those, too. They want to feel comfortable with the milieu and the story arc (no unhappy endings, for example) but still be surprised by the details, the dialog, the style, the characters. A hero should be heroic but unique, a heroine sympathetic but fascinating. The plot should have surprises while still staying within the parameters of a romance. Do you know how hard it is to achieve that balancing act?

KAREN KOSZTOLNYIK, *Senior Editor*
Warner Books

How can an editor keep a bestselling author on top of his or her game and in tune with the marketplace?

When you notice a bestselling author's career is stagnating a little bit, you have to recognize that and work with the author, suggest they try a different direction. Maybe they are writing sad books that don't work, but their happy books have sold well, so you would suggest they go in that direction. I'm simplifying here. Or suppose you see that novels that are part of a trilogy are selling well, so you might suggest that author might try a series of three. The editor has to determine what it is about the author's work that has run its course. It is important to be communicative and constantly be assessing. If one thing didn't work well, you talk to the author about going in a different direction. It isn't easy to let go of something that worked well and try something else, but sometimes that is necessary.

JENNIFER ENDERLIN, *Publisher*
St. Martin's Press

Why do you think some authors can turn out top-quality books that satisfy their audience, year after year, whereas other authors fade away after one or two popular titles?

I think it's because some popular authors get burned out. Some popular authors stop challenging themselves. Some popular authors let their egos get in the way, and they refuse to be edited; they refuse to take suggestions.

The ones who are able to sustain their careers the longest are the ones that are constantly challenging themselves and willing to work with their editors to make sure their books are the best they can be. They raise the bar higher for themselves each time.

I think it's a sheer matter of burnout a lot of times. It is very hard to write fiction year after year. I think sometimes their spirit gives up before their checkbook does.

So it's not that their talent wanes. It's just the mental energy it takes to keep writing is depleted over time.

That's right.

The two most uncomfortable perches in the publishing industry are occupied by the author trying to get a contract for a second book when the sales of his first were poor and the bestselling author whose sales noticeably slip.

JOHN BENNETT, *Owner*
Bennett Books in Wyckoff, New Jersey

How quickly can you tell that a bestselling author is slipping in popularity?

We see it pretty fast. An author on the kids' side of things, R.L. Stine of *Goosebumps* fame, had been a bestseller for a decade or more. Seemingly one fall, all the kids got together and said, "Enough of this stuff; he's writing the same book over and over again, and we're bored with this and are moving on to another author." He just stopped selling. You can see it almost immediately in the computer. You can buy the normal 20 or 30 copies of his book again and again, and then all of a sudden, you find a book that doesn't sell a single copy.

I've seen that on the adult side with Tom Clancy and Robert Ludlum, perennial bestsellers that, for unknown reasons, stopped selling. And it is not a gradual decline over a number of titles; it tends to be one book that just doesn't sell. Usually, publishers will come out with another book by that author and say, "We know that book wasn't as good, and here are the reasons why. But try this next book. It's going to bring that author back up to the higher sales level." On a few rare occasions that happens, but usually the public simply decides to move on to someone else. That author never gets back to the heights they attained.

That phenomenon is kind of scary.

It is. It argues for authors putting away their royalties in CDs and treasury bills and not counting on being a bestselling author forever.

BARBARA DELINSKY, *Author*

Why do you think some authors who have had a very successful first book sometimes fail to achieve that same level of success with their second book?

There's the distraction caused by touring and promotion. Some authors buy into their own hype. Some authors only have one book in them, and one book does not a real writer make. And then there's the author whose first book has a unique premise—how to *possibly* live up to that the second time around? So, given all these things, the challenge of duplicating a success is complex. The pressure, in and of itself, to match that first success becomes debilitating.

My books may be more or less unusual in their premise, but I feel that each is a good, solid read. An *author* is someone whose name appears on the front of a book; a *writer* is someone who can craft books over and over again. To me, the test of a real writer is being able to write consistently.

Not all authors have this ability to continue evolving in their craft, turning out one fine novel after another. Some extremely gifted authors only manage to produce that one, really great book, which makes the achievements of authors who write dozens of popular books even more impressive. Not only do these authors seem to have an inexhaustible wellspring of creativity, but they have incredible self-discipline to keep at the word processor day after day, year after year. They also have an uncanny sense of what will be popular with masses of readers at any given time.

DANIEL HALPERN, *Editor-in-Chief*
HarperCollins

Why do you think some authors write book after book, while some just write one?

Some people are abundantly talented. Joyce Carol Oates we know is prolific, but what makes her special is that each one is really good. On the other side, there are a number of one-book wonders—one great book and then . . . the big silence, which I don't think is the end of the world. Some of the biggest novels of the 20th century were by novelists who only wrote one book. One great novel is worth 15 lesser ones.

FAMOUS WRITERS' TIME IS NOT THEIR OWN

Popular authors face another form of stress: increasing demands on their time. You got where you are by spending every available hour writing, learning your craft, and revising and polishing your first manuscript until you couldn't stand the sight of it anymore. Now that you have reached your goal, you find that you are asked to do all these other things to help promote your books. Then there is the celebrity aspect itself. People want you. To appear at events. To help promote a charitable cause. To go to the A-list parties. We've seen a number of authors whose word output mysteriously declines when they are seemingly in their prime and in good health. Unfortunately, these authors have crossed the bridge into dangerous territory, where the ego satisfaction they receive from being recognized is more satisfying than the writing itself. Writing a perfect paragraph can no longer compete with the perfect night on the town, where seemingly everyone wants to meet you.

Fortunately, most bestselling authors recognize this danger and steer clear of it. But the other problem, demands on their time from the publishing industry itself, is more difficult to cope with.

SUSAN ELIZABETH PHILLIPS, *Author*

As you become more successful, does your writing career become more time consuming?

Much more. I was on the road for two weeks when *Ain't She Sweet* came out. I went for a month without taking a day off. When I got back home, I was in the kitchen with my husband and exclaimed, "This was supposed to be a part-time job!"

There are three aspects to a writer's career now. First the business aspect; there's just so much more of that, and it's good. I'm certainly not complaining. But it does interfere with writing. And now there's this Internet thing. Writing is not easy for any of us, and I really struggle. It's now so easy, when you can't think of your next sentence, to click onto the Web and check e-mail from readers or postings on your bulletin board. I have a couple of strategies to stay focused on writing. I keep a kitchen timer in my office, set for one-hour intervals. During that one hour, I don't get up from my chair, don't go the Net. The other strategy is to work on my laptop, which does not have Internet access. The Net is a real time sink. It's the devil!

You're allowed to take a day off . . .

I try to write at least an hour each day on weekends. If I take a full day off, even Sunday, I have to deal with that resurfacing or reconnecting time, because I've been pulled away from the book.

CHRISTOPHER PAOLINI, *Author*

What had been the biggest impact on your family from having such great success with *Eragon*?

Personally, I've ended up traveling a tremendous amount. I did an entire year of promotion with the self-published version of *Eragon*, then a couple of book tours with Knopf. It's fun to meet the fans, booksellers, librarians, and teachers who have loved and supported the book. But it is stressful being on a book tour, because you can't take much time to enjoy the places you visit. It's a pretty rushed schedule.

As far as the family at large, I would say the biggest change is the amount of attention we get from people who want books signed or advice, and dealing with the business side of publishing. Also, the financial security that has come with *Eragon*'s success has removed a lot of worries.

I remember when I had a choice of pursuing my art—I drew the map and the dragon eye for *Eragon*—or my writing. I chose writing, because I didn't want to become a starving artist. What I didn't realize is how many starving writers there are. Fortunately, that's not a worry I have right now.

Success is an elusive state of being, shifting from moment to moment and from person to person, almost as quickly as momentum changes in a football game. An author's perception of where they are on the success scale often changes over time. One author may consider it a success just that their book is published. Others may use the size of the advance, number of copies sold, or the prestige of being able to say they are bestselling authors as the true measure of success.

"For several days after my first book was published,
I carried it about in my pocket and took surreptitious
peeps at it to make sure the ink had not faded."

SIR JAMES M. BARRIE, *A Reader for Writers*

THE GLORIOUS FIRST SUCCESS

One thing is certain: the top-selling author never, ever forgets that very first sweet taste of publishing success—and the profound feeling of relief that accompanies it.

PETER STRAUB, *Author*

Could you take us back to your first big commercial success and tell us how it happened?

I remember it very, very clearly, because it did cause such a great change in my life. My breakthrough book was called *Ghost Story;* it was published in 1979. Before that, I had published one mainstream novel that did not sell very well because, in fact, it wasn't very good. Then I published two supernatural books that you might call Henry James-y, or English, in style. They did quite well but didn't get anywhere near the bestseller list. People liked them, though, and I made enough money to support us, and we could even buy a house. So we were doing quite well.

I still wanted very much to move up from getting $30,000 paperback advances to getting $300,000 paperback advances. I was getting more ambitious, and I started a novel that was much more ambitious than anything I'd done before. It had more characters than I'd ever dealt with before. It was on a much larger scale. I knew when writing it that it was going to make a much bigger splash than any of my previous books had done. So I told my agent about this book, *Ghost Story,* and she started to try to get my publishers excited. That book came out and rolled along tremendously, almost under its own power. I had the feeling I was riding this huge machine that was rolling downhill by itself, and all I had to do was steer it in the right direction and keep any little parts from falling off.

It did take a great deal of time to write it, but it was a very exciting and satisfying period. *Ghost Story* went on to make much more money than I anticipated.

What sparked the sales of Ghost Story?

Something happens when a publishing house gets excited about a book. There's an unmistakable aura that is communicated through the organization. It becomes the book the sales reps talk about, the book the publicist hammers home when talking to the press. There is a lot of noise about the book right from the start, and people have the feeling if they want to stay in touch in the book world, then this book is something they should read. And *Ghost Story* did get very good reviews in most places.

CHRISTINA SKYE, Author

Romantic suspense/paranormal author Christina Skye is an award-winning bestseller of 19 novels. A prestigious RITA award finalist (given by Romance Writers of America), her books consistently appear on the *Publishers Weekly, USA Today,* and *New York Times* bestseller lists and feature Navy SEALs. *Code Name: Princess* and *Hot Pursuit* are two of her recent titles.

How did you react when you made the bestseller list for the first time?

Making a national bestseller list is a pleasant validation for the largely interior battles that a writer fights every day to bring an imaginary world to life. The flowers from my publisher were gorgeous, and the congratulatory e-mails were nice too. But sooner or later, reality sets in. The job is still about writing strong books, no matter where on the lists your name appears. Most authors I know define their success against an inner yardstick—not by media reviews or price club sales but by how close to the heart they have cut with each story. In every sentence, the work is clear: to probe the human heart, conjuring up characters so real they whisper in your ear and leave their fingerprints all over the paper. When that magic happens—whether for the 1st time or for the 50th time—an author's life changes completely,

Making a bestseller list pales in comparison to those momentary flashes of creative power.

NICHOLAS SPARKS, *Author*

When does an author feel comfortable that he or she can replicate the success of their first book?

I never get comfortable, and I think you have to feel that way if you want to be a long-term success. You also have to make the right career decisions.

Basically, once you've been successful with a book, you can take one of two paths. People have been successful with both. One path is to write a book that is pretty much the same as the first one. The reader thus knows exactly what to expect when they pick up a book by the author. The second path is to keep some of the elements in the novels the same but change as many other elements as you can. That's the path I took.

I write love stories. They are set in North Carolina. The characters are very universal. From there though, everything about my novels is different. Some have been written in first person, some in third person, some in both first and third person. The character perspectives are different. *The Notebook* was written from the perspective of an 80-year-old man; *A Walk to Remember* was told through the eyes of a 17-year-old boy; *Nights in Rodanthe* was written from the perspective of a 45-year-old divorced woman and mother of three.

In addition, the length of each book is different, the characters are different, the settings are different. The dilemmas the characters face are different. Romantic evenings are different, the external story is different. The overall theme is different.

In the spirit of doing things differently, do you ever give thought to leaving the love story genre?

No. It's a very difficult genre to work in. It's challenging to elicit genuine emotional response without resorting to melodrama and even harder to stay original. Hence, I never become bored.

STEPHANIE LAURENS, Author

Could you take us back to your first big commercial success and tell us how it happened?

I've no idea how you define commercial success—hitting the *New York Times* list, the *USA Today* list, the *Publishers Weekly* list, the Waldenbooks list, or simply earning out the advance? If you mean earning money, then every one of my books has earned at least enough to fund a family for a year. Most have earned a lot more. But even my first book has been reissued and reprinted and thus earned relatively large amounts—all of my books are continuously in print and earning. This is the way of successful genre fiction.

How it happened? That's easier to answer. Because I wrote books readers want to read, and I did that book after book, year after year. In genre fiction, you build an audience, and then you just keep on at it. Writing genre fiction is writing entertainment—being successful means being always entertaining. That's it.

What did that success mean to you personally?

It meant I could continue doing what I loved to do—writing stories—while never having to worry about paying the bills. I suppose you could call that the ultimate freedom.

ANNA JACOBS, Author

What did your first big success mean to you personally?

Wild excitement at hitting the charts for the first time but, best of all, increased publisher support—they liked the book so much, they did a two-for-one, giving away my first book, *Salem Street,* with a purchase of *Our Lizzie.* It boosted my numbers on a regular basis. Since then, my publisher has gotten behind me more than ever before. In other words, I well and truly climbed out of the midlist. Before *Lizzie,* I was selling through and going into reprints, but with much smaller print runs.

A PERSPECTIVE ON LONG-TERM SUCCESS

DR. SPENCER JOHNSON, *Author*

You have enjoyed tremendous longevity—two decades of success—which is extremely unusual.

I remember at one point early on in my career, after the tremendous success of *The One-Minute Manager,* of being so conscious that no other bestselling nonfiction author I had ever heard of had been successful for 20 years. I wondered what else I should be doing to make a living. I certainly wasn't going to be writing one nonfiction bestseller after another. So, because ten books have become bestsellers, I feel I've been extraordinarily fortunate.

Has your attitude about success changed over time?

Enormously. In my early, ambitious days, I defined success by the size of the advance, the size of the first printing, which talk shows I got on, where I was on the bestseller list. However, one day my brother reminded me that *I* wasn't on the bestseller list. My book was. This is an important distinction. Every author ought to know that. It's been very helpful to me to remember that. Separate your ego from your work, and you are a lot more peaceful and happier.

PETER STRAUB, *Author*

Has your attitude about what constitutes success changed as you've gone along in your career?

Undoubtedly my view of what constitutes success is more subtle now. I used to define success for each book as allowing me to pay for the life I wanted for a couple of years. I'm not unhappy with that definition now. Other writers have redefined success to an immense pitch, so if you want to be John Grisham, you have to sell an incredible number of books each year, and you have to write a good book every single year. In a way, that has come to be the standard of success in the book world.

About the time I turned 40, I became much more conscious of style, and I began to revise my books much more heavily than I had before, line by line, to clean out all the fuzz and blow the dust off, to present things in the right order. My objective was to get a kind of fast-moving transparency in the prose. This is a great part of what I'm after in my writing—what I've been after for the last 20 years. Success now is bound up intimately with writing as clearly and as vividly as possible.

BARBARA DELINSKY, Author

How has your attitude about what constitutes success changed?

Early in my career, success was defined as signing a multibook contract. Then money became the measure of success. Then hitting the bestseller lists. Then hitting *high* on the bestseller lists. What can I say— I'm a competitor.

As far as the deeper, more personal sense of success, nothing has changed. I've always defined success as finding happiness with my family and having good health. Being with people I love and seeing them happy was the true measure of success for me 24 years ago, when I started writing. It's even more true today.

18

FINAL THOUGHTS

WISDOM FROM BESTSELLING AUTHORS, EDITORS, AND AGENTS

THE MAKING OF A BESTSELLER

WISDOM FROM BESTSELLING AUTHORS, EDITORS, AND AGENTS

IRIS JOHANSEN, *Author*

Can you identify any key turning points in your career that propelled you to the bestseller list?

No. Actually, my career has involved a very, very steady climb. There were no real overnight successes. I worked at my craft. I try to make every book a little better than the one before. I gradually developed an audience, and when it was ready to happen, my success happened.

What has been most satisfying to you about your literary career?

The work itself, the writing. When I first started to write, it was just going to be a creative outlet, and it developed into a career. Every day I go upstairs to the office, I go with great anticipation, though some days turn out better than others. There are times you find yourself saying, "This bridge just isn't working!" or, "I'm going to have to throw this character away, because he's not turning out the way I want him to."

JENNIFER ENDERLIN, *Publisher*
St. Martin's Press

Have the prospects for a first-time author to make the bestseller list improved or declined in recent years?

It is getting harder. The industry is very competitive. There are a lot of good authors out there. To become a bestselling author with your very first book is practically impossible. It's been done a few times, usually when the book has a very high concept, like *The Nanny Diaries* or *The Devil Wears Prada,* something like that. But most times, reaching the bestseller list begins with building a readership in hardcover, then in paperback, and delivering a good book every time so your readership grows.

RICHARD CURTIS, *Literary Agent*
The Curtis Agency

How has the consolidation of the publishing industry affected a new author's chance of making the bestseller list?

It's reduced 100-to-1 odds to 1,000-to-1. The industry now puts its money behind frontrunners, books that are commercial winners before the author has written a word.

SANDRA BROWN, *Author*

Do you think, for new authors and writers, that there are more or less opportunities to get published today?

Definitely less, because publishing houses are feeling the economic pinch just like every other industry. They have to be careful where they put their money. They're going to invest in authors who have a track record before they take a chance on a newcomer. Of course, a new author can come along tomorrow and totally dispel that last statement. Publishers are always finding new authors who become phenomenons. That happens.

There is very little midlist anymore. On a publishing house's order form, there used to be their number-one book of the month; then there might be two or three known authors, but lesser known than the block-buster author. At the bottom would be all their other imprints, their science fiction, romances, or Westerns and all their series books.

In the middle would be the midlist: new authors, quirky books, or maybe something a little bit different. The midlist gave new authors a chance. A book would be published with a relatively small print run, but it would be found and perhaps talked about, and the next time, the new author would get more exposure. Now that midlist virtually does not exist, because the publishers can't afford to take a chance. Their accounts, the bookstores, don't want to take chances with new authors either. Everyone is looking for a sure thing, as sure a thing as they can possibly get.

STEPHANIE LAURENS, *Author*

Do you think there are more or less opportunities for authors to get published today?

I think it's as easy to get published now as it ever was. If you write a fabulous book that readers will grab and devour and enjoy, some publisher will publish it. My one comment would be that for genre fiction, getting published in the United States is easier than anywhere else, because the United States is the primary home for genre or entertainment fiction and publishes more of it than anywhere else.

CHRISTOPHER PAOLINI, *Author*

Is there anything you wish to add about your tremendous success?

I'm very grateful to all the teachers, librarians, booksellers, and fans who have supported the book. Without their support, none of this would have happened. Some people look at the success of *Eragon* as though it was handed to me. They don't realize the amount of work that went into it. The success was the result of 90 percent work and 10 percent luck.

BRAD MELTZER, Author

Do you think that now is an easier time or a more difficult time for a writer to get published?

Absolutely more difficult, simply for the fact there are fewer publishing houses out there to submit to. When I submitted my first novel—and this was before *The Tenth Justice*—I got 24 rejection letters; at the time, I think there were only 20 publishing houses. And now if you look out there you have even less. It's simple math: if you have fewer places to submit to, it's going to be harder on a sheer numbers basis.

Everyone likes to think that the past is wonderful and spectacular—and that the present is the worst it's ever been. But it's not always the case. I think, over time, there is a race for bestsellerdom, a race for the blockbuster. Some of it is based on perception, and some of it is based on the reality of what people are buying. But those races certainly mean that it's just going to be tougher on the person who comes out with a brand-new novel and has nothing but their own name, which no one recognizes, to put on it. And that is one of the scariest places to be when you're a writer. And every single one of us has been there.

LINDA FAIRSTEIN, Author

Besides writing the best book you can, how do you think a popular author should contribute to the success of his or her books?

Someone once told me that you have to sell books one by one. I like the whole marketing process. I like being in bookstores and libraries. I love doing events. I like to go places to help sell books. It's easier for me in a sense, because I had a job that involved public speaking and I'm very comfortable doing that in front of crowds, whereas many writers are cerebral. It's a solitary job, and they don't like getting on the road and hawking their book. I'm one of those authors who love book tours. I'll go wherever they send me. I love book signings. I like talking to readers who show up in bookstores. I have heard writers being foolish enough to grouse about libraries because they don't see the individual sales. Libraries are a fabulous market. They buy thousands of books and put those books in readers' hands. Many people find you for the first time at their public library. Especially with a series, they read one and they buy your next hardcover.

It doesn't end when you turn in the manuscript and you're starting on the next book. I really love participating in the marketing of the book, and I think it's critical to the success of a book.

BARBARA TAYLOR BRADFORD, Author

When you were first starting out as a writer, what advice do you wish you would have been given?

I learned early on that it is extremely difficult to create a novel, especially a long saga, without having a story outline and individual character outlines. Of course, one can make alterations along the way, but having these outlines makes the writer's job so much easier. When you know where your characters came from and where they are headed upon the conclusion of your story, you will rarely be stuck for ideas. I was never taught to have this kind of structure at the outset. But then again, I wasn't going to writers' groups or taking classes on creative writing. I graduated from typist to journalist to novelist.

NICHOLAS SPARKS, Author

What advice do you have for writers who aspire to make the bestseller list?

If you want to be an author, you should make an effort to understand the publishing industry, to learn which books are selling and why. Writing well is only half the battle. The best clients for an agent are those writers who are diligent in their writing and productive—they don't take five or six years between books. They work well with their editor. They don't complain about suggested changes. They listen. They are willing to promote. They get along well with people. They interview well. They make sure their stories are strong and original before they even start writing them.

All of these things are just as important as writing well. Writing is an art, but publishing is a business. There's a big difference between having one book that makes it big and having a big career. There are as many one hit wonders in the publishing world as there are in the music world, television, or movies.

When I speak to people who want to write a book, and many are in wonderful writing programs around the country, I often ask a simple question: "Can you describe your book?" You'd be amazed at the number of people who can't do this in one sentence or less.

I then ask them: "How many want to write a great literary novel?" They all raise their hands. How many want to get wonderful reviews? They all raise their hands. How many want to sell millions of copies? They all raise their hands. What they don't realize is that these three things don't commonly go together. If you want to sell millions of copies, you should consider writing a commercial novel. And that is not to say that commercial writing isn't high quality. It simply means that the plot isn't secondary to writing style. In other words, in commercial fiction, you better have a good plot.

DR. SPENCER JOHNSON, *Author*

What is most gratifying about your career as an author?

Stories I hear from people about how the books have changed their lives. But I tell them, my book didn't change your life, you changed your life while reading my book. That's an important distinction. Some people read the same story and get absolutely nothing out of it. The credit goes to the readers who take something valuable from the story and use it to their advantage and to the benefit of the people around them.

You have to be passionate about what you're doing. Your passion is picked up by the reader. Somehow they know it. When I'm writing, there's really nothing else I'd rather do. If someone calls me and says, "Let's go do something fun and interesting," and I'm on a roll writing at the time, I tell them, "Are you kidding? I'm having a ball writing. Why would I want to stop?"

My experience as a writer is the opposite from others I have heard about. I don't find it difficult. I don't find it lonely. There are some times when it's pure work, but those are very rare. Most of the time, I'm thinking, "I get to do this for a living!"

In fact, if I am struggling and the writing is not going well, I quit for the day. When I was a very young writer, writing children's books, a fellow writer and good friend of mine once read a draft of one of my manuscripts. When asked what he thought of it, he said, "I don't think it was much fun for you to write this." When I asked why he would say such a thing, he said, "Because it wasn't much fun to read." Ouch. He was right on. How could he have known that I had struggled against meeting a publishing deadline in order to get enough money to pay the rent, and it showed? Somehow, it seems, readers can tell.

The older I get, the more I realize that being able to write is a privilege, and it is best when you enjoy it and bring joy to the reader.

THE MAKING OF A BESTSELLER

What we have learned over the course of conducting these interviews is that *bestselling author* is not a generic title. The authors' paths to the top of the lists were as individual as their literary voices and writing styles. Most of them were not the student prodigies from the writing programs in the fine universities. Many bestselling authors did not even begin to achieve any kind of success until they were 10 or 20 years removed from college—if they attended college at all. Writing is often a second or third career or a hobby that turns into a business. For novelists, what brings uniqueness and zest to their stories often turns out to be life experience, what they have seen and heard during the course of everyday existence, and what they have observed from friends, family, and through their careers.

So what does it really take to be a bestselling author? We began the book by suggesting they must possess a sort of magic. Perhaps they use word processing software, unavailable to the typical writer, which turns average words to gold, much as country club duffers suspect that the pros on the PGA tour are given clubs that produce golf shots with supernatural power and accuracy.

But it turns out that the metaphysical explanations are incorrect. The one trait all bestselling authors share is an extraordinary dedication to the craft of writing, distinct from the business activity of promoting themselves in the publishing marketplace. Simply, they would rather write than do anything else. Not every writer, in their heart of hearts, can make that claim. Bestselling authors love their job; passion is their sustaining element.

In most cases, bestselling authors can look back and identify a turning point in their career that enabled them to immediately and permanently separate themselves from the enormous "pack" of writers turning out books at any given time. Call it the big break, a stroke of luck, the end product of tremendous effort—the result is the same. The struggle is for the most part over, and for that author, great rewards await. Fate taps them on the shoulder, perhaps in the form of an agent who goes way beyond the call of duty in contacting publishers on the author's behalf. Perhaps an editor goes on an almost obsessive mission to make sure an author's work gets serious attention at a publishing house. Fate could even be assisted by another bestselling author who believes in a new author's work and helps them get through the gates of the mighty publishing house.

Certainly this is a wonderful time to be an established, popular bestselling author at the top of your game. A number of publishing industry trends have come together to send favorable winds to a top selling author's career journey. Industry consolidation and the bottom-line emphasis at large publishing conglomerates has led to an increasing focus on making sure that bestselling authors' books succeed, because they are viewed as a less risky proposition in the marketplace than the new or midlist author. A consequence of this focus has been that the financial rewards for bestselling authors have escalated tremendously.

Although bestselling authors take very different paths to the top of the lists, their careers are marked by certain readily identifiable characteristics, characteristics that up-and-coming authors can certainly emulate.

- Incredible diligence and work ethic
- A recognition of the need to constantly grow in their craft, expanding and refining their skills
- A keen understanding of the business side of publishing
- Nurturing and satisfying the needs and expectations of their fan base
- Watching trends in the publishing marketplace—what is selling and why
- The patience and stamina to write a number of books before achieving great success
- A willingness to listen to, and accept guidance from, the professionals within their publishing house

Thus, there is a fascinating duality to their lives. Part of their life is spent in the quiet cocoon of their writing space, meditating, pondering, and creating. But the majority of bestselling authors also have a keen understanding of the business of publishing. Books are products that are expensive to produce and market, and the ultimate goal of everyone involved is to make as many readers as possible want to buy the book. Authors who make the bestseller lists use every marketing tool available to them to create a brand name that stands out from the pack. They work with great zeal to build, grow, and maintain a large readership.

Maddeningly, an author can have all these factors mastered and still not ever produce a bestseller. There is no denying that small miracles happen to certain authors that raise them above their peers, for reasons even they don't fully understand. Equally maddening, or perhaps frightening, is how an author's fans can suddenly and without warning desert the author, deciding they are tired of those books and want to find an author with a new and different voice. There are simply no sure things in the publishing business, no exact success blueprint to follow.

The creation of a bestseller is clearly a finely choreographed team effort, where scores of individuals contribute to the book's eventual success, starting with the author, of course, but proceeding all the way down the line to the individual bookseller who hands a copy to a customer and gently suggests, "You might like this one."

We have seen that there is much more to the bestselling author's "job" than the fun part, the writing. Maintaining a public and media presence is extremely important. A friend of ours who worked as the events coordinator for a large chain bookstore told us that the traditional book signing event—author at a table with a stack of books and several pens—doesn't work as well as it once did. Increasingly, he looks for authors who can put on a "performance" of some kind. It could be a dramatic reading of the author's work, a lecture, or an interactive experience with the audience: a show, in other words, complete with props sometimes. Similarly, authors whose ambition includes selling millions of copies of their books have to be comfortable with appearing on television, with spinning stories and sharing amusing anecdotes, just like any film or TV star appearing on *The Tonight Show,* for example, would be expected to do.

This emphasis on creating demand for books through mass media has caused many people to question whether the quality of what we are reading is improving or on the decline. Recently, we received an advance reading copy of a new book in the mail, written by a well-known, obnoxiously self-promoting individual in the business world. We were surprised he sent a copy to us, because we barely knew him. It turned out he was sending these copies out, at his own expense, to practically everyone in the country he had ever had any contact with. He told us that the mailing was intended to create buzz for his book. Nowhere did he say anything like, "I wrote a great book. It needs to be read." For this author, making the sale was the thing. He had a new product. Now it was time to go out and hawk it. He has that magic sales touch, after all.

This fellow is probably in for a bumpy ride. It turns out that the best-selling author is the beneficiary of magic, not the creator of it. The best-selling authors are not gods and goddesses at all. The true power in the publishing field is not wielded from an author's Mt. Olympus or down the corridors of the mighty publishing conglomerates, but rather from the lone individual out there, somewhere in America—this person could be in a large city like Chicago, Atlanta, or Seattle, or perhaps in a small Midwestern, Southern, or Southwestern town—who loves to read and loves to tell friends about a great new book. That person tells another, who may tell five more, and a ripple of acknowledgement from one reader builds—sometimes so slowly it takes years—into a tidal wave of success, culminating in a spot for that author on the bestseller list. Then, once this coveted spot is earned, it is likely the author's next book will earn a spot as well.

The bestselling author's most valuable possession is an intangible one: the quiet tens of thousands, or millions, of people out there waiting expectantly for their next book. The great thing about these quiet millions is that they are not impressed with glitzy ad campaigns or recommendations from the self-appointed "literati" on the East and West coasts, who tell them what they *should* be reading. Most of these readers don't even notice the imprint of the publishing house on the book. Ink, paper, and an eye-catching cover design are the tools used by all the publishing houses, big and small. These readers' beloved authors are generally not the ones who get the great reviews from the major media; in fact their work is often disparaged, even dismissed by critics.

What the national press thinks about a book may be much less important than what appears in their local newspaper, the book review that appears in their church newsletter, or the impromptu book discussion around the water cooler at the office or the factory—or the recommendation from a friend who works at the local bookstore. What really impresses these silent millions of readers are the words on the page. The bestselling author who commits to delivering those meaningful, memorable words can enjoy a career of tremendous acclaim and almost unimaginable financial rewards.

The truth is, it's pretty hard to fail when you have legions of loyal fans like these behind you. That is why the most savvy bestselling authors stop and salute their fans every chance they get. The authors who neglect to appreciate their fans do so at their own peril. Whatever lofty position you occupy in the publishing world, there is another author—or hundreds—out there equally talented, possibly more talented, and certainly hungrier, waiting to take your place.

Above all else, what a bestselling author really is, is a writer who has innumerable reasons to be grateful. These authors have been chosen to receive a strikingly rare, special distinction by a bustling, competitive marketplace made up of readers they will, for the most part, never meet. As with earning knighthood, their names will forever carry a glittering preface: *Bestselling Author.*

Maybe the pen really is mightier than the sword.

A

Absolute Power, 184
Adams, Chuck, 70–1
Adaptations, film, 174–78
Advance reading copies (ARCs),
120–21
Advances, 26, 65
Advertising, 113
Agents, 79–90
advances/royalties and, 65–66
career building and, 84, 160–62
collaboration with editors, 73–74
competition for, 89–90
editors' perspectives on, 87–88
film adaptations and, 168–69
negotiations and, 65, 80–81
personal satisfaction, 8
role of, 79–87
Ain't She Sweet (Phillips), 48, 107
Amazon.com, 41–42, 43, 99, 100, 124
American Booksellers Association, 22,
103
American Library Association, 36
American Tabloid (Ellroy), 175, 200
Andersen, Susan, 113
Andrews, V.C., 116
Anne Frank, 167
Anonymous Rex (Garcia), 192
Author(s)
advances, 26
book promotion and, 129–31
bookstore impact on careers of,
102–4
as brands. *See* Brand image(s)
career planning and, 74–75
characteristics of bestselling,
237–41
evolution of style of, 203–6
lives of bestselling, 207–15

marketing and, 133–45
movie adaptations and, 165–78
as product spokesperson, 127–28
prolific, 222–23
unknown, 29
views on readers' tastes, 48–50
voice and, 28, 31, 115, 146
web sites of, 113, 123
Avon, 154
Awards, 57, 59, 114

B

B. Dalton, 99
Bachelor, The (Phillips), 155–56
Backlist, 152
Baldacci, David, 151, 184
Ballantine Book Group, 154
Barnes, William, 99
Barnes & Noble, 99
Barrie, Sir James M., 225
Benchley, Peter, 180
Benioff, David, 177
Bennett, Arnold, 16, 187
Bennett, John, 10, 93, 103–4, 221
Bestseller lists
explanation of, 18–24
future sales of books on, 15
history of, 16
media/blurb driven factors, 85
nonfiction, 17
point-of-sale trend, 21
publishers and, 13–14
recognized national, 18
statistics and, 14–15
"Bestseller Lists and Product Variety:
The Case of Book Sales"
(Sorensen), 15
Bezmozgis, David, 121–22

Share the message!

Bulk discounts
Discounts start at only 10 copies and range from 30% to 55% off retail price based on quantity.

Custom publishing
Private label a cover with your organization's name and logo. Or, tailor information to your needs with a custom pamphlet that highlights specific chapters.

Ancillaries
Workshop outlines, videos, and other products are available on select titles.

Dynamic speakers
Engaging authors are available to share their expertise and insight at your event.

Call Dearborn Trade Special Sales at 1-800-621-9621, ext. 4444, or e-mail trade@dearborn.com.

Dearborn™
Trade Publishing
A **Kaplan Professional** Company